WORKING
HOM

WORKING FROM HOME

HOME

201 Ways To Earn Money

Marianne Gray

PIATKUS

To all the self-employed

© 1982 Marianne Gray

First published in 1982 by
Judy Piatkus (Publishers) Limited of
Loughton, Essex

British Library Cataloguing in Publication
Data

Gray, Marianne
   Working from home: 201 ways to earn
   money.
   1. Home Labor—Great Britain
   1. Title
   658'.022   HD2336.G7
   ISBN 0-81688-152-4 (hardback)
   ISBN 0-81688-225-3 (paperback)

Designed by Richard Garratt

Drawings by Eljay Crompton

Phototypeset by Tradespools Limited,
Frome, Somerset

Printed and bound by The Garden City Press Limited,
Pixmore Avenue, Letchworth, Hertfordshire SG6 1JS

CONTENTS

THE JOBS

Working for Others
Homework
  Sewing and Knitting
  Typing
Homework and the Disabled
Direct Sales
Mail Order
Selling Over the 'Phone
Computer Work
Corsets
Distributing
Invigilating
Market Research
School-crossing Attendant
Somebody's Secretary from Home

Agencies
Accommodation Agency
Au Pair Agency
Building Repairs Agency
Business Services Agency
Domestic Cleaning Agency
Employment Agency
Foreign Student Accommodation
House-sitter Agency
Imports and Exports
Marriage Bureau
Minicab Agency
Settling-in Agency
Speakers' Agency
Travel Consultant Agency

Animals
Animalware
Animal Watch
Beekeeping
Boarding Dogs and Cats
Dog Beauty Parlour
Free-range Eggs

Goatkeeping
Training Dogs

Children
Babysitting
Child Escorts
Childminding
Children's Book and Toy Shop
Childware
Kiddy Packs and Lucky Dips
Playgroups and Nursery Schools

Clothes and Accessories
'Almost New' Emporium
Alterations and Mending
Clothes-selling Parties
Customising Clothes
Dressmaking
Handbags
Hatmaking
Kit Clothes
Knitting
Pattern Cutting Classes
Silk Lingerie
Specialist Clothing
Theatrical Costumes

Crafts
Basketry
Batik
Bookbinding
Bottle Chopping
Calligraphy
Candlemaking
Christmas Decorations
Crochet
Decorating on Glass
Decorative Wood Techniques
Embroidery

Enamelling
Flower Making
Handspinning
Jewellery
Leatherwork
  Saddlery
Macramé
Mosaics
Moulding with Polyester Resin
Ornamental Ironwork
Papermaking
Papier Mâché
Patchwork and Quilting
Picture Framing
Pottery
Silkscreen Printing
Soft Toys
Stained Glass
Weaving

Food
Baking and Cake-making
Confectionery and Preserves
Deep-freeze Cooking Service
Directors' Lunches
Fruit Baskets
Packed Lunches and Sandwiches
Party Catering
Party Organisation
Party and Picnic Packs
Specialist Cooking
Tea Room
Weekend Cooking

Furniture and Soft Furnishings
Caning
Curtains
Cushions
French Polishing
Gilding
Lampshades
Loose Covers
Making Wooden Furniture

Marquetry
Mirrors
Restoring Wooden Furniture
  Antique Dealing
Upholstery

Health and Beauty
Beauty Salon
Chiropody
Hairdressing
Keep Fit Classes
Massage
Natural Beauty Products
Slimming Treatments and Sunbeds

Plants
Compost
Dried Flowers
Farm Cropwork
Growing Decorative Plants
Herbs
Indoor Plants
Jobbing Gardening
Landscape Gardening
Market Gardening
Mushroom Growing
Office Windowbox Service

Repair Work
Bicycle Repairs
  Wheel Building
Car Repairs
Clock and Watch Repairs
General Repairs
Restoring Antique Dolls
Restoring China and Ceramics
Sharpening Shop

Services
Accountancy
Address Service
Astrology
  Taro and I Ching

Bed and Breakfast
Book-keeping
Car Washing
Compiling Crosswords
Computers
Duplicating
Graphic Design
Graphology
Home Economics
Home Laundry
House Guardian
Household Help
Househunting Service
Indexing
Kits
Letter/Typing Service
Minicab Driving
Model Making
Nursing
'On View' Advertising Service
Packaging
Painting and Illustrating
Photographic Processing
Photography
Printing
Proofreading
Public Relations/Promotions
Publishing
Reading to the Blind
Research
   Picture Research

Abstracting
Information Consultancy
Geneology
Shopping on Order
Sign Writing
Singing Telegrams
Spray Painting Cars
Still Life Modelling
Taking in Lodgers
Telephone Message Service
Tourist Guide
Transcribing Braille
Translating
Typing
Washing Windows
Word Processing
Writing

Teaching
Dancing classes
Driving Instruction
Foreign-language Conversation
Music Teaching
Teaching English: EFL and ESL
Teaching Lipreading
Teaching Literacy and Numeracy
Teaching Self-defence
Teaching Sports
Teaching Typing
Teaching Yoga
Tutoring

— INTRODUCTION —

'When I said "Why don't you make some money at home", I didn't mean this!'

This book is packed with over 200 ideas for jobs you can do from home. It is based largely on the experiences of people who have started out alone, working from their spare rooms, garden sheds or from corners of their kitchens. They all wanted to earn money. None of them became a high-flying multi-millionaire but all of them gained a sense of confidence and self-sufficiency, however tiny the project. Many of them were mothers with young children who would have given their eye-teeth to get out of the house but could find no job that would pay enough even to cover childminding fees; others felt less strongly about externalising and were happy to work alone from home; some simply could not bear the idea of having to work for a boss again, so became their own boss! And many of them were unemployed, redundant or retired.

Being your own boss has advantages and disadvantages. It isn't all the ringing of tills in your ears and the repeating images of £££££s signs in your eyes! To some, opting to work for yourself spells insecurity, and the thought of staying at home to do it is even worse. To others, it means financial survival and a way to gain independence. Working for yourself offers, above all, a chance to develop the personality – because, often for the first time, you are forced to be imaginative, decisive, inventive and *daring*! When you are working for yourself you make sure that your work is first-rate, that the rewards are fair and that they are extracted regularly from tight-fisted clients. When the buck-passing stops with you, you tend to make sure that there is no buck!

This book has been written to inspire and encourage those of you who itch to earn money, have time on your hands and, if not a training or a skill, a little energy to spare. There is absol-utely nothing to stop you going solo. You set the pace, the time and the place. In the following chapters I have attempted to outline the technical, personal and professional high points and hazards, reasons and regulations. The jobs described are for the skilled and the unskilled, the experienced and the inexperienced, and can be done either in the home or from it. Listed at the back of the book are the names and addresses of organisations who offer information, assistance and courses, the names and addresses of certain suppliers and a selection of books to read for reference and instruction.

When you read this book, remember that you won't be the first person to strike out on your own. All it takes is a determined first step with your best foot forward.

MONEY AND MOTIVATION
or The Case For Working From Home

Work, unfortunately, is not a cure for all ills but it certainly can help. It can end economic insecurity and be an antidote to boredom, uncertainty and grief. We all know we would be happier with more money. People who cannot find work or are tied to the home, those who have been pensioned off or made redundant, and those who have given up jobs to start a family or look after elderly parents will also find themselves confronted with that overwhelming and intangible desire to feel needed, to be a cog in the wheel again and be part of a work 'family'.

In the 1980s we need to work for our personal and financial survival. With fewer jobs, a higher and higher cost of living and less and less funds, any housebound spouse who turns a hand to making money is making a noticeable difference to the kitty. It is often thought of as the second income. One in eight of the British workforce is now out of work and this second income could very easily be the first.

Second income earners are usually

those who are limited for one reason or another in their choice of jobs and have to work either in or from the home on a project that is flexible enough to fit in with the domestic routine and practical enough not to upturn home life. Only a few years ago working at home smacked of sweated labour, but now the home-based worker has acquired a certain standing and a certain respectability. Being self-employed you are your own boss. You can choose what it is you are going to do, depending on how skilled or how experienced you are, how much time and money you can afford to put into training (if you need it) and how much finance (if any) you are prepared to invest in the project. The idea of not having someone to report to, and at the same time working from your own home – which may be a place you already consider a source of full-time employment – might sound pretty ghastly. However many people do not have an option and they either have to or want to work.

There is nothing to stop anybody setting up on their own and organising themselves and possibly others to earn money. The most important factor is motivation. If you have it, use it! Life is not a rehearsal so it is important to get it right the first time. Decide what you want to do, learn how to go about it and find out if there is anybody out there who will pay you for doing it. After the first flush of motivation, check that the job you have chosen *does* suit you and your talents. Examine your reasons for doing it and look carefully and positively at the problems that must be overcome.

If by working you are going to overload a routine already filled with domestic chores and commitments, will you be able to streamline your lifestyle so that you do not end up with a double burden? Are you prepared to make changes in your lifestyle and perhaps even changes in values? The home is obviously going to be affected by new developments in it, and the people who share it with you more so.

Are you working purely for money? Or are you working for the satisfaction of doing something useful or creative, or for mental sharpening, or for a mixture of reasons? If it is only for the money, then how much do you want to make? If it is for priming the mind, then how seriously are you going to take a job? Are you really sure you want to or have to work? Would voluntary work be more rewarding? Your reasons for working will affect your motivation and commitment to earn money and therefore the job you choose to do.

There are dozens of reasons why different people work but all these reasons fall into just two categories: 'have to' and 'want to'.

Some people have to work in order to pay the bills but cannot find the right jobs. The 'system' simply does not cater for mothers bringing their pre-school age children with them to work, and housebound women with toddlers have no alternative but to earn from home. The system is also insufficiently flexible to handle the possibility of redundant people working part-time with their former companies; they are given a golden handshake and expected to disappear. The same applies to retired people who are one day cast onto the 'scrapheap' along with a wealth of accumulated experience. And sadly, in Britain, it is hard for the disabled to find work.

These four groups – the housebound, the redundant, the retired and the disabled – are all potential workers who find themselves sitting at home wondering where the cash is going to come from to pay the rent, the mortgage or the heating bills.

The second category comprises those who have more esoteric reasons for wanting to work. Some have emotional reasons, like self-actualisation and the need to succeed at something. Some people whose children have left home find themselves desperately looking for something to quell the boredom. Others choose to work as freelance consultants using their past business experience. The more entrepreneurial, who know they have something terrific to offer the world, try to organise a project and steer it to success. And there are those who do not like working for anybody else and have always dreamed of being their own boss, miles away from monotonous office life.

As you can see, the reasons vary enormously:

Geoffrey knew that he was destined for far greater things than playing second fiddle to an incompetent superior so one morning he cleared his desk, went home and started to run an interior decoration consultancy from his living room. Today, he and his business are thriving.

Carolyn has two small children at home all day and very little free time. She manages to make and sell one patchwork eiderdown cover a month to help balance the family budget.

Julia, an executive's wife who is regularly expected to produce dinner parties and entertain her husband's business associates, often felt little more than chief cook and bottle-washer. She invested in a large deep freeze and, with a couple of friends, started a freezer-food cooking agency.

Angela knew her husband wanted to buy video equipment but could not afford it, so she started to design and make satin cushions decorated with seascapes, which she sold through smart shops, and many cushions later she bought the video. Next she wants to buy a piano and take lessons.

Douglas operates a small book-keeping business from his wheelchair. Apart from giving him a good income, it means that he does meet people when they call at his home to discuss the work.

None of the people I have mentioned, from either category, was sure where self-employment would lead, although if they had done some market research they would have had an idea. Their motivations were different: some worked to live, literally to make ends meet; others lived to work, to make a lot of money and become famous! Whichever way you approach it, the work will demand effort and hopefully the results will encourage and fire you to produce or do bigger and better things!

However, pensioners do have a problem and it would not necessarily be to their advantage if business boomed.

John and Avril retired the same year and almost immediately felt the need to join others on a joint project. This group of friends chose to make things for gardens: *'We'd always been active in our own gardens and between us we're producing concrete gnomes (Avril paints them) and welded ironwork to hold potted plants – and sometimes even the plants to go with them. We sell quite well locally, although none of us wants to sell too well or we will lose our pensions! We still believe that saying about being "never to old to make a million", but we keep our earnings below the limit permitted for persons on retirement pension. It suits us that way!'*

For women with children who are slightly older and go to school there may well be about four free hours a day in which to develop a profitable pastime. It's quite surprising how much can be done in half a day when the place is empty. If you think about it, it is equal to a very long half-day in an office, or a short full-day without tea-breaks and office chat sessions.

With six to eight hours a day available for work, you will find that you can actually put in more than you would during an average office day. It is unlikely that you will be caught napping or slowing down for the last portion of the working day because you want to knock off at 5 pm prompt. It is equally unlikely that you will want to take long lunch breaks to spin the day out. With six free hours a day on your hands you should be able to run quite an ambitious concern.

The following chapters take a look at the personal and practical aspects of working for yourself from your home base and give advice on how you should put your plan into action.

A LITTLE SELF-EXAMINATION
or Hardening Up Your Commercial Arteries

For the housewife, a division of loyalties is one of the harder aspects of turning professional. Home and childminding can have a blunting effect on a woman's mind. Only she can sharpen it. After years of being somebody's wife and somebody's mother, probably restricted to working inside the home as a housewife rather than outside it as a working woman, equality of the sexes doesn't mean that much. Confidence is low, potential underestimated and knowledge of what is available in the outside world limited. But running a home is very much like running a business. It takes management, decisions and practical skills and were the housewife paid only £1.50 an hour for her services to home and family, seven days a week, she would receive a respectable sum. So housewives, if you think you cannot do a job and run a home, consider that already you are the ultimate working women, performing a most important role, yet with no formal training and no negotiable status on the job market. To quote a businessman: 'Running a home is the same as running a business but harder because you have no staff – you are the boss, the teagirl, the secretary, accountant, manager and clerk.'

If your working experience has been gained in the office, bear in mind that there won't be any office 'chums' at home to commiserate with you when you have a cold or enthuse over the new outfit you're wearing. Your client certainly will not care: he or she is only interested in your product or service. Even worse, you might not have any clients in the early days – it takes time, luck and word of mouth to build up contacts, a good reputation and custom. Unless you have been talked about and can be recommended, potential clients will not know that you are taking your enterprise seriously, and that you are producing goods or supplying a service of good quality and at competitive rates.

Have you considered whether you are going to be able to cope with living not just above the shop but *in* it? That means spending every day and every night in the same place on both a professional and domestic level. It is a case of running your work with your right hand, the home with your left and doing both well. How successful you will be depends on your priorities. Some jobs affect home life more than others. Some consume it while others lightly overlap. You alone know how much time, energy and determination you can dedicate to your job.

The only work structure you will get at home is self-imposed. *You* have to devise a way to pace yourself and to motivate yourself. Even if you only intend to work for a couple of hours each day, you are probably going to have to trick yourself into getting going. Looking out of the window thinking about starting, nipping off to make another cup of coffee or cleaning the house from top to bottom is not good enough if you are supposed to be working. You are going to have to prune the domestic chores by simplifying the routine and sticking to essentials. A lick and a polish and a quick squirt from an aerosol can of furniture polish will fool friends and family – and, eventually, you!

Things have to change and you, too, have to change in order to make the transition to working from home easy.

Janet runs a catering concern specialising in directors' lunches: *'The biggest change for me was to cultivate a delicate and oh-so feminine look while thinking and pushing like a man! Because you're "merely" a housewife, people expect you to be inefficient outside the home, so you have to do twice the work, especially well, in half the time just to pass the test!'*

It takes a lot of determination to uncover and exploit your reserves of common sense, discipline and optimism when you first begin. See it as a challenge and muster all the forces you have available. Learn how to be single-minded about yourself and your aspirations. You will be the one who gives yourself a black mark for letting things slip, or a shiny gold star for every triumph.

Getting started can be a terrible time, heavy with doubt and despondency. Maybe all the redundancy money, or family savings, has been used to set up your venture and you are in the middle of the Initial Squeeze period, waiting and wondering when and if the cash is going to flow in. This is a common complaint known as cash flow. Take heart: it should go away if you have planned your work properly. It is unavoidable unless you are doing a job that requires no investment and is sold for instant cash. Most forms of work which prove profitable in the long term involve some initial investment, then a production period followed by a time lapse between completing the product and selling it. Even then, buyers might take up to three months (or more) to settle their bills with you.

Once the job is ticking over nicely, most people who work for themselves get a wonderful warm feeling of success. After all, ambition and free enterprise is good for you and good for the economy when it is successful. But success, too, has its problems. These may concern increased responsibility or the need to move into bigger premises. One solution is to employ others or to work outside the home. What will happen if your project turns into a meteoric success? Can you see yourself the head of a sprawling empire? Would you be able to join forces with others? Could you drive a hard bargain? Does it excite you to think of yourself possibly making more money than your partner?

If you think you could handle the success then you've been overlooking your potential for far too long!

Try the brief test below and see how well you will fare in business on your own. Delete the characteristics which do not apply to you. Be honest with your answers – we all know which is the 'good' column.

?Are You:

Energetic	Lethargic
Persuasive	Uncertain
Punctual	Always late
Friendly/cheerful	Shy/often depressed
Patient	Easily niggled
Tidy	Messy
Determined	Disheartened quickly
Tactful	Always putting your foot in it
Accurate/reliable	Careless/vague
Adaptable	Inflexible

?Do You:

Radiate confidence	Cringe in the background
Have plenty of ideas	Seldom have any ideas
Like working alone	Need people around

Long for an element of risk	Hate insecurity
Take the initiative	Loathe decision-making
Excel under pressure	Go to pieces and dither under pressure
See problems as a challenge	Complain loudly
Organise well	Try and avoid having to organise
Thrive on efficiency	Love pandemonium
Accept advice/criticism well	Get snappy when criticised

If all the deletions are in the right-hand column, you should have been working for yourself years ago! If most of them are in the left then working alone at home is possibly not for you. Perhaps you should stick with the job you've got (if you have one) or try sharing an office job with somebody, part-timing or, if you can arrange it, doing your previous work for that same company but from home. If the deletions are fairly mixed, you have got a good chance of going solo successfully but you should choose work that will suit your personality.

Choosing the right job has to be based on what you do best, what you think you could do well or what you would like to do, and on how well you could organise yourself. Keep a hawk-like eye open for other people's good ideas and take note of the things you do or make which cause others to praise you. Not everybody has a skill, qualifications, training or experience, so if you are to work for profit you will have to concentrate on a job which is appropriate to you. Everybody has something to offer but usually you have to put something in to get some-

thing out. In this case the 'something' would be a short training course, either full-time, part-time or evening. Alternatively, teach yourself by reading the relevant instruction books (see Contacts). Not all courses are expensive, but they will call for an investment of your time.

The right job must also depend on whether there is a need for it. Would anybody buy it? You have to spot the dead-end projects early on. Spend time doing market research and preparing costings.

When you have decided what you are going to do, go out and talk to friends and anybody else who will listen to evoke feedback and reactions. (They'll say you're brave or mad.) Talk to the Citizens' Advice Bureaux and information centres. They will advise on formalities (if there are any) and how you can check the market. By the time you've gone through the subject over and over again you'll know whether you believe in it, in yourself, and in a future.

Once you have confidence in your plan and your ability to carry it through, start thinking about the practicalities that surround it.

HOME IS WHERE . . .
or The Practicalities

Once you have decided that you are going to work from home there are two things which must be sorted out quickly and without fuss: the family (unless, of course, you live alone) and the space you are going to call your own.

It is far easier to organise your busier life with a little help from the family than it is to be faced with complaints about how inattentive you are to their needs. Tell them about your project and how the home is to be run in glowing, positive terms and from Day

One try to have them toeing the line! Whatever your role is in the family (mother, father, offspring, grandparent), you will find that any change you initiate in a domestic situation is likely to cause upset to somebody. As long as there is order to the new routine, everybody will know where they stand. It will make it easier for them to accept your new role and lessen the stress for you.

If you have children who are old enough to do all those things which allegedly 'any child could do', well let them! Bedmaking, washing up, doing a spot of laundry or cleaning might not be every child's idea of fun, but why should Mum have to do it if she is spending as much time as possible working to finance the next family vacation or a car to take them there.

It is very important for everybody's morale to give work based in the home the respect it deserves. If you are *working* you are not *playing*. If the man opts to work from home or if the woman does, it should be taken seriously from the start. The biggest source of potential help and encouragement should be one's partner, and although it might be hard for a person firmly entrenched in the nine-to-five mould to make concessions to fit in with the new routine at home, the financial benefits should become clear. Many women who try to earn money from home have pointed out that their husbands and children do not take their work seriously and think they are only doing it for fun. Some men say that they encounter hostility from friends and family if they attempt to work at home, and that they are often considered to be failures. Nothing could be further from the truth.

Before you announce to the world that you are going into business, work out how important and relevant your proposed project is in practical terms. How much of an upheaval will be required? Will people want your service or product? How much can you sell it for? What will the rewards be after everything else has been taken into consideration?

Do a feasibility study of your own and find out. (See page 24.)

A workplace

Ideally, a job run along reasonably professional lines should be performed in a room away from the domestic running of the home. However, most homes do not have a room to spare and you might have to settle for a quiet corner in your bedroom or just a couple of drawers or a cupboard, depending on the project.

Barbara, a hairdresser, found her way round the space problem by setting up her salon in the sitting room: *'When our daughter was born two years ago I had to start working from home. Although my husband wasn't too keen on the idea he realised how much the money was needed in order to pay for equipment for the baby and a new washing machine, so he built a conservatory off the kitchen area which we now use as the lounge. I set up all my hairdressing equipment in the sitting room and plumbed in a basin.'*

If you are lucky enough to have a spare room, attic, basement, garage or garden shed which can be converted into a workroom, check that the ventilation, light, heat and access is suitable for the job you have in mind.

Check with the neighbours that your work will not disturb them. A noisy or smelly machine in a garden shed or constant delivery vans in the street would probably make them complain to the Council, who would, in turn, probably ask you to stop using the offending equipment or vehicles.

You should ask the landlord's permission if you want to work in rented property. If you own your home you should be aware of certain formalities pertaining to some freehold house deeds and mortgage agreements which do not permit businesses to operate from the premises. You should be aware, too, that legally you should contact your local authority and apply for change-of-use to change part of your property from domestic to business use. If permission is granted it might affect the rateable value of the house. It is a fact that the majority of small concerns start off 'without the benefit of clergy', as a representative of the Alliance of Small Firms and Self Employed People put it rather succinctly. Planning permission, personal consent and licences to work at home are dealt with on page 36.

If the job you intend to do involves employing others to work in your home, you must apply to the local authority for planning permission or a licence. If planning permission is not immediately granted, you do have the right to appeal.

Market research

The next step is to find out who will want your product or service, whether there is a demand for it in your area and what people will pay for it. If there is no *local* demand, you will find yourself spending a percentage of your profits on transport and postage. Of course, you may find that your idea does not appeal at all, or it is so appealing that dozens of people are already doing it. It is inevitable that an attractive article or an efficient system will be copied.

Start your market research by looking in the local newspaper or church magazine, and at corner shop and community centre notice boards to see what products or services are advertised. Enquire at shops whether your product is one they would buy and make some samples to show to the buyers. If the buyers are not interested, ask them why. It could be the colour, the quality or the packaging. Buyers are used to being approached and it is their job to buy just as it is yours to sell. Buyers can be snappy (who can't) but they are usually very courteous.

If you intend to give a service, you obviously can't produce a sample to show people, but you can always produce a brief questionnaire to find out if people would use it and if they know of or use any similar services. If the service is already available in your area you will have either to undercut it, improve on it or move to a different area.

A professional market research company (see the Yellow Pages) will test the market reaction for you for a fee. It may be quite expensive, but it is not as costly as sinking money into a project which nobody wants. If they reveal that your product or service is not that uncommon, then if you cannot find ways to make it less so, you should drop the idea. There is always a gap in the market waiting to be filled by the right concept.

Finally, do not automatically believe your friends when they say your brainchild is a winner. Few friends will

21

want to criticise objectively another friend's pride and joy.

You now have some facts and, assuming that they present no insurmountable problems, settle down to do some sums. Calculate whether your product or service can be offered at a price below the going rate. Work out realistically if, in the final analysis, it will actually be cheaper for you to do whatever it is than not to do it. A common mistake is to overestimate your sales figures. Err on the side of caution.

Outlay and overheads

The size of your outlay affects the size of turnover you must achieve and the time and effort that must be spent on the project to make it viable. If you have to spend money on large items try to arrange credit terms and spread the load. Consider the following points carefully.

Assuming there *is* a room in your house which can be used as a workroom or office, how much will it cost to equip it with second-hand furniture and equipment? If your work requires clients to visit you at home, how much will it cost to decorate and organise a reception room?

You may need to buy a typewriter or adding machine, spinning wheel or greenhouse. Calculate the investment required. Is the money available for this initial (deadweight) investment or must it be borrowed and repaid, with interest, over a given period? There

might be services you'll need regularly, like weekly deliveries of parts and provisions, or monthly rates for legal, accounting or secretarial assistance, to add to the overheads. Consider what you will need to spend on the business to set it up and to run it properly.

Remember that if you work from home you will have to pay for extra heating and lighting, postage and telephone. If you have to deliver your product, consider the cost of transport. Do not forget to add the cost of stationery, advertising and insurance, and allow something for sundries. If the family cannot be relied upon to take efficient-sounding messages you might have to invest in a second telephone or in a telephone answering machine.

Take all these points into account and tot up the cost, then see if the estimated total tallies with the amount of capital available to start you off.

Warning: Think carefully before plunging savings into equipment which is too sophisticated for your experience. It is far better to start small and build up your business as your experience and profits increase.

Costing it out

Too many small business concerns flounder almost immediately because nobody bothered to do their sums right. Pricing brings in a sink-or-swim element. If the price is too high nobody will buy the goods; if it is too low everybody will wonder why – and you won't make a profit.

The amount you are going to charge

is arrived at following this formula: the amount spent on materials plus the cost of your labour at 'x' per hour, added together and doubled (for 100% mark-up), plus VAT (if this applies).

The materials should be costed down to the last reel of cotton or pot of paint. Your labour charge should include the time taken getting the order in the first place and the time spent doing the work. If you have to deliver goods or run up mileage acquiring materials, do not forget to budget for or charge for transport. The AA provides a service which tells you how many miles it is from A to B. If you are going to spend a quarter of your time collecting and returning work, it is only fair to charge for mileage *and* time. These finer details should be agreed with the client before you undertake the job. The 100% mark-up covers a percentage of your initial investment on equipment, which can be spread out over several years, a percentage of overheads, advertising costs etc, and it should allow you a small profit. When you have worked out what the true sales figure is, find out what professionals are charging for the same goods or service. Can you charge slightly less and still make your venture viable?

Some people offering services find the simplest way to arrive at a price is to reduce an agency rate for similar work by 10–20%. The amount you decide to charge for your labour is entirely up to you. It would be pointless to charge £5 an hour if it prices your product or service out of the market. Do not be tempted to pursue a project if you cannot make it pay.

You should aim to charge per job rather than per hour if you can, as in the long run you will make more money this way. There are time-costing books designed for various careers – ask at your local Business Library or the business section of your local library, or see if the British Institute of Management can advise.

So if you were making, for example, silk cushions, you would cost it out like this:

Material	Labour	Total
(fixed cost)	(2.50 per hour)	
£8.00	£5.00	£13.00
Plus 100% mark-up		£13.00
		£26.00
VAT (if necessary) 15%		£ 3.90
		£29.90

Shops, if you are selling to them, will probably charge the customer double the buying-in price of your goods. They have to cover their tremendously high overheads and also the risk of not selling the item, so it is clearly in your interests to try and keep the price down at first when you are selling to a shop. When they come back for more, raise the price gradually. Whatever you do, don't mess about. Once you have decided to put up the price, do so with conviction!

Feasibility study

○ How much time can you devote to your work? (Take into account interruptions by the meterman, the children being ill, school holidays, delays caused by the washing machine breaking down, etc.)

○ What is your anticipated income? (Be realistic.)

○ List your materials or ingredients. (Don't forget small items such as string, wrapping paper, nails, glue.)

○ List any labour-saving devices you need for the house to save you time, and note their cost.

○ Estimate your living expenses, operating costs and overheads. (Beware of underestimating living expenses. Include a proportion of the household electricity, telephone and insurance bills, rent and rates, etc. Will the rates be increased if you are granted planning permission for change of use of part of your home? Work out how much the equipment costs in fuel, hire costs and maintenance.)

○ Calculate how much capital investment is needed to cover equipment and setting up. (Consider entering hire purchase and leasing agreements which are paid monthly).

○ Estimate the cost of promotion and advertising, both to start up your business and to keep the orders coming in.

○ Calculate how much money is available and how much will have to be borrowed. Calculate the interest due on borrowed capital. (Don't forget to arrange overdraft facilities at the bank in case of a short-term cash flow crisis.)

○ Balance income against expenditure and if the project seems feasible then think about leaping in. If you are in any doubt, ask an accountant to advise you.

○ Once you have sorted out practicalities – and the family gives you the go-ahead – accept the challenge!

GETTING STARTED
or Manoeuvring Your Way Through The Undergrowth

In order to start trading the buyers have to know what you are selling. If you're ready to move into the market place, be bold. Go out and flog your wares with conviction. Tell the world by being noticed in all the right places.

Advertising and promotion

It goes without saying that the best advertising and self-promotion is free.

The more you spread the word, the more the word-of-mouth network will work for you. Speak up loud and clear (beware of becoming a bore) to make sure that you don't become the 'little woman or little man around the corner', about whom nobody is any too sure. You can always make the system work for you by persuading your local newspaper to do a story on you. If you can present your work to the news editor in an interesting enough manner or if you do something sufficiently newsworthy to merit a few paragraphs, the response will undoubtedly be greater than it would if you advertised for weeks in the same newspaper at so much per line. Recently a woman dressed up as a witch and took free sample Sand-Witches around to local offices. She not only triggered off a sizeable story in the local gazette, but she also acquired an enthusiastic clientele. Specialist publications, too, could well be interested in your project. If you are making beautiful ceramic flower pots, perhaps a glossy magazine with a home and garden section would be happy to write a short piece on them. Send a well-phrased letter to the editor, enclosing a couple of *good* photographs of your product.

An ambitious, but not impossible, idea for promoting your speciality is to approach a company and suggest that they use your product as a special offer. For example, if you have developed an ingenious clothes-line, try a washing powder company. Alternatively, apply for space to give away samples or demonstrate your product at an appropriate exhibition – for example, at the Boat Show if you've invented a shoe-covering to prevent heels marking the deck.

If you are operating on a smaller scale, place notices in the library, Citizens' Advice Bureau, and clinics. Pin bright advertisements on the boards in shop windows, clubs, schools and colleges. It is not expensive. (It is advisable to put your telephone number, not your address, on an advertisement, just in case some crank sees it in a shop window and plagues you at your home.) You can also put a sign in your front window (see the leaflet *Town and Country Planning Control of Advertisements Regulations, 1969*, available from the Planning Department at your Town Hall) or have cards, brochures or leaflets printed advertising your work which you can slip through letterboxes.

For a wider market, place advertisements in specialist magazines, trade journals and national newspapers and send out personally written letters to the right people in the right places. Business Publications Limited publishes the *Advertisers' Annual* which lists trade journals etc. There should be a copy of this and other similar books in the public reference library. For example, if you are specialising in word processing services write by name to the managing director of a company which you think is likely to require such a service. State exactly what you are offering, at what price, how quickly it can be supplied and in what quantity. The letter you send will tell the potential customer a lot about you and your business. A nicely designed letterhead and logo and a well typed and well displayed letter will have far more impact than a letter sent out on a piece of tatty notepaper.

Do not overlook the Yellow Pages where anybody with a business telephone line can be listed under a specific heading. Listing is done through the local telephone operator who will connect you to the Yellow Pages sales section. It is a free service. Also free is inclusion on the Telegraph Information Service list, which requires you to send them a résumé of your work. The country's major telephone marketing service is Teledata which works 24 hours a day, seven days a week. Teledata charge a basic fee plus a small amount for each order negotiated through them.

To find the right market, sometimes you need to be your own travelling salesman, persuading people to buy. Try showing your product to buyers for shops (remember their huge mark-up), or rent a market stall and sell direct to the public or go to offices and demonstrate your product there. Why not arrange to give a talk on your craft or skill at a local club and then sell your wares afterwards, or organise a selling party at your house or at the home of a friend? Selling parties are becoming very popular and effective.

Frankly all these approaches take grit and backbone! You have to steel yourself to do it but once you have done it – and done it well – selling becomes second nature!

Renting a stall is a marvellous way to sell. It means that you, the house-bound worker, get a chance to meet other, usually like-minded, workers. The Women's Institute have more than 400 markets up and down the country run along business lines with efficient goods control and high standards. (A list of markets can be obtained from WI headquarters.) The Rural Crafts Association also runs markets, and most towns have craft centres and marketplaces where it is possible to rent stalls at a reasonable rate and sell direct to the public. Ask at your nearest Citizens' Advice Bureau or local Social Services Department.

Free advice on marketing abounds. There are books on the subject and information centres that will advise, as will the Marketing Society, the Institute of Marketing and the Market Research Society.

Whatever it is that you are selling, you will always have to keep jogging the public's memory. If it is linked to a certain time of year, like Christmas or summer, Ascot or winter, make sure that you are circulating samples or information about it six months beforehand, so that buyers have enough time to estimate demand and place their orders. It also gives you time to make the goods!

Warning: Make sure that every claim you make about your product or service is true, to the best of your knowledge and belief. You can be prosecuted under the Trades Descriptions Act if those claims are not true.

Packaging

Your product will probably need to be packaged, unless it is something huge like a boat or a model steam engine. Presentation is very important and it is worth spending time surveying the wholesale packaging companies in your vicinity (see the Yellow Pages) and designing your packaging to suit your market. If you make face creams from natural products, for example, your packaging must reflect health and purity and you could use natural colours and rough spun materials. If it is something very functional and streamlined, then wrap it accordingly. There are books on package design and magazines on packaging (*Packaging News* and *Packaging Review*) which give guidelines if you are at a loss for inspiration!

You must present your product with flair. If the customer does not like it you must develop an ability to survive disappointment. You cannot force anybody to buy something they do not want or do not like.

Getting paid

When you sell goods or a service either the customer will pay you there and then, in which case give a receipt, or you must send the customer an invoice. Receipt and invoice pads can be bought from a stationer's; keep a copy for yourself. Invoicing should present no problem provided you have kept an accurate record. It is very important to keep a list of everything you have spent on a project, together with a note of the length of time you have spent doing it. Keep a book listing your outgoings and expenses and also what you are paid for each transaction.

Most people pay their bills within about six weeks. Others are not so prompt and you will have to send a statement. If the statement has no effect, firmer steps have to be taken.

Valerie, who runs a small printing concern from her back room, has cracked this problem of non-payment: *'I send out a formal letter saying that if payment is not received within x days I will put the matter in the hands of my solicitor. They have, officially, been warned. If they still don't pay, my solicitor sends a fixed fee letter demanding the money and then they usually pay up. The one that didn't I sued successfully through the County Court.'*

The fixed fee letter is exactly that: a solicitor's letter sent to the errant customer for a fixed fee. It is not necessary if one intends to take legal action anyway. A citizen with a small claim can sue and defend actions through the County Courts without the help of a solicitor. These courts are concerned with private disputes and are quite separate from Magistrates' Courts and Crown Courts. They publish an excellent guide on DIY sueing (available from County Courts and some Citizens' Advice Bureaux) and normally it is quite straightforward to sue this way. If you win, it costs you nothing; if you lose, you are not footing the solicitor's bill. Either way, you will come out of the experience a slightly tougher person – possibly a good thing if you are still learning how to cope with your own affairs in the working world. Remember, nobody would let *you* get away with not paying a bill!

DOWN TO REAL BUSINESS
Rules And Regulations

Small businesses run from home are, like any company large or small, subject to a mass of rules and regulations and you should be aware of those affecting employees, tax, national insurance, pensions etc.

Your status

Before embarking on your project, decide whether you want to go it alone, whether you need to find a partner and whether you will have to employ people to help you if and when business expands. Sometimes joining forces with others on a cooperative or complementary basis makes more sense than struggling along on your own. These decisions are very personal. One person might be escaping from the staff problems he or she experienced in a former office job and sees taking on a secretary as stepping back onto the treadmill. Another person might find that operating within a self-starting or already established group of workers is the most sensible way to produce the best. In these self-help or cooperative groups the individual workers share the administrative work, complement each other's skills and at the same time learn new ones.

You have various alternatives.

You may choose to become a sole trader and to work alone. The difference between being a sole trader and simply being yourself is that you can choose to work (or trade) under a name other than your own. Jo Smith, who knits, might prefer to be known as Jolly Jumpers, and this is perfectly possible provided that she complies with a general statutory duty to divulge her name and address, thus protecting the customers.

In the past, anyone who traded under a name that was not their own had to register with the Registrar of Business Names so that the name and address of the owner could be traced. In February 1982 the Registrar of Business Names was abolished and replaced by a general statutory duty to divulge the owner's name and an address within the UK where the service of a document would be effective. This means that if you choose to operate under a name that is not your own you must display your name and address on all your business stationery – letterheads, orders for goods and services, invoices and receipts, and debt payment demands. You are also required to display your name and address prominently in the place where you do business, and to give your name and address, in writing if necessary, to customers and suppliers when demanded. The London Chamber of Commerce is now running a Business Register, but registration is simply for convenience and is voluntary – and you are charged a fee.

Sole traders are personally liable for all their business debts, so if you go bankrupt, the creditors can claim all your personal possessions.

Alternatively, you could form a partnership with one or two friends, but ensure that the relevant partnership documents are drawn up by an impartial lawyer. All the members of a partnership are personally liable for its debts, even if these are run up by one partner's mismanagement unbeknown to the others. You no longer register the name of the partnership with the Registrar of Business Names, instead the same statutory duty to give names and addresses applies.

Both sole traders and partnerships have attractive tax relief.

You could also form a limited company and you may like to consult the Department of Industry's Small Firms Information Service for advice. A limited liability company is of benefit to those who are in a bigger league than the average small-timer beavering away at home. A limited company costs a fee to set up and must be registered with the Registrar of Companies at Companies House. This can be done through an accountant or a solicitor. You will have either to pay yourself a salary or take money out of your company in the form of dividends. The law requires you to submit annual returns and audited accounts to the Registrar of Companies. You should bear in mind that even fairly straightforward accounts are expenive to audit. You no longer have quite the same tax relief advantages as before and profits are subject to Corporation Tax, but you are saved the risk of personal bankruptcy. The company's assets, not yours, would be grabbed by the creditors should your business fail. Obviously, it would be advisable to form a limited company if the financial risks were high.

What you ought to know

National Insurance: As soon as you start being self-employed and earn more than the odd pound here and there you should visit your DHSS office to sort out your stamps. They are your responsibility and you pay Class 2, a flat weekly rate of £3.75 (in 1982/83), *and* Class 4, which is at present 6% of your profits between £3,450 and £11,000 each year. Class 4 is payable by men under 65 and women under 60 and is collected by the taxman at the end of the year, so put it aside. It is possible to apply for exemption from Class 2 contributions if your gross annual earnings are (or are likely to be) below a certain amount (£1,600 in 1982/83). Otherwise you will have to get a card from the social security office and stick on your stamp each week (or arrange for direct debit from bank or giro account). You get no unemployment benefit and only minimal sickness benefit. To help you through the maze, the DHSS issues leaflets NI.141 – *National Insurance guide for the Self-employed*, NI.27A – *People with Small Earnings from Self-employment* and NI.208 – *National Insurance Contribution Rates.*

You may find that you are entitled to some state benefits because your income is low or because you have dependants and the DHSS leaflet FB.2 – *Which Benefit?* expands on this.

Pensions: If you intend to remain self-employed you should consider putting as much money as you can into a private pension plan because the State is not going to look after you very well in your old age. While the rest of the working population is entitled to two pensions, the basic pension plus an earnings-related pension, the self-employed only qualify for the former – which is considerably less than the national average wage. *Self-Employed Pensions*, a handbook from the magazine *Money Management*, lists 90 pension plans and details the circumstances they suit best. Pensioners receiving retirement pension can earn, as a right, a limited amount set at regular intervals by the Government without losing the benefit.

Tax: The self-employed are taxed under Schedule D. This system allows you to claim tax relief on your running expenses, which you cannot do as an employee paying PAYE. It is perfectly possible to be self-employed and to work solely for one person or company. There is a simple way to tell whether you are truly self-employed or whether you should be an employee. If you have a contract *of service* and you work *under supervision, direction and control* and are paid on an hourly basis then you are an employee and should be paying tax through the PAYE system; if you have a contract *for services* and charge a fee then you are self-employed. Only if the dividing line is very faint will the fact that you work for one person affect your status.

A single person can normally earn up to a specified amount without paying tax. As soon as you start working for yourself you should let your local tax office know, and a convenient way to do this is to ask the Inland Revenue for their excellent pamphlet *Starting in Business* (IR.28) which includes a copy of form 41G, the one needed to inform the Inspector of Taxes of your new status. This pamphlet gives all details on self-employed tax, etc. From Day One start keeping your accounts in order because you are going to have to submit annual accounts to the Inspector giving details of your trading profit. Keep a note of your income and expenditure and keep all your invoices and receipts. (It's a demanding but not impossible task; many people prefer to use an accountant to keep their accounts in order for tax purposes.)

Wives earning money in a self-employed capacity will find that their husbands normally have to pay the tax due on their gains. They can choose to have their earnings taxed separately and should apply jointly to do this six months before or not later than 12 months after the end of the relevant tax year.

VAT: This depends on your anticipated turnover. If it is in excess of a stipulated amount you will have to register with HM Customs and Excise for value added tax. They issue a fully-explanatory leaflet – *Should I Be Registered for VAT?* (700/1/81). Some goods and services are exempt from VAT, othes are zero-rated and the rest are taxed at a specified rate. If you are registered, you can usually claim back some of the VAT charged to you for materials etc.

Insurance: If you are working at home to make a profit then you should check your household insurance policy and step up the fire, theft and damage cover if necessary. Ask your insurance broker for advice on the following and their application to you:

Permanent health – should you be unable to work for a few months through sickness or accident.

Public liability – should somebody have something happen to them, like break a leg, on your premises or due to your equipment.

Product liability – should someone be poisoned by the food bought from you or be electrocuted by the burglar-alarm kit sold by you.

Motor liability – your existing policy probably only covers you for domestic use.

Employer's liability – compulsory if you employ anybody (except your family), to cover bodily injury and/or disease.

Employing others: You should apply to the local authority for planning permission if you want to employ one or more people to work for you in your home. Permission may be refused, in which case you can appeal against the ruling. The Planning Department may issue you with a licence to work at home and to employ one other person. (See page 37).

If you intend to employ somebody to work for you for more that 16 hours a week, once they have been with you for more than 13 weeks you will have to draw up a letter of appointment or a contract of employment. They are both legally binding provided they state all the terms and conditions of employment – rate of pay per day, hours of work plus terms and conditions, holidays and holiday pay, sick pay, pension and pension schemes, job title, notice periods on both sides, grievance procedures and any disciplinary rules relating to the job. The Wages Council or the Low Pay Unit will advise on the minimum legal wage allowed – although, as a self-employed person yourself employing other self-employed persons, you should play fair and pay a decent wage for services!

As the employer, you must pay employer's National Insurance contributions to the Inland Revenue and deduct the employee's contributions and tax from the wages you pay. An employee of pensionable age is no longer liable to make NI contributions, and some married women have reduced contribution cards. The employer must deal with tax under the PAYE scheme.

Outworkers or homeworkers, however, are not employees. They are classed as casual labour and are responsible for their own tax. However, there is a campaign to have all homeworkers classified employees by law. The way the law stands at the moment, if a homeworker has been working solely for one person or company for several years and the flow of work dries up the homeworker will find that, as he (or she) has been self-employed, he is not entitled to unemployment benefit, redundancy payments etc. That person can appeal through a Citizens' Advice Bureau or Legal Advice Centre and may learn that in his particular case all the 'tests of employment' apply – ie hourly rate, working under supervision, direction and control and under a contract of service – and he can, by law, be retrospectively reclassified as an employee. This obviously can mean serious repercussions for the 'employer' who had not realised his position and will not have issued the statutory warnings of termination of employment or paid employer's National Insurance contributions etc. In some cases, people have found themselves taken to an Industrial Tribunal and required to reinstate the employee or make redundancy payments, back payments of Class 1 National Insurance contributions, etc.

An employer is obliged by law to take out an approved insurance policy to cover bodily injury and/or disease during the course of the employee's employment (see page 32).

The Health and Safety Executive provides a short guide to the Employer's Liability (Compulsory Insurance) Act, the local tax office will issue the *Employer's Guide to PAYE* and the local social security office has an *Employer's Guide to National Insurance Contributions*.

There is however a simpler way round the complex labyrinth of responsibilities and regulations: employ people who already work on a freelance basis (ie they retain their self-employed status and pay their own tax and NI contributions), or enlist members of your own family, who can be recompensed in kind or be paid at a level below the minimum for tax and National Insurance. The second approach might arouse suspicion when the authorities check up on you and your business so do find out exactly what is permitted and what is not. Obviously paying a relative 50p less than the minimum needed to qualify for National Insurance contributions would be asking for investigation!

Who you ought to know

There are always people and organisations you ought to know about who could help to smooth the path of progress. You might never need to call on them but it pays to get advice, even if you have to pay for it!

A friendly bank manager: If your own savings can't stretch to financing your endeavour try your bank manager for a loan. If he turns you down it's always worth trying another bank. Banks have become more receptive to lending money to individuals and small concerns since they discovered that small businesses form one of the central pillars of the economy. When asking for a loan make your case clearcut: state why you need the money, what you are going to do with it and

how you are going to repay it. The National Westminster Bank has issued a guide for those who ask for financial aid. In brief, it says you should present a sound proposition well. That means a watertight workability report delivered by a person offering facts and figures, not shrugs and grins! In any event, you *should* open a separate account for your earnings, not just to keep home money and work money separate but to boost your morale as well.

Warning: Avoid at all costs being taken in by outfits offering special loans at 'special' rates. If your bank can't help you they will be able to offer advice on specialised help.

If you borrow money, you will have to pay interest and conform to the terms of the creditor. You will probably be asked to provide some security like shares, a life insurance policy, or possibly your house.

A good accountant: If you are going to earn enough to pay tax and run a small but successful concern, an accountant will know how to get the best for you out of the tax system, and will advise you on how to keep the books. (He might even know of a backer for you!) It is important to find an accountant who understands the problems of the self-employed and, if possible, your specific business. Make sure he's registered with the Institute of Chartered Accountants or the Association of Certified Accountants. If you can't find an accountant through personal recommendation, you can always ask those two bodies to advise.

A nearby solicitor: You might never

need a solicitor's services but what will you do if your custom-built product blows a fuse and the roof off your house (or the purchaser's house) and you are not insured? A solicitor will also help you to get planning permission if you need to change the use of part of your home, and also help with contracts etc. The Law Society will recommend a solicitor in your area.

Assorted advisers: Many counselling and 'help' services have been set up by the Government and other agencies.

The Department of Industry runs the Small Firms Information Service which is willing to help you whether you are making next to nothing or have a small business with a big turnover. They'll help you with queries on tax, VAT, National Insurance, raising capital, and training. They have a selection of leaflets for further information and also specialists for counselling. There are Small Firms Information Centres in all major cities in Britain.

In rural areas there is the Council for Small Industries in Rural Areas (CoSIRA) which has the facilities to help with counselling, training and even finding finance and premises.

The National Federation of Self-Employed spends a great deal of time fighting for rights for the self-employed and is marvellously helpful. Members are automatically insured when they join to cover accountants' fees of up to £1,500 if they find themselves subject to a Revenue investigation, and a full professional advice service is given if they are ever faced with an Industrial Tribunal. The Federation will pay a substantial part of any award should members follow the advice, still get taken to the Tribunal and then lose the case. They will also pay up to £10,000 worth of lawyers' fees if any of their members get into trouble with the Customs and Excise (VAT) or Health and Safety at Work regulations. They also help in connection with motoring problems as they are the first to appreciate that a van or car can be vital to the success of a small business.

The Alliance of Small Firms and Self-Employed People (ASP) was formed to keep the self-employed out of trouble and offers not only advice but legal aid and insurance schemes too.

The Cooperative Development Agency (CDA) exists to promote cooperatives. It is an advisory body, carrying out feasibility studies and helping to find finance. Church Action with the Unemployed and the Industrial Common Ownership Movement also offer advice.

Your local Citizens' Advice Bureau is a good place to start from if you are not quite sure what you should be enquiring about!

People with money: Raising money is often the toughest hurdle to leap. If the bank has refused you, other sources of capital may be available in the form of development grants and loans from public bodies. Your library or Town Hall should know of the local ones. The Chancellor of the Exchequer recently launched the Business Opportunities Programme and the Loan Guarantee Scheme to regenerate and create small businesses. The London Enterprise Agency, backed by a consortium of large companies, encourages small businesses in the inner city area of London. Industrial and Commercial Finance Corporation Ltd (ICFC) was established by the Bank of England to put long-term money into small businesses and it has area offices throughout the country. The Department of the Environment has formed Enterprise Zones with varying benefits to attract new businesses.

The law and working from home

Although you are unlikely to have interference from the law if you are running a small, discreet business concern you should know how you could be affected, what your rights are, when you should fight and what the legal remedies are. Consult a Citizens' Advice Bureau, who will be able to point you in the right direction should you fall foul of the law.

As already stated, your working plans must be discussed with your landlord if you live in rented accommodation, or your housing officer if you live in a Council house.

Planning permission: Planning legislation is fairly standard throughout England and Wales but there are minor variations in interpretation from local authority to local authority. It is complicated and affects most people who make money working at home.

You may need planning consent if you want to alter the outside of your property, but you may not need it if the alterations do not affect the front of the building or add more than 75 square metres (760 sq ft) to the floor area. However, structural alterations must have building regulations approval, or byelaw approval if you live in London, before you carry out any work.

The planning law requires you to apply for permission to change the use of your dwelling or property from residential to business. The dividing line between residential and business is set by the local authority and there are usually no restrictions on jobs or hobbies that earn you pin money. In many cases it is difficult to differentiate between a profitable hobby and a form of business. Obviously, if you want to erect an aerial on your roof to run your minicab business or if you plan to fill your garden or yard with motorcars awaiting repair, then permission must be sought. Employing people to work for you in your home will probably mean you require planning permission, and so can erecting signboards advertising you and your goods or service.

Most planning authorities have a policy aimed at preventing people turning their homes into offices and it is a sad fact that the majority of people who apply for permission to change the use of part of their home from domestic to office or workroom are turned down. If, in fact, consent is given, you should remember that the rateable value of your house and the amount you pay in the pound will be increased. There is one rate for domestic use, one for commercial and one in a range for properties which fall between these two uses. When you come to sell, if you were successful in your application for change of use, a proportion of the profit will be subject to capital gains tax.

Clearly, the planning authorities are in a position to dash your dreams of success. Happily, they usually turn a blind eye to people working at home but if there is a steady stream of delivery vans or customers to your front door, or if the sound of your knitting machine or typewriter clatters on late into the night then the neighbours might complain. Once the authorities receive a complaint they must take action. However, if an enforcement notice is served you are entitled to apply for planning permission and appeal to the Minister if you are refused. The law is so slow that it can take up to two years before you have to stop altogether. You may be able to get a personal consent or licence from the local planning authority which will enable you to carry on with your business provided it does not get any bigger.

Most people who work from home do not apply for planning consent and simply try not to attract the attention of the planning authorities. However, if you want to play it by the book you should speak to your local Planning Department and see if they have any strong objections to the type of work being carried out in your home. Assuming that a formal application for planning permission would be turned down if you live in a residential area, you can always apply for a licence to work at home. This is granted more frequently than a full planning consent and it covers you as an individual or you plus one other person. It may limit your expansionist activities but it means the authorities are happy as the granting of a licence controls the use to which the house is put. In effect, the 'use' of the house does not change, and you may work there and also employ one person to help you.

Selling: The laws surrounding selling are varied and changeable. For example, you need a licence to sell food to the public, a pedlar's licence (available from the police station) to sell from the back of a van, and you may need a licence to sell in a street market, door to door or from your front room. Frequently the law is not enforced and it has numerous exceptions to the rule, so make sure you check this with your local authority.

Safety: If you intend to run a workshop or studio that is open to the public or involves other people (employees) 'to make, alter, repair or finish things', you should contact HM Factory Inspectorate's district inspector to inspect your premises for potential hazards. You will also have to be inspected by the Fire Officer who will check for safe fire precautions, fire fighting equipment, exits, ventilation, wiring etc. (Ask the Town Hall for details.)

Mail order: A Mail Order Protection Scheme is run by the Newspaper Publishers' Association to cover consumers who buy through mail order advertising. They publish a free leaflet detailing the particulars and you can obtain this from the Mail Order Secretariat. Other matters concerning mail order can be referred to the Mail Order Traders' Association.

Trading standards: If you want to know where you stand when you buy or sell anything, read *Fair Deal – a Shopper's Guide*, issued by the Office of Fair Trading and available through the Trading Standards Department of your local authority. It details the rights of consumers and the duties of suppliers. Alternatively consult your local Citizens' Advice Bureau.

Patents: If you have invented a gadget or machine or method and want to stop others exploiting your idea, you should patent it. You have to file an application (which protects your invention for a year) which leads to

publication and granting of the patent, and you pay various small fees throughout the procedure. There are agents who will do this for you. If you wish to do it yourself, the pamphlet *Applying For A Patent* is available from The Patent Office.

Warning: Do not tell too many people about your invention or sell it before filing an application. Unscrupulous people will steal a good idea and patent it for themselves.

Bankruptcy: This is a lengthy, painful and costly procedure, so for small debts try to coerce your creditor into some alternative arrangement. Bankruptcy is very sordid. More details can be gained from the County Court or High Court. Ask your bank manager, Citizens' Advice Bureau or the Small Firms Information Service if you need help or advice.

WORKING FOR OTHERS

'... As I was saying – the benefits of double glazing are enormous ...'

Not everybody wants to, or is able to, leap in at the deep end and embark on a business venture utterly on their own. Sometimes working at home but with an 'outside' employer who will bear the responsibilities when the going gets tough can be an attractive prospect. It can also provide a bridge spanning the gap between leaving the office routine and going solo. This halfway stage can be divided into homework, which is not to be recommended except where it concerns the disabled, and freelance work. Freelance work divides loosely into two: selling or working for others on a commission basis and providing a specific service for a regular wage. There are several sectors in business where the boss will happily pay a skilled worker to operate from home instead of from the office. It is cheaper for the company as it reduces overheads, and it is more convenient for the worker. You may even be able to work for your present company from home.

Homework

A homeworker is a person over 18 who works in domestic premises, is provided with work and who returns the completed articles to the provider or to a third person. There are upwards of 150,000 homeworkers in Britain. They are usually responsible for their own tax and National Insurance contributions. Homework reeks of sweated labour and frequently involves unscrupulous outfits who expect 'a token of goodwill' (money) upfront before sending you outwork or piece-work. This often ends up as naked exploitation.

Very low wages are illegal. Although not all homework is regulated by the Wages Council, of the sections it does cover the buttonworkers are on the lowest legal minimum wage.

Low pay *is* better, admittedly, than *no* pay. Some people are prepared to work for peanuts and many feel that they earn quite well when they receive little more than £20 at the end of the week. Often this kind of work is not worth more to the employer. Light and easy work that can be done at home unsupervised includes jobs like sticking labels on boxes, grading needles, assembling watchstraps, making Christmas crackers, folding cards etc.

If you *are* considering taking on homework it is vital to assess the overheads and possible problems like storage, fumes from glue, irritant substances, noise and so on. Always read the very small print as you may find a binding clause about how you foot the bill for the whole batch if there is one jammy fingerprint or one tiny error.

Homeworkers are, in theory, protected by the Health and Safety at Work Act but they are not included in the legislation incorporated in the Employment Protection Act. There is a compaign to have all homeworkers classified employees by law, and some homeworkers who have worked for years for the same 'employer' have been retrospectively reclassified employees. (See page 33.) Sweated labour does still exist. It is the job of the Low Pay Unit, a body set up in 1974, to put pressure on the Government on behalf of homeworkers. The Low Pay Unit will tell you the legal minimum wages.

Sewing and Knitting Employment agencies do not handle outwork but the local newspaper does. In the advertisements section employers are crying out for knitters and machinists. If you take on knitting or sewing outwork, beware of the employer who tries to persuade you to buy the necessary machine; any employer worth his reputation should supply one. Try to find out how much work there will be, how often you can expect it, and whether the firm will deliver the materials and collect the finished work. If not, make sure, your travel expenses are reimbursed. Bear in mind that it could cost you a lot to run an industrial sewing or knitting machine and that running costs come out of your pay. The Environmental Health Department or the Planning Department might step in and consider you to be a nuisance to the neighbourhood if the machine is too noisy, or if they regard the use of machinery in your house as 'development'.

There is a legal minimum wage set by the Wages Council for women's light clothing workers. Try to find work through a friend's recommendation if you are new to the game.

Most important: watch out for fly-by-night companies. These are usually un-unionised, unregistered and bad, bad payers.

Brenda recently started homeworking for a huge multi-national company machining skirts for 35p each: *'The recruiter told me that top machinists manage three skirts an hour and I reckoned I was pretty good, having worked as a machinist for 20 years. But I never made the three an hour mark.'* Instead she now sews collars for coats and can do 40 an hour which earns her more. She is happy with her lot. Her employer has installed an industrial machine at her home, delivers and collects daily and pays her 10% of her average weekly wage when the factory closes down for a two week annual break each year. *'At the end of the week I take out spending money from my pay packet, put a percentage of every pound away for tax, and keep a list of overheads for the accountant to claim off tax.'*

Rose replied to an advertisement for an experienced knitter: *'Someone came and left some wool with me and said they wanted an amazing Aran stitch jumper knitted for £3.50. Working every evening after the babies were asleep, it took a week to knit, about 20 hours for £3.50 (about 17½p an hour).'*

Typing Advertisements in local newspapers sometimes read 'Earn Up to £xxx A Week – working at home spare-time, no experience required'. Those who write off for details usually receive a printed letter saying that it is possible to earn less than half that amount by writing addresses and mailing commission circulars 'in just a few hours a week *if* a small fee is sent to cover administrative costs'. And they would then send the first work parcel...

Helen, on retiring from being a secretary at board level, bought herself a typewriter and took on some envelope and label typing work which was advertised in her local paper. The rate was not much more than ½p an address. Although many of the addresses were written in illegible handwriting, she managed to streamline her system to produce 100 envelopes an hour. She had to pay for wear and tear of the typewriter, new ribbons, lighting and heat ...

There is no legal minimum wage for typing and there is very little you can do about exploitation. A small advertisement placed by you in the same paper offering your typing services for manuscripts, theses, letters, scripts etc would earn you far, far more.

Homework and the Disabled

REMPLOY (parent body, The Manpower Services Commission) has five homeworking units dotted around the country (in London, Barking, Birmingham, Bristol and Perth) which organise homework of the light assembly and packaging kind for the housebound. Wages are based on an hourly rate and interpreted on piece-rate, so you are paid on results. If you are registered disabled and want to find out more, contact REMPLOY or the local job centre.

If you are disabled and on social security, anything earned over a few pounds a week will mean that the allowance is reduced on a pro rata basis. If you are entitled to invalid or sickness benefits, you need special permission from the DHSS plus a letter from your doctor saying that work would be therapeutic. You can then earn more a week without losing the benefits. If you are registered as being unemployed, special permission from the Manpower Services Commission is required. The only benefits that remain with you through thick and thin are the mobility allowance, war pension and, hopefully, your spirits!

Direct Sales

The Direct Selling Association will send you a list of their members (there are more than two dozen including Kleeneze, Pippa Dee Parties and Tupperware), all of which manufacture products and distribute direct to consumers in their homes. The Association also prints one code of practice for sellers and one for buyers in order to combat malpractices in direct selling. Direct selling is becoming an increasingly popular form of retail distribution. Buying guaranteed products in the comfort and convenience of your home or somebody else's home makes sense, and being a direct sales representative is very much a matter of being your own boss and reaping financial crops in direct proportion to your sales.

If you want to become a selling party organiser you should go along to a party and talk to the organiser. No experience is needed but it helps to have a welcoming, gregarious nature and a wide circle of friends and contacts. Most of the direct sales companies will give you a brief training, lasting only a few hours, and help you with your first few parties. They issue you with the goods, you collect the payment on sales and receive a commission.

A couple of good parties a week could bring in the equivalent of about five or six hours' work.

Suzanne works as a freelance salesperson for a home care products manufacturer. She expands on another aspect of direct selling: *'Apart from selling the goods one can also sponsor and train others to sell. I find this side of the business really challenging – helping people to reach their full potential. For someone with drive and ambition it is quite possible to make substantial headway – and a lot of money.'*

With some small items, for example Avon cosmetics, selling is done door-to-door. Each person is allocated about 100 houses to canvas, from which around 30 customers are gleaned. Armed with a bag of samples and pamphlets, you take down the orders and then deliver the goods and collect the money when the manufacturer has supplied them to you.

Barbara, who says she would have died of boredom if she hadn't gone out on the road with Avon, has been door-to-door selling for a few months: *'The selling season for cosmetics is bad in summer and very good before Christmas. I alternate my selling approach. Either I go out and sell in the evenings or I do a weekly blitz. I only put in about 15 hours a week. I could put in far more time – the only drawback I can see is that it entails a lot of walking in all weathers. Your customers like you to be reliable, come rain or shine. On the days you deliver the goods and collect the cash, I think it is a good idea to have somebody accompany you. People in the neighbourhood quickly learn how you operate. For me, the ultimate highspot is seeing just how much I can sell – with persuasion! I've certainly become much more of an extrovert, and also more strongwilled because it's very hard not to spend what you make on Avon products on yourself!'*

Barbara paid a small fee for the right to sell Avon's goods. They gave her a bag with a few samples to start her off, and little by little she purchased the full range of samples to use for demonstration purposes. Orders are then bought from Avon, who give you 30% commission (minus VAT), which Barbara reckons works out at about 22% commission. *'The first few weeks were nerve-wracking! I'd never gone knocking on doors before. I lost pounds (of weight) in anxiety!'*

Judith, in contrast, prefers to run an agency from her garage selling carpets for a local mill. Agencies are pretty common and most large companies producing suitable commodities will consider ventures like this. *'I keep a dozen different carpets in stock and a three foot high pile of samples. I advertise through the local newspaper, and in good weeks I make quite a bit on the 6–10% commission. The time I spend on selling varies by the customer – they always ring up very early in the morning or very late at night and want to see the goods immediately! You quickly learn not to arrange your life around the carpets! I claim postage and advertising from the mill, and charge the customers for delivery. One can usually find this sort of agency job in the newspaper, but you should 'phone round to check if it's legit.'*

Mail Order

This is a hard way to make money: the agent gets only 10% of the sales (or the equivalent of 12.5% if you take your cut in goods). However, more and more people are buying from catalogues nowadays and the reason is twofold: it is convenient to receive the goods on the doorstep, and you pay in weekly instalments.

Agents are paid commission by the mail order firm on the orders they send in and, time permitting, can be agents for more than one mail order firm (keep the accounts separate) to broaden their field of sales.

By writing to a mail order company or by filling in coupons found in some newspapers or circulars which are pushed under the door, you can join the mail order ranks. The Mail Order Traders' Association has a list of members and a code of practice, and is there to take up any complaints. The two main catalogue firms are Littlewoods and Great Universal Stores, each of which have six different name catalogues under their wings. The firm provides the stationery and the catalogue and delivers to you the items you order (although big, bulky orders might go direct to the buyer). You are responsible for chivvying the buyers into making their weekly payments and you are expected to pay the weekly amounts to the mail order firm regularly. There is, thankfully, a service for taking action against customers who get into arrears or become difficult!

Warning: have goods and money in safekeeping at your home between deliveries, payments, etc. Make sure your premises are both safe and suitably insured.

Selling Over the 'Phone

Being a telephone salesperson – ringing old customers and finding new ones – is probably the most flexible job for the truly housebound person who is not inclined to make cakes or sew curtains from home. Dubbed as the 'Rent A Married Woman Scheme', many concerns have found it cheaper by far to appoint a person with a nice telephone manner to drum up interest in the firm (so that one of their reps can then pay the interested party a visit) than to maintain a squad of road reps who would have to drive round the country looking for business.

Judy started being a telephone rep for a hygiene-in-industry company in order to raise funds for Christmas presents, but found the hourly rate and the commission for each call that resulted in a rep visiting the interested party was alluring: *'I was sent on a telephone training course, which taught me how to deal with uncooperative switchboard operators, how to evoke interest, arrange meetings, tailor needs, sound convincing and handle "funny" conversations. I find it very stimulating to sidestep irrelevant questions and talk people through something they think they're basically uninterested in, and win them over! I work eight hours a week and can cover up to 100 companies! The firm I work for gives me a list and lets me do as much as I like. They pay postage and a fee per telephone unit, which I calculate myself. The only frustration is when the person you need to contact isn't available and you have to keep on trying them because you always call them back. You never give your number!'*

If this sort of work interests you, contact Sales Force Ltd. They work nationally and will put you on their books for work in your area.

Computer Work

Computer work is one of the few jobs management actually encourages people to do at home, but you have to be an experienced computer person with at least three years' experience behind you.

Off-site computer work includes jobs for systems analysts, software designers, datapreps, technical authors and programmers. Major concerns are tending to expand their off-site workforces – it saves on overheads. British Telecom's normal telephone lines link special terminal systems to large computers etc, and all the equipment is usually provided. The pay is excellent.

The British Computer Society has information and advice on computer work.

Micro-computers

Micro-computing is quite simple and can be learnt at home from books. You do not need qualifications or a lot of experience to do this work.

Jan does programming and data input on a micro-computer she has at home. She feels the secretarial and accounting sides of small businesses could be developed greatly if people realised that micro-computers were as simple as they are to operate: *'It's like sitting in front of a typewriter. I have a small one which was very easy to instal. I just plug it in and off I go! You need to know what goes where, which is something one acquires in a week's training. For programming, it is possible to teach yourself but you need a micro-computer, lots of time, and knowledge of the particular subject to programme it properly. There are courses at polytechnics and evening classes.*

Data input, by contrast, is a fairly young industry. In basic terms this is typing to screen and then storing the data on diskettes.

Before thinking about microcomputer work read magazines like Which Computer? *and* Practical Computing *and, if you feel confident, go round dealers and small businesses asking for work. You need a regular market to recoup costs and make money.'*

She added that one of the added delights of having a microcomputer installed at home was showing her two children, aged five and seven, how to play games on it!

Corsets

Archaic as it might sound, corsets are still with us, and corset manufacturers still need agents: women who measure customers and send off the specifications. The agents then buy the finished item at a wholesale rate to sell to the customer at whatever mark-up they choose.

Most people don't need more than one corset a year so to make money you have to advertise your service extensively. The firm will send you promotion material on their garments (bras, girdles, corselets and other foundation wear) and an initial supply of garments for display purposes. You will need a warm, clean room in your home for fittings.

Corset agent jobs are advertised locally when the manufacturers need somebody in a particular area. They train you for about two days a week for three weeks for a refundable fee and they supply you with stationery, promotion material and display wear. The job can become quite interesting if you make the effort to read up a little on health matters to add to the customer–agent relationship!

For further details you should write to the Corsetry Manufacturers' Association.

Distributing

If you have strong shoes, long legs and like the great outdoors, distributing coupons and samples will present no problems. It takes no experience, you work your own hours (when the kids are at school) in a defined area and slip whatever it is through the letterboxes of the houses on your patch. The only hassle, apart from the rain, is the dogs!

A contractor with a car will deliver the items for distribution, and there is usually a fixed (not high) sum for each round. For jobs look in the Yellow Pages under Circular and Sample Distributors and also in your local paper.

Invigilating

Invigilating can either be carried out in a large hall overseeing dozens of examinees or on a one-to-one basis in a pupil's home, for example for the Open University. It is not possible to find regular work, but invigilating is pleasant to do.

June has been invigilating on and off for years. *'We used to have to be post-graduates and wear gowns but now authorities are much less fussy. They tell you what to look out for, and as long as you keep your eyes open and are alert you can spend up to three happy hours reading a good book or doing your own work. The pay per session is moderate, but you are also paid travel costs. Try to avoid shoes that clatter – it's too awful if you have to clatter all the way down a huge hall to attend to a student,* and *back again!'*

For invigilation work get yourself on the Open University and local university and colleges lists.

Market Research

Although virtually everything is now computerised, there is still no substitute for a person with a pen, clipboard and questionnaire who collars respondees on draughty street corners or in crowded shopping malls.

Designed to provide detailed findings of public opinions on products, people and talkpoints, market research is, as the man from National Opinion Polls said, 'the talking to all sides of society on all kinds of topics!' It can be done to research a sales angle or for the purpose of population surveys, to find out which is the most popular television programme or the least popular political party.

You need tenacity and a fairly thick skin combined with great speed when approaching people – it is so easy to lose your interviewee!

Payment is based on an hourly rate, on the number of completed questionnaires or for the assignment as a whole.

For more details approach the Market Research Society, who publish a booklet listing their member firms who employ free-lances. You could also approach your local BBC and ITV offices for audience research work or the Office of Population Censuses and Surveys for social survey work.

School-crossing Attendant

You need to like children and be an impeccable time-keeper to be a Lollipop Person. The job applies, rain or shine, during termtime only. You have to pass a medical and be under 74.

It seems that there's a constant shortage of people wanting to do this job. Ask at the local police station for details and they will find you a crossing as near as possible to your home.

Somebody's Secretary from Home

There is a thriving population of secretaries whose bosses preferred to keep them on, working from home, when they would otherwise have left their jobs to start a family. The secretary who has done specialist work and knows the office ropes is invaluable. It is by no means impossible to create a working system whereby tapes, letters and files are dropped off at your home and collected later, and the boss's telephone is linked with yours at home. This way the boss knows that the system, which the secretary often knows more about than the boss, will not be disrupted.

Susan was secretary to an MP until she had to leave her job at Westminster to have her first child. She is, however, still his secretary: *'I'm lucky because my boss lives nearby and drops in once a day to give me dictation and sign the letters. His post is redirected to me, and he gives people who want to contact him my 'phone number. Sometimes I take dictation over the telephone, which can be difficult if the baby's crying or there's something going on at home, but now that most people know that I work for him from home they accept the background noises. For me, it works exceptionally well. I am well paid for doing a day's work, which I organise to suit myself. I keep my desk and filing cabinet at the bottom of our L-shaped lounge so I'm part of the house but not "in" it.'*

To work this way, you should sit down with your boss and discuss the pros and cons. If you are worth your salt, you'll win your case!

AGENCIES

'So that's Flo and Maisie to Woburn – and Mrs. Nibbs to no. 14, Lobelia Ave ..'

○ All agencies concerned with employment have to have a licence from the Department of Employment (renewable each year on inspection). Your agency must also have the blessing of the local authority, and they can have it closed if they feel that the constant stream of people visiting you is causing a nuisance to your neighbours.

○ If your agency is going to issue contracts, make sure you get comprehensive legal advice in the drafting of them. Any agency dealing with people who work for others should have a professional indemnity insurance policy against accidents.

○ You must display your name and address (if different from that of the agency) on all stationery and also on a notice visible to the public.

○ On a more personal front, running an agency from home will often mean an intrusion into your private life; clients tend to collect and deliver work or drop in to make enquiries at all hours of the day and night because they know you will be at home. Most agencies are full-time commitments.

○ You will possibly need to install a separate telephone line and doorbell. Be prepared to keep accounts and timesheets, pay salaries and wages and extract payments from clients, unless you employ an assistant to take over that side of the business.

○ In agency work contacts are your most important asset so it is well worth your while to cultivate them!

○ Your fees should include overheads, stock and stationery, as well as your time.

○ Anticipate using two rooms, one as a waiting room, so that you can cope with more than one client arriving at the same time.

○ See Contacts for addresses and reference books.

Accommodation Agency

Accommodation is always in demand, especially in university and tourist towns and places with seasonal events, such as the Edinburgh Festival, when the city is bursting with tourists and theatrical folk.

Find the accommodation by looking at advertisements in local newspapers, and by making enquiries in the area. Slip a 'Dear Landlord' letter into the letterboxes of houses and flats in the vicinity, explaining your service and stating that your charges for selecting the tenant, taking up references and drawing up the letting contract will be the equivalent of one or two weeks' rent.

One successful accommodation bureau in London states: 'We have always suitable applicants registered who are looking for accommodation. We let to a very wide range of people – professional, students, companies and overseas visitors. They require bedsitters, flatlets, studios, self-contained flats and houses.'

Try to see each property yourself, and make a note of exactly what facilities are available. Remember the reputation of your agency rests on recommending suitable accommodation, so try to provide a personal service matching individual clients to the different rooms on your books. The more landlords you can find the better, as it gives you more choice and you are under no financial obligation to the landlord. When you place a tenant make sure that there is a satisfactory agreement drawn up between landlord and tenant. (Ask a solicitor to help you.)

Inspecting the accommodation means that you will be out and about quite a bit, which is ideal if you like to go out and meet people and you can choose the hours to fit in with your commitments at home. If the agency turns into a flourishing business, it could be worth installing a telephone answering machine. Otherwise you need very little in the way of an office or space, simply a desk and a telephone and a good filing system.

Advertise for tenants in newspapers, what's-on type weekly magazines, colleges, embassies (short-term foreign tenants can be far more appealing than possible sitting tenants who have no plans to leave the country, let alone the premises) and travel agencies.

Once the ball gets rolling, expect a good profit margin.

Au Pair Agency

Apparently the British have the reputation of treating au pairs better than other countries. Consequently there is a constant stream of foreign girls waiting to enter Britain to work as au pairs and to learn the language.

Agencies are needed to place these girls, under the supervision of the Department of Employment. Agents have to be licensed and they are inspected annually by the Department, which keeps a record of every licensed agency in the country. Au pair employers have to adhere to stipulated wages, hours and provisions concerning the girls, and the girls themselves have to conform to certain regulations concerning Common Market status. Any complaint about an agency or from an agency is referred to the Department, which acts as arbiter.

Before you can begin business there is considerable groundwork to be done. Interviewers (or agents) have to be found abroad (through contacts or au pair agencies there) to deal with candidates so that the agency knows what it is getting. Girls should have references, a clean bill of mental and physical health (there have been many reports of au pairs coming to England to take advantage of the National Health Service), a modicum of English and, if possible, some experience with children. The girls arrange their own transport, but no girl should come over unless there is a suitable family waiting. As the agent, you will also have to interview the host family and see the home. The family should, in turn, see details and a picture of the au pair.

A two-week trial period is standard among good agents, with a refund or replacement in cases where the arrangement fails. Keep an eye on families who regularly complain about au pairs, and don't do business with families if you are suspicious of them. As agent you are morally obliged to the au pair and to the family, but remember that the au pair is on foreign ground and will turn to you for help – expect to have the occasional unhappy au pair sleeping in your spare room from time to time!

Agents charge the family a set fee for their services, and the law now allows them to take a smaller fee from the au pair as well.

Beware of the temptation to place dozens of girls to make money instead of giving each match your personal attention. This liaison work can easily operate two ways by sending British girls out to countries where you have links with other au pair agencies. In all these transactions, it obviously helps if you speak some foreign languages.

Advertise in magazines like *The Lady*, and in areas where families are likely to want an au pair.

Building Repairs Agency

Harassed householders are constantly in need of reliable people to repair burst pipes, broken windows, slipped tiles and burnt-out wiring, so there must be a market for a central agency co-ordinating all these services. The agent builds up a force of self-employed plumbers, electricians, carpenters, bricklayers, roofers, plasterers and so on, whose work can be vouched for and who, because they are self-employed, are able to work at short notice.

Roger, a retired architect, runs such an agency: *'I find the tradesmen through their advertisements, meet them, go and see their work and generally check them out very carefully. When clients ring me (I advertise in the local weekly newspaper) I take down their details and, that evening, contact the best man suited who is on my register. I go and look at the job to be done and hand over to the client the information I have on the tradesman, if I think he is the right person to do it. The client takes it from there. I am paid an introductory fee by the client.'*

An agency could also be operated along the lines of finding the right tradesman for the job and hiring him out at a fixed hourly rate, for which the agent takes a percentage of the total bill.

To run an agency of this type you must have some knowledge of (or at least an active interest in) the building trade. It is considered an employment agency, so the Department of Employment licence applies. It would be highly advisable to take out a professional indemnity insurance, just in case one of your tradesmen proves not to be the reliable person you thought he was.

Business Services Agency

Before embarking on a business service agency explore the staff market in your area. If it is already packed with freelance typists and book-keepers you will have to offer a wider and more specialist range of services, such as translating, legal or medical typing, mailshot writing, sorting out VAT and PAYE, typing dissertations or theses, taking minutes at meetings or operating a delivery service, depending on the skills of the people available. If there seems to be no demand for some aspects of the services you intend to offer, keep them in cold storage because as the agency grows people will be encouraged to rely on it for a wider range of requirements.

This sort of agency forms a clearing house through which temporary or part-time workers operate on an hourly basis as instructed by the agent (you), who is in contact with the customer. Fees are per hour, the agent paying the worker a set amount and receiving a larger set amount from the customer.

The regulations for this kind of agency state that temporary employees must not be prevented from taking up direct employment with the hirer should they wish (the agency is then paid a fee by the employer), and that permanent staff must not be approached in an attempt to persuade them to become temps. Your staff must always be paid, even if you have not been paid by the hirer, and they must not be asked to do the work of people on strike.

Joan runs a freelance secretarial agency. Most of the people on her books are mothers wanting to earn money while their children are at school. She started seven years ago with one telephone, and now has a telex, a word processor, photocopier and three golfball typewriters on the premises (her home) for people who prefer to work away from their own homes: *'I vet my workers very carefully and if there are more than two complaints from a client about somebody, that somebody is out! It's terribly important to keep the standard high. I try to match clients with special requirements with workers with abilities to match those requirements, and I make a huge effort to spread the word of the variety of work we offer. The latest project is to plan conferences for customers, starting from booking the hotel through to providing a high-powered secretary to take notes for the chairman.'*

Try to join professional bodies like the local Chamber of Commerce. If your agency expands into the overseas market (translators, conference facilities, bilingual secretaries, and so on), become a member of the London Tourist Board, or your local Tourist Board.

Set about finding clients in the same way as you would for an ordinary employment agency (see page 56), concentrating on businesses that are likely to require the skills you have to offer.

Domestic Cleaning Agency

Many people prefer to find domestic staff through an agency rather than take into their homes someone they know nothing about. To be able to trust a cleaner is particularly important as most domestic cleaners work alone in homes and offices when the occupants are out. Most domestic agencies also undertake to supply a replacement if one of their cleaners is ill or cannot work.

When you start your agency, you might have to go out and do some cleaning jobs yourself until the business is well enough established for you to stay at home and run it. (A telephone answering machine is therefore a very worthwhile investment.) When you advertise, mention all the domestic chores your team will tackle – including polishing silver, washing walls, cleaning carpets, scouring ovens, shampooing upholstery etc. In private homes the client provides the equipment, but for bigger contacts, like office blocks, larger industrial equipment will have to be supplied by the agency. Rates are estimated per hour, with a set fee for the agent, and the client pays the cleaner's travelling expenses.

Lindy, who is disabled, runs a domestic cleaning agency from her council flat: *'I think people doing this sort of work like doing it through an agency as it gives them a sort of identity. It's not, after all, very glamorous work. I interview thoroughly everybody who comes to find work and the ones I feel I can be responsible for go on my books. I try to keep a good selection of people available for work, from gardeners to decorators, so we can offer the fullest service. If you're advertising cleaners you may as well advertise allied jobs like gardeners!'*

This sort of agency does best in affluent areas where people are prepared to pay others to do their dirty work, or in business areas where buildings occupied all day need to be cleaned at night. There is a growing demand for cleaners and the opportunity for making a profit is definitely there.

Employment Agency

There is a lot of money to be made out of selling other people's labour. Under the terms of the Employment Agencies Act of 1973 there are three distinct employment services: an employment agency (permanent jobs), an employment business (hiring out temporary labour) and work contractors (working for a client using your own personnel).

Employment agencies fill vacancies for clients, who specify the details of the job and the sort of person they want. Often employers prefer to let an agent refer a few suitable candidates from his books for a final interview rather than spending time on advertising and answering applications, and holding interviews. If you do not have a list of suitable candidates, *you* can advertise and then sift through the applicants and interview the most suitable, finally recommending a short list to the client. If a candidate is appointed, you charge a fee based on a percentage of the recruit's starting salary.

To run an employment agency you need a good personal understanding of both workers and clients. Once an agency knows the sort of worker a client is looking for, his custom is assured. It takes a certain kind of person to extract the relevant facts from applicants. You must relate well to people, and be able to learn the art of interviewing. Ask for references and make a list of candidates' special aptitudes. Give them clear instructions about the job they are going to, and if you are in any doubt as to their abilities set them a quick test.

You may decide to run a general agency if yours is the only one in the area. Alternatively, specialise in secretarial or computer staff, or in nannies, nurses, models, actors, accountants – or indeed in any of the professions.

All employment agencies need licences granted by the Department of Employment. If you are operating from home they can advise on requirements, and you can also ask advice from the Federation of Personnel Services.

When advertising, make it quite clear that you are an employment agency. It is the responsibility of the agency to check that the employment offered is legal. The prospective employees must not be charged for the agency's services, nor can they be bribed to use them. Above all, your function is to ensure that the employee is qualified for the job concerned.

Advertise for workers and clients locally and in appropriate trade journals. Leave your card at every available business outlet in your area and scan both the Jobs Wanted and the Vacancies sections of local newspapers. Don't knowingly leave an advertisement for an exciting, well-paid job in your office window after the vacancy has been filled, because to do this is against the law.

There have been many success stories in this line of work. People today are always changing jobs, so why not be the entrepreneur who makes it possible?

Foreign Student Accommodation

From March to September young foreigners arrive in droves to study English, or to tour Britain in groups organised by travel agents specialising in 'student operations'. These travel agents depend on agencies to find economically viable accommodation for either long- or short-stay students, where they live in friendly surroundings with an 'authentic' English family.

To match the student with the host, the agency must interview the family and have at least a photograph and full details of the house, the room and the facilities available. It is advisable to have a couple of references from people like the family doctor. The rates of pay received by the family depend on the kind of accommodation offered and the number of meals provided.

Most families can be found by advertising in newsagents' windows, in college or school journals, and by watching the Accommodation Vacant advertisements in the local newspaper. Once you have a sizeable list of vetted, suitable host homes, introduce yourself to the travel agents dealing in student operations (via the London Tourist Board). Also approach schools of the ARELS (Association of Recognised English Language Schools) list, the British Council and colleges and student organisations abroad.

Agency fees are normally set on a per capita per night charge, with extra if you are prepared to meet the students on arrival or to organise social functions. It is pleasant work, especially if you enjoy the company of young people and know some foreign languages when their English fails them! It obviously helps to be near a college or cultural centre which attracts foreign students. Although London is fairly well covered, there is a shortage of friendly homes for foreign students in the rest of the country.

House-sitter Agency

This is a field where impeccable credentials are all important. Running a house-sitter agency means recommending someone to live in and look after a house while the owners are away, so it is the responsibility of the agent that the sitter is totally reliable and that he or she will respect the owner's property, as well as feeding the dog and watering the plants.

The client should present the agent with a list of instructions relating to the central heating system, fuseboxes, burglar alarm circuit and so on. The agent undertakes to repair any damage that may be caused to the property during the owner's absence (refundable) and to replace broken or missing items on their return. It is therefore essential to have professional indemnity insurance and to get references before you employ a new house-sitter.

The sitter lives rent-free and is housed by moving from job to job. A small band of hand-picked sitters is ultimately a more workable system than having a long list of sitters to choose from, as you may have to help them find temporary accommodation.

This is seasonal work, at its peak during school holidays. Advertise for houses to sit in the holiday sections of magazines and newspapers and approach travel agents, foreign companies and big businesses with foreign interests. Finding sitters is the main problem because there are not many mature people who are prepared to lead such a nomadic life. Visitors from abroad who are here to study or work for a limited time are good candidates, so advertise in embassies, post-graduate departments and overseas visitors' clubs.

Imports and Exports

This may sound rather complex as there are numerous rules and regulations to be complied with, and you need to understand the various tariffs and quotas involved in the import and export trade. But all these are clearly set down in the handbooks published by organisations like CoSIRA and the British Overseas Trade Board, and with a little homework and some market research you could set up a very profitable business.

The market research is important, so do not skimp on it as the rest of your business career will follow directly from it. You need to find a commodity which is expensive in your area and cheap elsewhere, or vice versa – depending on whether you are importing or exporting! Trade fairs and international exhibitions provide an ideal opportunity to test a sample of the goods you are thinking of handling, and also to take orders once you are established. Try to anticipate future trends so that you are not competing in the same field as other people, but don't take any risks until you are sure you understand the market.

You will need some capital to pay for your first consignment, and you may be able to borrow this from a sympathetic bank manager. Try to get orders and deposits in advance, and spend time getting to know your customers so that you can predict what they are likely to buy in future. The trade delegation sections of foreign embassies are also worth cultivating, as they can often help with business contacts in their home countries and smooth over any problems you may have, for example delays at Customs. Be prepared to travel, maybe at short notice.

Before you start, you should make sure you are fully covered by insurance and can offer guarantees. This is one occupation where it is in your interests to seek the advice of a solicitor from the outset, as you could run into all sorts of problems if the goods are faulty or one of your clients does not pay on time. (Importing toy camels carrying anthrax will mean more than just the end of your business!)

Jean imports cars from Belgium to Britain: '*I found it the easiest thing in the world to start up in importing, but I do know of a few people who carry the scars of import/export disasters. It is vital that you have – and retain – your own reliable* honest *contacts and that you keep on the look-out for new markets. It's risky and takes guts – putting the money in and then hoping and waiting for the returns. I find the whole business so* exciting!'

If you do your market research thoroughly, build up personal contacts, find the right commodities to handle plus the right buyers, and provide a reliable and efficient service, then you can make a very good living. It could become big business.

Marriage Bureau

The success of this venture depends very much on you yourself, whether or not you can make people feel they trust you enough to tell you personal details about themselves, and whether you can accurately assess their characters and compatibility with others. It helps if you already have a background as a social worker or marriage guidance counsellor, otherwise read as much as you can about the subject. (The personal and Agony Aunts columns of women's magazines are full of information on people, their hopes and their relationships.) The National Council for Marriage Guidance can offer advice.

The atmosphere of the agency is very important, so aim at creating a relaxed living room setting where clients (strangers but potential partners) will feel at ease. Keep everything as 'tasteful' as possible, right down to the stationery. Ask clients to fill in a questionnaire which is probing but straightforward (if in doubt, look at the questions asked by other agencies and computer dating services). The questions will let the people registering with you know what angle you are taking in your attempt to match them successfully.

Payment can be either a registration fee or an annual membership fee, with an additional fee if the client marries someone they meet through you. Be prepared to be investigated by the Office of Fair Trading as some marriage bureaux have given the business rather a bad reputation.

Advertise in local newspapers and maybe specialise in a certain area, for instance older people or professional people. If you speak foreign languages, remember that foreigners who come here to work are often loveless, lonely and lacking in confidence.

It is obviously very rewarding when two of your clients marry and live happily ever after!

Minicab Agency

If you enjoy company and are looking for a home-based job which involves plenty of social contact, running a minicab agency would be ideal – and a lot of fun. Its success will largely depend on where you live, so do some market research before you start. The next step is to get planning permission, as you could well be reported by neighbours if you were suddenly to start having minicabs drawing up outside your house at all hours.

You can work from the living room as all you need is a two-way radio and a couple of telephones, but a separate office would mean less disturbance to the rest of the household. The minicab drivers will also probably use your house as a base to wait for calls, in which case you will need lots of chairs and be prepared to make endless cups of tea.

Two telephone lines are essential. If customers cannot contact you the first time they call they will go elsewhere. Both you and the drivers will need to be equipped with two-way radios, for which you need an aerial. The higher the aerial the farther the radio will carry, but for a local service in a built-up area you can site the aerial on your roof. Contact your local radio supplier (see the Yellow Pages) for details of both radio telephones and aerials. Base station radios can be bought new or second-hand. Usually the agency supplies drivers with radios.

The drivers have their own cars and pay the agency a regular fee for supplying them with a radio and work, so you need to be sure you can keep them employed before taking on too many cars. Drivers' earnings are linked directly to the number of miles they drive and they will leave if they don't get enough work. Advertise for owner/drivers in the local newspaper, garages and car accessory and spare parts retailers. Inspect the cars regularly. One dirty vehicle or one sloppy driver or a breakdown could lose you a lot of business. There are no hard and fast rules in this business.

Advertise the service in hotels, restaurants, pubs, clubs and so on, and try to get regular contracts with local businesses. Leave cards everywhere – from telephone kiosks to private houses and high street shops. Consider offering a chauffeur service and VIP transport as well. The more drivers you have, the better your earnings.

Settling-in Agency

This agency is used by people who have to move lock, stock and barrel from one city to another without having a chance to sound out their new home town. Business executives are often called on to move at the drop of a hat, and so are university and hospital staff.

Moving house is always a headache, especially if you have a family. To find out about temporary (or permanent) accommodation, local schools, shops, leisure facilities, entertainments and public transport means researching an area before you move into it. A settling-in agency offers an *in situ* research service, using people living in or near the towns on which information is required. Working to a specified list of requirements, they send their information to the central agency, which presents it to the client and gives appropriate advice. The researchers are paid a set fee and the agency charges the client according to the size of the job. Large companies are often prepared to pay for this service if it helps their executives to start work in their new jobs without outside distractions.

Advertise in the more upmarket trade journals and contact companies direct. You could also consider having a link with a countryside removal company, and offer to handle the actual move. You will need some capital to start with, to cover the cost of advertising and research which can be expensive in this field.

This is a good business to get into for, as yet, there is little competition.

Speakers' Agency

If your circle of acquaintances is full of interesting eloquent people who know more than a little about a given subject or can deliver a witty, well-structured speech suitable for entertainment at a private or professional function, you could be in business with the many organisations and societies that are always looking for new speakers.

To find speakers, start by making enquiries in your area. Look through newspapers and magazines, following up authors who have written an interesting book, travellers who have returned from an exotic foreign trip, or housewives who have started an enterprising business. Approach organisations like the Women's Institute and the Commonwealth Institute to see if they have experts available to talk, and remember that anyone with something to promote (that includes authors) will be willing to talk.

When you have built up a circle of speakers, make a list of subjects and give details about each speaker on your books – where they live, whether they will travel and the sort of talk or speech they can give. Take this round to organisations which hold regular meetings, such as colleges and clubs, and to businesses, for annual dinners. The client is charged a fee, which will vary from speaker to speaker, and the agent receives a percentage of the fee. Fees can be anything from two-figure amounts to five-figure amounts, with most media celebrities hovering somewhere around the three- to four-figure mark.

Travel Consultant Agency

You do not need a qualification to be a travel consultant, but you must have an intimate knowledge of the business, including at least two years' experience of working for a travel agent and plenty of contacts.

A travel agency needs a licence and a shop front and it should be a member of the Association of British Travel Agents, all of which means capital, business guarantees and stringent requirements. As a travel consultant, however, you can work from home, operating through an agency on a commission basis. You need good, dependable contacts and you must be very up-to-date on all the travel brochures. Advertising is frowned upon, so you will have to rely on your reputation for business.

> Susan retired from the travel agent business to become a consultant: *'When people have saved all year for their holiday, they need and expect guidance from an agent. They want to know how far the hotel is from the beach and how often the buses go, which the person sitting in the agency booking tickets probably won't know. A consultant should have all the details and make suggestions to help people plan their trips. It's a completely different service from just selling the tickets! My customers phone me at all hours and I go to their homes to see them when both spouses are back from work, or at weekends when they have the time to talk about their holiday. Once settled, I make their booking through an agency (always one that's a member of ABTA) and my earnings are part of the commission the agency receives from the operator. It's lovely work provided you know your subject!'*

If you are dealing mainly with tourist holidays, the work will be seasonal and will not provide an income all year round. To add an extra string to your bow, you could become a representative for tour agents or hotels, carrying their publicity material and working on commission. There are also plenty of opportunities for acting as a consultant to businesses who need someone to handle all their travel arrangements and to find suitable locations for conferences and conventions.

ANIMALS

'My first tip!'

○ Before taking on any job with animals, first make sure that you are fully aware of what is involved. On a personal level, you have to like animals and *enjoy* caring for them. Animals represent a considerable amount of routine work and are a constant tie.

○ If you intend to house animals, estimate the expenditure needed to feed and clean them, and also to provide heat, light, suitable accommodation and veterinary care. Check with your local authority's Planning Department and the Environmental Health Department about regulations on buildings and living conditions for livestock.

○ If you have neighbours, discuss the project with them first – they can prosecute if your endeavour presents a health hazard, noise, smell or other offensive disturbance. They can also take action against you if the animals are being neglected or ill-treated.

○ If your property is rented, check your lease or consult your landlord to find out whether you are permitted to keep animals.

○ To *board* animals, you need a licence from your local authority. You will have to keep a register of the animals open for inspection by either an authorised veterinary surgeon or an inspector from your local authority.
○ If you are keeping other people's animals, take out an insurance indemnifying you against liability. The Equine and Livestock Insurance Company will advise you on insurance matters.
○ Above all, make sure you know how to look after the animals before you start – ignorance and mistakes might mean not only the end of your business but the end of the animals as well.
○ See Contacts for addresses and reference books.

Animalware

The person who invented the magnetic cat flap must have made a fortune. There are many other things in the animalware line which, with proper marketing, would appeal to the millions of people who dote on their pets. Here are four ideas:

David makes cat scratching posts. He nails and glues carpet remnants to a piece of timber which is attached to a solid base.

Paul makes self-assembly kennel kits. He produces three different styles, each made up of wooden sections and a collapsible frame.

June sews coats for dogs, using waterproof material and old blankets. She gets pieces of material free from a local factory, and she can line up to 15 coats from one blanket.

Geoff has made a supply-when-pressed pellet feeder for cats to use when their owners are away. He is now working on a flow-when-pressed milk releaser.

Remember to patent your innovation as soon as it has been proved reliable and commercially viable.

Animalware can be sold through animal clubs, kennels and pet shops on a commission basis, or by mail order through advertisements in newspapers. If you hit on a good idea, it could prove very profitable. Sometimes the simple ideas are the best.

Animal Watch

Many people would rather not board out their pets while they are away on holiday. Apart from the expense, some animals are utterly miserable away from home and, even worse, may pick up some infection. For people who keep a vast family of pets ranging from rabbits, birds, fish, dogs, cats and hamsters to boa constrictors and bees, there are not many neighbours or friends prepared to take on the responsibility of looking after the menagerie for more than a day or two. This is where the animal minder comes in. The work can involve anything from taking a ferocious hound for a walk once a day while the owner is at the office, to visiting a house twice a day for a month, while the family takes its summer vacation. You would be expected to look after the animals, feed them, groom them and clean up after them.

Do not contemplate offering an animal watch service unless you really like all breeds of animals. You will need to produce a couple of personal references because you will have access to the client's house, and you should also be able to demonstrate to the client that you know how to care for his pets. The RSPCA prints pamphlets on looking after domestic animals and, if in doubt, ask any animal welfare society for advice. Adult education institutes do a course in animal care and nursing.

Make sure the owner leaves you with instructions on routine procedure, a telephone number or address where he can be contacted in case of emergency, and the details of the local vet and the nearest animal clinic. Owners should provide the food and litter. Charge for your time plus any extras you incur such as milk, fresh food and vet's bills.

There is no financial outlay involved and the money is reasonable for enjoyable work. It is still fairly uncommon practice however, so your service will need plenty of advertising, by word of mouth and in the local papers, smarter magazines, pet shops and veterinary clinics.

Beekeeping

Beekeeping is a fair-weather business. A long spell of bad weather can upset the bees and you can end up spending more money than you make. As the initial investment is high and there are many risks involved, beekeeping is a specialist job which should be well researched. The British Beekeepers' Association publishes literature and keeps a list of beekeeping groups. They will also advise you about local bye-laws and courses. Some local education authorities have an officer available to supply technical information on the subject. You may need his help with swarm control if you have no experience of beekeeping.

You will need a good-sized garden, properly equipped hives (seond-hand ones must be sterilised before use), a veil, gloves, smokers, a one-piece bee-proof boilersuit, and assorted honey extracting and storing equipment. Spring is the correct time to buy your bees – try to obtain them from a source close to their new home so that they are used to the climate. A colony can be five combs or more, depending on how many you feel you and your garden can handle. The honey yield of six to 12 combs is 20–40 pounds annually. Honey has to conform to certain standards and must be sold in either plastic containers or screw-top jars. (See HMSO leaflet SI 1976 No. 1832.) Sell the honey through local food shops. Old combs can be rendered down and the resulting beeswax sold to make candles and polish.

Bees need regular, but not daily, care. In winter they have to be fed with sugar syrup to help them over the colder patches. The income varies from year to year but can be very good.

As Hilary, a London beekeeper, says: *'You have to "exploit" your bees to take their honey. Sometimes you become almost too attached to them to be able to bring yourself to "steal" it!'*

Beekeeping is not very suitable for people with small children, unless the hives are well away from the house.

Boarding Dogs and Cats

Either board dogs or board cats, but not the two together! Both need a warm, dry place to sleep, good regular food, clean water, grooming, exercie and love. Their kennels should be in a large, heated, well-lit outhouse, which is easy to clean. However large your property, more than 40 occupants is too many. Dogs must be taken for daily walks or allowed to run in an exercise area. Cats should be provided with separate, enclosed, exercise runs. Consult the Kennel Club and the Feline Advisory Bureau for guidelines. Under the Animal Boarding Establishments Act of 1963, boarding animals for payment requires you to register with your Environmental Health Office, who will inform you what requirements have to be met. There are regulations concerning accommodation, food, hygiene, health and safety, and the premises will be inspected. You will have to pay a licence fee, and you also need planning permission for the change of use of your premises and for building runs or pens for the animals. Take out insurance for your liabilities, and consult the neighbours before you start.

You will need to have a good knowledge of veterinary matters because if you are not able to care correctly for the animals in your charge, most of the profits you plan to make will disappear in vets' bills. There are several animal care courses run by animal welfare societies and adult education institutes, but even after taking a course you should always call in the vet if you have any doubts about the health of the animal you are looking after.

Be sure that all animals are in good health when you accept them. Ask for a vet's certificate if you are in doubt and you should never accept a cat or dog without vaccination certificates. Note the animal's details, in particular any idiosyncracies, and ask the owner to bring its equipment, too. By law you have to keep a register of animals arriving and departing.

To conform to the anti-rabies restrictions which apply to most mammals, you will need a separate area for animals which are in quarantine. These animals must be looked after under the supervision of the vet, who will inspect them daily. The requirements laid down by the Ministry of Agriculture, Fisheries and Food are strict.

Advertise your service locally through veterinary surgeons, pet shops, clubs and clinics and also in travel agencies and newspapers.

You need to be energetic to look after animals and it is an all-consuming life-style with considerable outlays if you are to do it properly. But if you are an animal-lover it is very rewarding emotionally as well as financially.

Dog Beauty Parlour

All dogs need seasonal trims and occasional clips, and many breeds, such as poodles, require expert grooming and attention. The salon should be in a room or shed outside the house, equipped with a large low sink, running water and electrical points. Fix non-slip matting to the bottom of the sink and attach a shower spray to the taps. Dirty dogs will need to be washed in the sink with anti-flea soap or dog shampoo (remember that the wrong soap can cause skin-irritations). Eye protection and a muzzle for the dog might be necessary, for many animals do not take kindly to bathing. After a bath, dry the dog with a warm hairdryer.

Brushing and trimming should be done in a dry, warm and light part of the room. You will need a range of brushes, scissors and clippers to cater for all kinds of coats. Equipment is available from pet shop suppliers (see the Yellow Pages), and you can get advice from a local kennel club or dog-training organisation.

John and Mary run a salon from their converted garage: *'We have found that it has been vitally important to teach both ourselves and the animals how to relax. If you're tense and make a small mistake when clipping, it is very frightening for them and really rather dangerous for us. You have to understand and like the animals. It is a source of great pride and satisfaction to use the psychological approach on a difficult animal and to find it works. Half the joy in this job is dealing with animals. The other half is turning them out correctly groomed. It is important to know what you are doing – there are many, many books to refer to.'* They also run a disc-engraving and accessory sideline: owners well-pleased with their beautiful new hound take little persuasion to buy a bijou rhinestone collar!

There are profits to be made in this field if you operate in the right area. Advertise in *Dog News* and other dog magazines, and locally in shops, veterinary clinics and newspapers.

Free-range Eggs

In many respects, ducks are easier to keep than chickens. They do not perch, they lay their eggs on the ground and they do not normally go in for high flying. They do, however, need a pond and a regular supply of clean straw to lay in. A good layer will produce more eggs per bird than a hen and the eggs fetch a higher price too. Ducks, however, cost more to buy than hens.

Hens must be housed in huts with perches, nest boxes and, as laying is linked to light, good lighting. Their runs will need fences up to 6 feet high to keep them in, and their wings should be clipped. In the case of both ducks and hens, the runs will have to be foxproof, which means you need to sink the fence to about 6 feet below ground level. Over and above the cost of poultry houses and runs, you must budget for eating and drinking troughs, food (bought monthly to retain freshness and vitamin content), disinfectants, vaccines and medical care and, of course, the birds themselves. Although day-old chicks are cheaper to buy than adults, they will have to be reared in a warm, dry, light place and will not be ready to lay for up to five months. The smaller the bird, the smaller the egg. In winter, both hens and ducks lay considerably fewer eggs.

Read a guide on poultry-keeping and check with the authorities whether you are (a) permitted to keep poultry on your property and (b) allowed to sell your produce. Consult your local Environmental Health Department, the Ministry of Agriculture, Fisheries and Food and the British Poultry Federation for advice and information on the stringent hygiene and EEC egg-marketing regulations.

This project is not something to be entered into unprepared, and you should bear in mind that ducks and hens can never be left to run themselves. The profits on eggs are good and there should be no problem in finding a market: take a market stall, sell to health food shops and restaurants, and display a sign outside your home to attract passing trade and local people, who will probably buy from you regularly. You can also sell the manure to gardeners.

Goatkeeping

The demand for goats' milk has increased since it was realised that people who suffer from certain allergies do not react as badly to it as they do to cows' milk. Goats' milk yoghurt and cheese are also very popular in health food shops.

To have a continuous supply of milk, you need two nanny goats, kidding in alternate years, and one young one. They need milking twice a day, producing a milk supply varying from 2–14 pints daily. Obviously, you will have to learn how to milk goats and, as you cannot leave them unmilked for even a day, you will have to find somebody in the locality who can milk them in your absence. There are several books on goatkeeping.

Goats are gregarious, skittish animals and you should not keep just one on its own – a lonely goat is a noisy goat. Goats need a warm, dry stall to sleep in, preferably with a washable floor covered with dry, clean straw. They can either roam free in a field by day or live in a large pen and go for grazing walks on a chain. They eat practically anything, but as they are ruminants it is important to give them plenty of bulk foods (fresh greens and hay). They also need a constant supply of drinking water.

Goats are not expensive and can be bought through the local goat club, which the British Goat Society will introduce you to. Check that there is no restriction to keeping them at your home and find a vet to give them medical care when needed. (Foot and mouth is a disease to which goats are highly susceptible, and infected animals have to be slaughtered.) Consult the local health officer about the regulations for sterilising milk bottles and so on. There is no price control on goats' milk and it, and the by-products yoghurt and cheese, may be sold to shops and dairies.

The work is hard but very pleasant and goats are affectionate creatures. The income is good, and to cut down on overheads you can always collect leftover fruit and vegetables from the markets to give to your goats.

Training dogs

Most dogs owners love to watch Barbara Woodhouse training dogs on television, but they can't or won't be bothered to knuckle down to the time-consuming task of teaching their own dogs obedience and discipline. If you have a patient but firm attitude, a collection of good instruction books and the space for a training course, anybody with experience of dogs and their psychology can take dogs (and their owners) for training classes. Charge for a full course of classes.

Planning permission is needed to open a dog training school, and you should be licensed by your local authority. The Kennel Club will advise on the best way to go about it.

Advertise in the local newspaper and at the veterinary clinic. It is a pleasant way to make money, provided you like and understand both dogs and their owners; it is not a good job if you have small children running around. In any case, take the precaution of insuring yourself against injury.

CHILDREN

○ Working in a child's world should not be attempted unless you genuinely like children! You should be energetic, enthusiastic and patient, and if you are going to work with children in your own home forget about being house-proud. Good health is imperative.

○ As more and more mothers are going out to work and single parents are usually obliged to leave the house to earn, surrogate mothers are on the increase during working hours. The pay is not high, but then the motivation to look after children should be on a human rather than an economic level.

○ See Contacts for addresses and reference books.

Babysitting

Babysitting can be a plum job, particularly if you babysit in the evening when the children are asleep. Often there is nothing to do but watch television or read. Generally, there is a meal or a snack provided. This service has now been extended to 'granny' sitting, which can require the sitter to read or talk to the elderly person or just to be in the house in case help is needed.

Arrange fees (on an hourly rate) in advance and, if the work is likely to run late into the night, transport home. Make sure you note the telephone number where your employers can be contacted in case of an emergency, and ask for details concerning your charges and make a note of any potential problems.

Work can be found through agencies (see the Yellow Pages: Babysitting Services). Agencies will require a reference, but once you are known as a reliable babysitter work should come directly to you. Advertise locally in shop windows and newspapers as well.

Daytime babysitting is needed by parents who work and want somebody to collect their child from school and give them a meal. For this sort of work, you can often take your own child along too.

Child Escorts

So many Britons work abroad and send their children 'back home' to school that the need for child escorts has grown considerably over the years. The service also includes accompanying a child to special classes or to hospital appointments when parents and adult relatives are unavailable, and escorting children by car or public transport from the country to a town or city.

Child escorts work either through agencies (see the Yellow Pages: Employment Agencies – Universal Aunts in London is the biggest), which need a reference and pay set hourly rates plus transport and expenses, or privately, at negotiable rates, through local organisations and boarding schools. The busy seasons are half-term and the beginning and end of term. If the parents are abroad, the child might also need a bed for the night.

It is amusing work (provided you enjoy the company of children) and requires one to be punctual, patient and enterprising enough to sort out possible hazards and last-minute problems.

This is very suitable work for ex-nannies, and for parents and grandparents who are missing the responsibility of bringing up their own children. It can be a lot of fun!

Childminding

If you have small children and your house already resembles a bomb-site, minding other people's children can make sense.

A childminder is somebody who is paid to look after one or more children for more than two hours a day. Childminders should register with the local Social Services Department after the Department has checked that the home is suitable and the applicant has had the compulsory chest X-ray.

A childminder may look after three or four children under five including her own (depending on the locality), at a rate per hour set by the parent and the minder. The National Childminding Association provides guidelines on fees, childminding requirements and childminders' entitlements. The work is not highly paid. Childminding rates charged in cities are far higher than those charged in country areas.

> Carolyn has been childminding for 12 years: *'I'm already so involved in the routine of my own children that a few more for the day doesn't make much difference. In fact, it gives my kids live-in playmates, which means that they never get bored. I find it a rewarding job and reckon there would be many more battered children if there weren't people like us. It is essential to have a tolerant husband who is not going to lose his temper every time he comes home and trips over somebody else's child happily ripping his wallpaper!'* (Wear and tear is deductable off tax.)

Adult education institutes run courses in childminding and many social services have voluntary groups and training schemes for new childminders. Charges vary depending on how much the childminder has to do: nappy changing and bottle feeding the very young, or providing tea for an older schoolchild and a table for homework.

Fostering The natural extension to childminding is fostering (shared care between the foster parent and the authorities, who pay you for your services), but this sort of occupation is not profit-motivated and should definitely not be considered as a way to wealth. The National Foster Care Association provides all the information on the subject, as well as running training schemes for prospective foster parents.

Children's Book and Toy Shop

Outgrown toys and books are found in roughly the same places as outgrown clothes – in attics and cupboards, and at jumble sales and markets. Working on the principle that most discarded toys can be repaired and made to look almost new, it follows that it must be worth trying to resell them.

If you have a mini-van, a hatch-back or an estate car, you can take your goods to the buyer – to schools, fairs, clinics and other places where parents and children congregate. You will need an easy-to-assemble display stand, which you can make yourself, and the strength to carry boxes of goods. Hand out cards in the right places giving your proposed selling route for the next few weeks and you should not need to advertise your travelling shop. News of unusual enterprises does spread very quickly by word of mouth. You will need a licence from the Council to sell in this way.

Those who are not mobile could always turn a room at home into a small shop and put a notice in the window. It could be run as a library, with parents paying a fee to join and a small amount for each item borrowed. You will need planning permission to run a shop from home, and maybe to advertise in your front window.

New books and toys are bought from wholesalers, and you will need to have capital as security. Think carefully before you decide to deal in new items, particularly in books. Experience as a librarian would help and some experience of wholesalers and selling is important.

Outlay is on a display stand, crates in which to shift the goods, stock, transport and advertising. It is very pleasant work for those who enjoy browsing around market stalls and are interested in children. Even if you do not charge prices high enough to make you rich, you and your children's circle of friends and acquaintances will increase tenfold.

Childware

People with children often do not have enough storage space to keep the pram, cot, playpen and buggy of the first child until the second one is born. They either pass them on to somebody else who is about to start a family, or they sell them in the 'Under £10' advertisement section of their local newspaper. Most of these things are still in good condition, and would cost very little to buy and refurbish.

Keeping well away from the jumble sale image, there is a market for hiring out children's equipment or renovating it to sell. You need a spare room, shed or garage in which to display the childware and, to offer a complete service, a suitable vehicle for delivery. Advertise locally in toy shops, health clinics, schools, libraries and other centres where people with children might go. If you are hiring out you will need printed forms stating the terms, stressing that extra costs will be incurred if damage is done to goods. Make sure you ask for a deposit if payment is to be at the end of the hire period, and insure against theft. It is worth printing a little stick-on label 'Hired from . . .' to display (prominently) on the equipment and, as with most things, spend as much time as possible *talking* to people about the service.

Good money is to be made if you can catch the eye of the bargain-hunting parent market.

Kiddy Packs and Lucky Dips

Parents are usually putty in their children's hands: a few pence for the lucky dip or for a surprise pack is quickly given.

The main work in this project lies not in making the contents but in preparing the packaging. As the excitement for the child is in the promise of the unknown, every whistle, paper hat, sweet and keyring should be done up in a different wrapping and all the parcels presented in a colourful bag or cardboard box. For the contents, you want *inexpensive*, unusual knicknacks of the Christmas cracker variety, so start by contacting good wholesalers (see the Yellow Pages: Toys and Games Wholesalers).

The market for kiddy packs is found at children's parties, amateur pantomimes and school fêtes, and for lucky dips at more public places, such as toy shops. Take examples round to shops and to organisers of children's activities. Work on a 100% mark-up.

Playgroups and Nursery Schools

If your area has not got a playgroup or nursery school, then consider starting one or both.

To run a playgroup for children of pre-school age requires no formal training, but you have to register with the local Social Services Department and the premises (large house or village hall) have to comply with standard regulations concerning safety, health and hygiene. This involves safety catches on doors and windows, ventilation, light, heat, lavatory facilities (one for every eight children), catering, toys and play areas. The ratio of adults to children differs from area to area and is determined by the local authority involved. The Pre-School Playgroups Association has all the information needed and adult education institutes run playgroup training courses.

The same regulations apply to starting a nursery school, but there must also be a qualified nursery nurse in charge. The British Association for Early Childhood Education has the details.

Before considering launching either a playgroup or nursery school, check that the neighbours are not going to object to the noise. Local fund-raising through fêtes, bring-and-buy sales and sponsored walks helps to spread the word, and should encourage people both to donate toys and equpment and to send their young children to the school.

There are fair profits to be made in nursery schools, but only modest ones in playgroups. In both cases your children go to work with you and have a wonderful time! In many areas there is a lack of good playgroups and nursery schools, so you should not go wrong. But you must really like small children because in these jobs you will be required to concentrate full-time on their amusement, their appetites and their natural functions!

CLOTHES AND ACCESSORIES

○ Making a living out of clothes depends on your flair for fashion and style and your ability to sew or knit exceptionally well, working quickly and expertly.

○ You should inform the local authority that you intend to use a room in your home as a workroom and, if you are going to sell clothes, you must apply for a licence. Selling is governed by many changing and inconsistent laws, and it is advisable to check exactly where you stand legally (ask your local Citizens' Advice Bureau or go direct to the authorities). Conducting a small home-based business is unlikely to raise problems but you must be aware of the law. For example, there are often restrictions on running a business from Council property or privately rented accommodation.

○ Write to your local adult education college for details of courses. The City and Guilds Institute has a scheme which includes clothing, and many private colleges up and down the country also offer training.

○ Check the code of practice laid down by the Mail Order Traders' Association if you intend to sell by mail order.

○ See Contacts for addresses and reference books.

'Almost New' Emporium

Every parent wants his or her child to be well-dressed, but most parents blanch at the prospect of having to buy new clothes for their fast-growing children every couple of months or so. 'Almost new' clothes, sold at roughly half the price of the new article, must be the answer.

Operate your second-hand children's clothes shop from a room well supplied with shelves and hanging racks. Remember that presentation is a major part of selling: the room should be clean and tidy and the clothes neatly stored or displayed. You will need a sewing machine if you want to repair and modernise the clothes, and you should wash and iron them before deciding on size and price.

Clothes can be picked up inexpensively from jumble sales and market stalls. Encourage parents to bring their children's 'almost new' clothes to you to be sold on a commission basis (25–30%). Try to be imaginative and buy ahead, for example at the end of the summer buy clothes for the following summer.

If you run your 'shop' on an appointment-only basis or sell through 'parties', you are unlikely to break the law on selling. You might need planning permission and a licence to sell if you convert your front room into a showcase of saleable merchandise. So, however small the business, if you wish to set up a shop in your home, find out about the legal requirements before you start.

The outlay and overheads are low and the profits could be high. Spread the news by word of mouth, advertise in schools and tell local organisations such as the Brownies and Cubs.

Alterations and Mending

This is a much underrated service, which is becoming harder and harder to find. It may sound unglamorous but there is money to be made: drycleaners need people to do invisible mending, individuals and dress shops need alterations carried out, and many people need somebody to replace a zip or alter a hem if they themselves don't have a sewing machine, the time or the inclination. And it's almost impossible to find somebody to dye clothes nowadays.

Joan has a large family and only a few free hours a week: *'Altering clothes and mending is not nearly as dreary as it sounds! I get my rewards from knowing that I've saved something from being thrown out. Anyone can do it – you just need to think up the best way to solve the problem.'*

Offering an express service means that you can charge more, and extra money can also be made by providing special services, for example adding lace to a cuff, enbroidering a collar, lining a jacket or dyeing the article. Charges should be per hour, unless they are fixed per job. Don't forget to charge extra for materials such as buttons and zips.

Advertise through cards in the windows of shops, laundries and drycleaners. Visit local boutiques, tailors and dressmakers to tell them of your service. It is an aspect of sewing they themselves do not go in for, and they could therefore recommend you to their clients without losing their own business. And remember the schools market: children can outgrow uniforms and clothes in a term and alterations are constantly needed.

This work is easy to fit in with the home routine as each job is small. The money is good if you are well organised.

Clothes-selling Parties

Clothes-selling parties fall into several categories and, if successful, can often lead to opening a shop selling clothes. Starting small, you can use the sitting-room to sell in and the guest-room wardrobe for storing the merchandise. Either act as an agent for clothes companies or sell for yourself, buying the clothes wholesale or second-hand.

Selling clothes for others, as an agent, can be followed up through the Direct Sales and Service Association (see page 42) and works on a commission-per-item-sold basis. Private enterprise selling, provided you know your market, can reap far higher rewards.

Joyce buys direct: *'I go to the wholesaler and buy what I reckon my friends and their friends will want to buy. I put price tags on the dresses, with a 50% mark-up, and deliver them to the home of the person who has agreed to hold a selling party for me. They, in turn, receive 10% of the profits. I could do three parties a week, circulating the unsold dresses with the new stock so that eventually everything is sold and no group of buyers sees the same clothes twice. My guideline is: if I like a dress, I buy it!'*

Daphne runs 'Once Worn' parties: *'I started because I was bored. First I raided my wardrobe which contained lots of lovely frocks I no longer wore. I cleaned, mended and ironed them with care and invited friends round. They bought them all and I made quite a lot of money! Now I buy in and also sell friends' clothes for them working on a 60–40% split profit basis. I try to keep the standards high, dealing only in nearly-new items.'*

Elizabeth buys 'scrummage' lots: *'I sort, repair, alter, wash and iron the clothes and sell the best ones to my neighbours. Often one item earns me more than I paid for the lot. With the profits I have bought a three-wheeled moped. I go to markets and sales three days a week and spend the other three preparing the clothes for resale. I advertise in the local papers and* Exchange and Mart, *offering a refund if not satisfied, but most of my customers send for more parcels.'*

Customising Clothes

Customising clothes can be sewing the name of the local football team in felt letters onto their tracksuits or designing a promotional logo to launch a new product. Either way, it is a matter of displaying the name as attractively as possible. In the first case, the client may say he wants the name stitched in blue on an article of clothing which he provides; in the latter, you suggest a design and provide the article of clothing. This second method is preferable, as clearly profits will be greater if you can buy the article of clothing wholesale (see the Yellow Pages: Sportswear/Clothing Manufacturers and Wholesalers).

Approach possible companies with a selection of samples and a price list. To work out the prices, first contact suppliers of clothing used for promotional or group activity projects. Ask for their catalogues and lowest prices, and see if you can persuade them to give you a larger discount for a repeat order.

Once your sums are right, there is money to be made in this currently burgeoning market. You need a room in which to store supplies, plus access to a variety of printing methods. Advertise in sports and business magazines, clubs and sports shops, and approach the promotion/publicity/personnel managers of likely organisations with samples and suggestions. Anyone can do it – it just needs ideas!

Dressmaking

People go to dressmakers for a variety of reasons: they have some material they want to have made up, they cannot afford the time to shop around, they have odd-shaped figures, they don't like public changing rooms or they simply live miles from the nearest dress shop.

To be a good dressmaker you need to be a skilled seamstress with a good knowledge of pattern-cutting and design. There are many reference books on dressmaking and there are courses at colleges and adult education institutes. You will need an electric sewing machine with all the attachments, a large cutting-out table, dressmaker's scissors, a tailor's dummy, a steam iron, a full-length mirror, hanging space and pattern books. The sewing room should be warm, light and large enough to hold you, your equipment and the customer. It should be well away from family intrusions.

Price is worked out on an hourly basis, including the time spent on fittings and shopping for the customer. The cost of the materials, unless the customer provides his or her own, is extra. (The left-over scraps of material can be used for patchwork.) If the customer is providing the material, make sure that she (or he) buys and studies the pattern *before* selecting the material. So often customers expect a dressmaker to 'run up' a little number from insufficient, unsuitable fabric.

Dressmaking need not be restricted to working for individual clients: boutiques are always looking for good new designs, and production can be increased by joining forces with others and separating the roles of pattern-cutter, designer, machinist etc.

A high standard is expected from a private dressmaker, and your income is directly related to the speed at which you can work. Nobody is going to pay you for a superb seam that has taken hours to sew, but on the other hand they won't come back if you do a rough job!

Advertise in local newspapers, and fashion magazines and put cards in the windows of fabric shops and drycleaners and on club notice boards.

Handbags

The range of handbag styles is enormous, and today they are made from all kinds of materials. If you have a novel idea, like cylinder box-bags in glitter silver plastic, there is nothing to prevent you making them.

Handcrafted leather bags (see Leatherwork) are always popular, whatever the fashion, and you can make soft leather clutchbags, stylish pouches and envelope bags simply using an ordinary domestic sewing machine. Concentrate on plain, classic shapes in good-quality leather, or alternatively opt for the latest fashion and make witty, fantasy styles to sell in boutiques and craft markets like London's Covent Garden Market.

Quilted fabric is popular for roll bags and small purses, and you could extend your business to include toilet bags and cosmetic purses, which sell well in chemists. You can buy the fabric ready quilted, or quilt it yourself which takes longer but works out cheaper on materials. Canvas is another fabric ideal for satchels and large shopping bags, and would also be suitable for a range of lightweight travelling holdalls. PVC fabric now comes in many different designs and makes practical, waterproof shopping bags. Several plastics can be made up on a sewing machine; clear plastic is useful as you can cover other more delicate materials which wouldn't stand up to much wear and tear.

If you invest in an industrial sewing machine and some tools, you can work with tougher materials. Adult education institutes and the Cordwainers College in London give technical training in handbag making. If you want to make more traditional bags using frames, clasps and fastenings, these can be bought from craft shops and through handbag manufacturers.

For a proper finish, handbags should be lined, though this depends on the material you are working with. It also helps to provide useful pockets, and you should pay attention to strong handles and secure fastenings.

For really exotic bags, concentrate on evening purses which can be made of more delicate materials such as silk and velvet. Fabrics such as lamé and brocade can be bought quite cheaply from theatrical fabric suppliers, and you can get quite carried away with decorative effects, such as braid, feathers and beadwork. Even everyday bags can be decorated with appliqué shapes, fringes, plaited straps and so on.

Outlets depend very much on the kind of bags you produce. Craft shops and stalls in markets will be best for most bags, but for really exotic and ultra-fashionable styles approach boutiques and shops selling fashion accessories, or the handbag department of large stores. There is definitely a market for unusual and interesting bags.

Hatmaking

You don't have to be David Shilling to make wonderful hats, but a flair in this field helps as hats are worn less today than ever before.

Experience in the millinery trade is recommended, otherwise it will take a long time to master the equipment (to shape the hat) and to learn how to get the best out of the materials. Financial outlay on equipment is high (purchase from wholesalers: see the Yellow Pages), and if you move into the half dozen peacock feathers per hat market, materials can cost a lot too.

This is challenging, creative work with very little competition from made-to-order hats. And the range open to you is endless – knitted hats, straw hats, felt hats, turbans, bridesmaids' crowns, little net and feather numbers, beach hats and, of course, The Wedding Hat which every woman needs at some time or another.

Show samples of your designs to shops and advertise in magazines like *Vogue*, *Tatler* and *The Lady*, whose readers still spend substantial sums on buying hats for social functions. And wear your hats whenever you can.

Either train with a professional hat maker, or take an adult education course on millinery. Some of the books on the subject are rather old-fashioned, but the techniques have not changed in decades, only the materials. You can be quite revolutionary with hat materials and design, but you *must* know the techniques.

Kit Clothes

Many people enjoy sewing but can never cut out the fabric correctly. Others find that standard-size off-the-peg garments are always too big or too small and have to be altered. Some just enjoy making something the easy way, which is what kit clothes are about. The customer sees an appealing outfit advertised in a newspaper or magazine, writes off for it and sews up the already-cut garment, which can always be altered to fit. The finished article naturally brings enormous satisfaction to the customer as he or she feels that they made it themselves.

To prepare kits, you need to be a good pattern-cutter and should have a sewing machine with a swing needle to seal off raw edges. You will need plenty of space in which to cut out the fabric, and a packaging service or room where you can pack the kits in strong, damage-proof wrapping. Establish connections with wholesale material suppliers who deal in good-quality cloth, and charge a 50–80% mark-up on each kit. Mail the kits recorded delivery, and include with the instructions a contract exonerating you from any responsibility if the customer fails to follow the instructions correctly. The Mail Order Traders' Association will give you advice on this, and it is worth consulting a solicitor over the wording.

Kit clothes can be anything from anoraks to fancy dresses made from crêpe paper, and from wedding dresses to children's outfits. Your kits can become quite exclusive if you join forces with a crafts person who could, for example, screen print each T-shirt, make a lace collar for each blouse, or provide hand-painted buttons, hand-carved buckles or hand-tooled belts. There is plenty of opportunity to experiment, putting bright ideas into practice. Remember always to wear one of your own kits!

Advertise your mail order service in newspapers, and try to interest magazine fashion editors in promoting your kit as a special offer. It is also worth renting a market stall where you can display both the kits and the made-up clothes.

Knitting

Over the past ten years there has been a knitting revolution, caused partly by the versatility of advanced knitting machines and partly because knitting has attracted many bright young designers. It takes a fraction of the time to produce a garment by machine than it does to knit the same garment by hand. Many modern machines have programming devices, which does mean that you should have a separate room in which to knit so that tiny fingers cannot meddle with the programme! Some manufacturers offer a brief instruction course in the customer's home when they buy a machine, and most evening institutes run courses. However, some people do experience difficulty mastering the more advanced models. Knitting machines are expensive to buy new, so keep an eye open for a good second-hand one, or hire. Do not buy a machine without seeking advice from experienced knitters. If you are still unsure, contact the Citizens' Advice Bureaux who have researched the subject. There are machine knitters' clubs country-

```
```

wide and many, like the Worldwide Machine Knitters' Club, provide their members with advice, special offers, courses and patterns.

Handknitting is much more of a craft, and a realistic price for the time it takes to knit a lovely lacy cardigan or a traditional Fair Isle sweater is often prohibitive.

In either case, knitters need to spot fashion trends and be able to produce original, exciting designs for their sweaters, scarves, gloves, hats, dresses, babywear or whatever. Unless you want to specialise in clothes made from expensive handspun threads, keep the price down by buying wools and yarns direct from the mills. Ask the Wool Secretariat for advice.

The best way to advertise your goods is to wear them! Sell to your friends and they will wear them too! You can also take samples of your knitting around the shops, but remember that most clothes shops add on a 100% commission fee. If you work out a terrific pattern, show it to a magazine fashion editor and offer to produce a pattern as a special offer for their readers.

There is plenty of profit to be made on machine knitwear. The technique is not difficult to learn, and the work can be very creative. It is up to you!

Pattern Cutting Classes

Many dressmakers need some tuition, either in the basic principles or in particular areas, such as sewing with special fabrics; more advanced dressmakers often want to make their own patterns, particularly as commercial patterns are now so expensive. As well as the tuition, classes held in someone's home are popular as social gatherings and to teach dressmaking and pattern cutting is a very pleasant, sociable way to earn money.

You do not need to be qualified to hold these classes in your home, but you should have a good deal of knowledge and experience if you are going to be able to do the job properly. The City and Guilds Institute issues a certificate following certain courses in dressmaking and pattern cutting.

You need to invest in a tailor's dummy, but you can expect the students to bring their own sewing machines and sewing equipment, although you may need to advise them what equipment to buy. The size of the class is largely determined by the size of the room you work in, so it helps to have a fairly large workroom and enough chairs and table space for everyone. (You could always hold classes in your living room but make sure you have a large, *very old*, table. After one class of pattern-cutting, the table will look as if it's contracted galloping woodworm!) Remember that some students will be cutting out material, which takes up a lot of floor space. Provide tea or coffee halfway through each class.

Jane runs a pattern-cutting class in an area where the demand is for children's clothes: *'I take six people at a time for two hours a week over a period of six weeks. I won't do one-to-one classes as it's so demanding and it doesn't pay. This way the courses evolve and we concentrate on quick methods and things that actually interest the participants rather than the usual run-of-the-mill pattern-cutting classes. Inventiveness is all important.'*

Charge for each course rather than for individual classes, to make sure that students do not drop out halfway through. If you have more students than you can teach in one session, hold separate classes for beginners and advanced dressmakers. Advertise locally in fabric shops and sewing machine suppliers, and also in the schools in the area.

Silk Lingerie

Silk lingerie is very special. Prices are high to very high as silk is expensive and the work is fiddly and time-consuming. Those who can afford it buy from specialist shops and from private dressmakers who are either recommended by word of mouth or sought through mail-order channels.

Customers may want to come for fittings, so make sure your workroom looks as appealing as the end product! Advertise in colour supplements and the more exclusive fashion magazines. (Beware: their rates are expensive!) Buy the silk direct from silk merchants and keep a selection of laces and trimmings in stock. It is essential to have a good training in pattern-cutting. Keep several books of patterns so that customers can choose exactly what they want – when working in silk, nobody can afford to make a mistake.

You will need good eyesight and exceptionally nimble fingers.

Specialist Clothing

If you know of a line of clothing which will sell well and which you can produce speedily and inexpensively, then it would be a waste of time to ply your trade as an all-round dressmaker. With well-placed advertising you could make a niche for yourself producing, for example, Victorian nightdresses, dolls' frocks, wedding dresses, maternity wear, children's party clothes, quilted jackets or silk ties.

If you know your product is good, make up samples and show them to the appropriate shops. Invest in illustrated pamphlets and advertisements in colour supplements and magazines. Really push your product. Specialist clothing will require an all-out selling campaign to get it off the ground. But remember, people don't like to see the same old stock year after year so, when sales pick up, start branching out with variations on the theme. This way, your style and idea remain constant but the product is enhanced.

Equipment and premises are the same as for dressmaking, although if you are making ties you would not need a tailor's dummy! When business improves, you should consider out-workers to speed up the production line.

There is a fortune to be made if you come up with the right idea.

Theatrical Costumes

You must know your period dress for this job, and a collection of reference books on costumes through the ages will help not only you but the client as well. Start working for the local amateur dramatic society until you feel confident enough to approach professional theatres and film production companies.

Bargain bundles of fabric can be bought direct from textile mills (see Contacts and the advertisement columns of relevant magazines). These fabrics are good to have to hand as certain costumes, like those for the back row of the chorus, require less splendid materials than do those for the stars of the show. Get to know the tricks of the trade (like using Velcro instead of zips and fasteners, using fabrics for their textural effect, painting fabrics and making use of unusual materials and trimmings to bring out small details).

Advertise in show business publications, as well as writing personal letters to individual companies. For inspiration, visit exhibitions and leading theatrical costumiers. If you have the space and contacts, consider buying back your costumes cheaply when the show is over and starting a costume hire business.

CRAFTS

'Oh no, I never have any trouble getting hold of the empties!'

O There are no legal restrictions on doing craftwork at home.

O Approach the Crafts Council, the British Crafts Centre and CoSIRA (the Council for Small Industries in Rural Areas) for general information on setting up a workshop and selling to the public. (Try to get an entry in the CoSIRA book, *Craft Workshops in the Countryside*.)

O Adult education institutes run courses in the various crafts, as do the Women's Institute, who also sell craftwork through their weekly markets in towns all over the country. There is a wide range of craft books on the market, both for beginners and for the more advanced, and the Crafts Council publishes a magazine, *Crafts*, in which courses, suppliers and outlets are advertised.

O Be prepared to enter a field already filled with diligent enthusiasts doing crafts for fun as well as profit. Whatever you make, it must be competitive both in terms of workmanship and originality. On the other hand, there is a large market for hand-made

89

craftwork, both practical and decorative, and there are plenty of outlets through which to sell your work.

○ Visit craft exhibitions (there are many galleries throughout Britain) to see what professional craftsmen are producing. Although much of the best craftwork is traditional, there are new styles in crafts as in everything else, plus new developments in techniques and materials.

○ The Hand Crafts Advisory Association for the Disabled will give advice on crafts and equipment suitable for various disabilities, and they will also advise on outlets.

○ See Contacts for addresses and reference books.

Basketry

If you are contemplating taking up basketry you will be entering a market already filled with inexpensive, imported baskets from the East and also beautifully made baskets woven by the blind, so try to strike out with bright new ideas and designs. There is still a market in Britain for traditional hand-woven baskets, particularly heavy log baskets, cradles and cat and dog baskets. The equipment needed is minimal – mainly basic tools which you may already have. The only investment is in materials so this is an ideal craft if you live in a part of the country where there is a plentiful supply of willows, rushes or reeds.

Baskets can be made from a variety of materials, virtually any natural fibre which is strong yet pliable, even sturdy fibres like root, vine and fern. The challenge comes in the method you use and the complexity of the design and the colours you choose. There are several different techniques, including weaving, plaiting, coiling and caning (see Furniture). Adult education institutes and the Women's Institute run courses and advice can be sought from the Basketmakers Association. There are also several excellent books on the subject.

Tools vary depending on which materials you are working with, but you will need tough shears, knives, scissors, an awl and round-nosed pliers. If you do not have a local supply of materials, they can be bought from suppliers.

Basketry is soothing to do but very hard on the fingers, so take it gently to begin with. It is one of the crafts most suited to blind people, and there are special shops selling their products. Try to find an unusual angle so that you are not competing with cheap imports, for instance you could make hanging baskets to sell

Crafts

through florists, and tablemats, trays and shopping baskets for kitchen shops. You could also specialise in making corn dollies, which is a similar technique, and these sell well at agricultural shows and in craft shops. If you also make home-made sweets or potpourri, you could make up attractive gift baskets covered with cellophane and tied with ribbon. Sell these to gift shops or on market stalls, for instance at the Women's Institute markets. Advertise cat and dog baskets in the local vet's surgery and in magazines for pet-owners.

Basketry is one of the oldest crafts and pre-dates both weaving and pottery. It is very enjoyable work and leaves plenty of room for experimentation.

Batik

Batik is an ancient craft which originated in Indonesia. It is a method of dyeing known as wax-resist. The design is painted onto the fabric with hot wax, and the fabric is immersed in the dye; the waxed areas resist the dye, so that the painted design comes out in negative. The fabric is then plunged into cold water which hardens the wax and it cracks, giving the marbled effect typical of batik. The process is repeated for each colour. The wax is finally removed by ironing the fabric between layers of absorbent paper. Batik takes time and patience.

Silk and cotton are the most suitable fabrics, though with practice you can branch out and experiment on different materials. You can use batik wax or beeswax, available from craft suppliers, and chemical or vegetable dyes. You will need a long table to spread the fabric out on, a *tjanting* (the traditional wax pen), an alcohol lamp and stand, a pan in which to melt the wax (preferably a double-boiler, for safety), brushes and stamping tools for repeat designs.

There are courses in batik at adult education institutes, and batik is usually covered in general craft books as well as more specialist books.

Batik can be used to create beautiful and original clothes, scarves, wallhangings and furnishing fabrics. Try to join forces with a dressmaker who will design clothes for the designs you produce, and take them to craft shops and 'ethnic' boutiques. Each length of batik fabric is a 'one-off' so you can claim they are really exclusive. Remember, though, to keep a note of the 'recipe' (the strength of dye and the time the fabric is immersed) if you need to

91

produce more than one length of fabric in the same colours, for example, for a pair of curtains or set of floor cushions.

This is very enjoyable work to do, and if you happen to drop wax accidentally onto the fabric you may even improve the randomness of the design!

Bookbinding

Traditionally an apprenticed trade, bookbinding is now learnt by many people from books and can be combined with a part-time course at an adult education college. Contact the Society of Bookbinders and Book Restorers for further information.

Paper, cloth and leather are the most usual binding materials. The price of leather and the extra skill you need to work in it will probably deter you from using leather until you are more experienced. The equipment consists of a press, a sewing frame and a set of brass tools for lettering (try to buy them second-hand). Materials include adhesive, paper and thread. You do not need a special workroom, but make sure children or pets cannot get at the desk or table where you work.

Charge by the hour, plus materials. Bind according to the value of the book – a £5 book with £5-worth of binding will not sell for £10.

Sell your service to second-hand booksellers, restorers, and private collectors. Advertise in specialist journals, whose readers might want the separate issues bound together, and in academic magazines offering to bind theses. Write direct to the publishers of limited editions.

This is interesting work, the returns are moderate to good and it would suit those with design skills. Rebinding an old book is very rewarding, and it is equally stimulating to design a new binding for a limited edition of poems or prints. You could specialise in tooled leather bindings (see Leatherwork). As well as books and journals, you can bind items like writing paper folders, games boards and boxes, which all sell well through expensive gift shops.

Bottle Chopping

Bottles and jars are usually non-returnable and end up in the dustbin, when with a bottle chopper and a little imagination they could be turned into vases, ashtrays, storage jars, candle-holders or hanging baskets. The technique is very simple.

The only equipment is a glasscutter and sandpaper (silicon carbide paper) to finish off the rough edges. You should wear goggles and gloves for protection. Cut the bottles somewhere away from children and be sure to sweep up carefully when you have finished.

The wheel of the cutter scores a line around the bottle and you then tap along that line until it breaks. It is very simple, requiring practice rather than force. Cutters are available from hardware shops and last for ever, so the overheads are very low and the supply of bottles and jars is free. You can buy cork stoppers in different sizes for storage jars.

Sell to gift and kitchen shops and take a market stall at Christmas, maybe filling the jars with herbs or sweets.

Warning: Cut bottles should not be used as glasses for drinking from, even with the most thorough cleaning and sanding.

Calligraphy

Calligraphy, the art of handwriting, is becoming increasingly popular. It is one of the simplest crafts to take up, requiring very little equipment, and it can easily be done for profit in a quiet corner at home.

Calligraphy is much in demand for invitation cards, letter headings and posters. Introduce yourself to your local printers, who can recommend your service to their customers, and also advertise in more exclusive stationers and craft shops. Approach colleges and universities in your area and offer to design their certificates and diplomas. You could also produce a printed range of labels for home-made preserves or wine, or 'Ex Libris' cards to go in the front of books, and at Christmas you can make elegant greetings cards.

Calligraphy has now become an art form in its own right, as well as a means of conveying written information, and there are many decorative techniques, such as illuminated or gold lettering. Once you have gained enough experience, you may find your work is good enough to display at exhibitions and to sell as framed works of art, and you can then work to commission for private collectors and societies or organisations needing special display work.

Calligraphers often cut their own quills and mix their own ink, but pens, nibs and ink can all be bought from specialist shops. The best calligraphy calls for beautiful paper and again there are several specialist shops selling a wide range of different papers.

Adult education colleges hold courses in calligraphy, and the Society of Scribes and Illuminators will arrange for tutors to give classes. There are also several excellent books on the subject.

Candlemaking

Candles have become so popular that there are now specialist shops selling nothing but candles in every conceivable shape, size and colour. You can have great fun experimenting with unusual moulds, making joke candles in the shape of fruit or eggs, decorating them with dried flowers or adding different fragances to the wax.

Candlemaking is quite a messy process, especially to begin with until you get the knack. You will probably have to work in the kitchen as you need a stove on which to melt the wax. Wax is inflammable, so an electric stove is safer than gas. You will also need somewhere to hang the candles while they are solidifying.

There are three kinds of wax: beeswax (expensive), paraffin wax and stearin wax (you should use a mixture of 9 parts paraffin to 1 part stearin). Buy in bulk. Apart from wax, you need wicks, a metal saucepan to melt the wax in, a thermometer, wax-soluble dyes and fragrances. Moulds can be improvised from paper cups, tins and glasses or bought from a candle supplier or craft shop.

If you are going to make candle-holders to go with your candles, be sure they are made from non-flammable material. Mention your candlemaking activities to the insurance broker, as it could be worth increasing the policy to cover fire risk. There are several courses and books on candlemaking and it is not a difficult craft to learn. Prices are good, especially for the more unusual scented or 'novelty' candles, and you can charge more if you include a candle-holder and candle together in an attractive gift package. Sell to gift, craft and kitchen shops or take a market stall.

Warning: Remember to keep small children out of the kitchen while you are heating the wax.

Christmas Decorations

Obviously this work is seasonal so cannot be viewed as a big money-spinner all the year round, but you can expand to include Easter and Valentine's Day.

Decorations can be easily and cheaply made from almost any material: expanded polystyrene (cut out or layered), wood, straw, plastic, fabric, papier mâché, plaster of Paris (for miniatures and figurines of the Nativity), or simply paper (ruffled, cut, painted, collaged and glued for crackers and paperchains). Some of the most attractive traditional decorations are made from natural materials which you can collect free – miniature Christmas trees made from branches, pine cones, logs, holly and mistletoe.

Start work around June and take samples round to buyers soon after so that the decorations are in the shops by October or November when Christmas shopping starts.

For ideas, look around the shops and through the seasonal issues of magazines. There are also several practical books on the market. It is really a case of turning out something which is irresistibly pretty, well made and which captures the spirit of the occasion. Refer to craft books for the different techniques, such as papier mâché.

Provided you supervise them, this is something that can involve the children as well – and keep them amused.

Crochet

Crochet is quick to do, and the only equipment needed is a crochet hook and the yarn. With just a couple of stitches, you can produce lovely intricate patterns which look deceptively complicated.

Crochet can be done with one hand, using a wooden hook holder, so it is suitable for anyone who is partially disabled (consult the Hand Crafts Advisory Association for the Disabled).

Dorothy crochets during the week while she childminds, and sells her work at the weekend on market stalls: *'Even when it's not in fashion, crochet is good for collars and cuffs, ponchos and shawls. For every item I sell I get an order for something else. Because it's sometimes impossible to keep up my stocks, I often employ older women who crocheted when they were young as a matter of course – they are thrilled to be back in harness. The only problem is that yarns can become costly as wholesalers tend not to send small amounts to individuals working from home, so it is important to hunt out cheap yarns in markets, sales and out of the way places.'*

There is a Knitting and Crochet Guild and courses are held at adult education colleges. Take samples of your work to boutiques as well as selling direct to the public, but remember shops will charge a high commission, or put on a high mark-up, although they will proably sell the work for very much more than you can charge on a stall.

Decorating Glass

Several things can be done to glass to enhance its appearance and increase its value.

Painting on Glass   Painting glass is the simplest way of turning an ordinary piece of glass into something special. If you are artistic, you can draw directly onto the glass freehand, otherwise you can mask off areas to create a geometric pattern, giving a stained glass effect. Delicate designs look best on wine glasses and decanters but also think big and bold for larger areas. A glass-topped coffee table could have a chessboard painted on it. Mirror surrounds could lend themselves to dramatic Art Deco effects. Try to obtain special commissions to work in people's homes and offices, painting a 'view' on a window which looks out onto a brick wall.

You need very basic equipment: paint, brushes, thinner, masking tape and a craft knife. Make sure the glass is clean before you start. Techniques and ideas for designs can easily be acquired from craft books.

Etching   This is a process in which controlled amounts of acid are allowed to eat away selected parts of the glass surface. It can transform an ordinary wine glass into a collector's piece, and is often used for lettering on glass.

You will need etching fluid, stop-out material (to stop the acid running off the pattern), a brush, tweezers, a spoon, thinners and a craft knife. Acid is dangerous, so its use must be controlled very carefully. Keep it away from children.

Engraving   This is the most skilled glass-decorating technique and you need some artistic talent, although you can buy designs to trace. It also takes a very steady hand!

Engraving involves cutting into the surface of the glass, either with a wheel or using a diamond or steel point. Mistakes have to be polished out, a time-consuming process, so practise on cheap glass. Not all glass is suitable for etching – the lower the lead content, the more difficult it is to etch.

As well as the engraving tools themselves, you will need a good lamp, goggles and a dark cloth to work against. Keep children well away from your work area, and be very careful to clear up the fine grains of powdered glass after you have finished.

There is a Guild of Glass Engravers which runs engraving courses and publishes a pamphlet, *Starting from Scratch*. Some of the larger adult education institutes do part-time courses, and there are specialist books on engraving.

Create your own designs to sell through gift shops, but also try to work to commission, offering a personal service for anniversaries, wedding presents and commemorative plaques.

Decorative Wood Techniques

Following on from the enormous popularity of stripped pine, there is now a renewed interest in the traditional techniques of wood decoration. Uninteresting pieces of furniture can be transformed into works of art, and ordinary everyday kitchen spoons and chopping boards can suddenly become decorative gifts.

Painting on Wood   This is extremely popular in Germany, Russia and Scandinavia, and in England we know it mainly in the form of 'canal boat painting' which has recently come back into fashion for decorating wooden kitchen and garden ware. It is equally effective on tin, and is often seen on trays and watering cans. Chair backs, mirror frames and spice racks need only a few brush strokes, or you can execute a really complex design on a blanket chest or chest of drawers. The materials are straightforward paints and brushes which can easily be obtained from artists' suppliers.

Stencilling   This technique is ideal for those with no artistic talent, as ready-made stencils can be purchased separately or in book form. Alternatively you can cut your own, using special stencil paper or heavy paper or card coated with glue or varnish. The paint can be sprayed or applied with a stencil brush. As well as decorating kitchen utensils, boxes and pieces of furniture, you can also work to commission stencilling floors and walls.

Pyrography or Pokerwork   This is the technique of burning designs into wood with a heated metal instrument. You can simply use pieces of wire twisted into different shapes and heated with a blowtorch, but a special pyrography machine is a small and fairly inexpensive piece of equipment. It consists of a heated 'pencil' with which you draw the designs, attached to a control unit. Pyrography can be used to decorate many kitchen items, such as salad bowls, bread boards and spoons, and it is also used to decorate leather.

Découpage   This technique appeals to devotees of Victoriana, of which there are many. Cut-out paper shapes are glued onto the wood and then coated with varnish. It is ideal for covering worn or stained surfaces, so you can work on old boxes and tables bought very cheaply in junkshops. Again the materials are very cheap and readily available from hardware shops and artists' suppliers.

There are several other traditional wood finishes, such as stippling, marbling, graining and lacquering (see Gilding), all of which are now coming back into fashion.

As yet, there are few courses in these specialist techniques but there are several craft books which will give you all the information you need. Often a section on these subjects is included in general crafts books and magazines.

Sell your work through craft shops and pine furniture dealers, and try to get commissions for individual designs, such as babies' cots or children's toy chests.

Embroidery

There are many different embroidery techniques – patchwork and quilting are also forms of embroidery, although they are treated separately in this book as they are so popular and have their own separate organisations and suppliers. Most embroidery is time-consuming and the materials are often quite expensive, so you must be sure of your market if you want to take up embroidery for profit as well as for a hobby. You cannot compete with the cheap embroidered clothes imported from India, so you need to think of a specialist or unusual approach or to work to commission.

Adult education institutes run courses in the various techniques, and so does the Women's Institute. The Embroiderers' Guild promotes all aspects of embroidery and publishes the magazine *Embroidery*; you can join one of the Guild's local branches, which hold regular meetings.

Specialist embroidery suppliers advertise in *Embroidery* and other crafts magazines, and many offer a mail order service. Very little equipment is needed, mainly needles and scissors. For some forms of embroidery, you will need a frame or hoop which supports the fabric and keeps it under even tension. Completed pieces of embroidery are often 'blocked', which means dampening the fabric and stretching it out on a board so that it dries in the correct shape (stitching often distorts the fabric).

Canvaswork Also called needlepoint, this form of embroidery is done on evenweave canvas with the stitches completely covering the surface. It includes the very popular Florentine embroidery (or bargello) which consists of zigzag geometric designs, usually worked in woollen thread. Florentine work is used extensively in upholstery, for chair seats, footstools and firescreens, and you could therefore approach antiques shops and upholsterers and offer a service replacing worn embroidery on furniture. You could also work through interior designers, creating designs to fit in with the colour scheme of individual rooms.

Canvaswork is also suitable for small items, such as needlecases and belts, and for many beautiful designs on cushions and wallhangings. Small items can be sold through market stalls and craft shops, but you will probably find that you cannot charge a realistic price for larger pieces of embroidery which take longer to do. There is, however, a growing demand for designs supplied in kit form, with the design painted on the canvas for the embroiderer to follow. If you have a good eye for design, you can run a flourishing business from home supplying kits either by mail order or through embroidery outlets and department stores. Take samples of your designs to likely outlets (there are many specialist embroidery suppliers through the country) and exhibit at the various trade fairs (for instance, the International Craft and Hobby Fair held each year at Wembley) and craft shows.

Embroidery threads and canvas are available from specialist shops, but if you are operating as a business you would do better to buy in bulk direct from the manufacturers. If you are producing your own designs, you may be able to sell them to an embroidery manufacturer to market themselves, which would save you the chore of packing and posting hundreds of individual kits. You could also send samples of your work to craft and needlework magazines, which pay well for the copyright of an original design. In this case, you will need to supply the completed piece of embroidery together with instructions.

Appliqué This is the technique of 'applying', or superimposing, one fabric on top of another. It was traditionally used on quilts and today is frequently seen in the form of individual motifs used to decorate children's clothes and babywear.

The swing needle electric sewing machine is a great boon in appliqué, as you can sew the motif directly onto the background fabric using a zigzag stitch to cover the raw edges. Another modern innovation is iron-on interfacing, which strengthens the appliqué shapes and is quick and easy to use.

To keep down costs, buy remnants of fabric in sales and use offcuts from dressmaking (ask friends and relatives to pass on their unwanted scraps of fabric as well). Simple shapes work very well, for example, a colourfully patterned butterfly on the bib of a little girl's pinafore dress or a row of ducks on a bathroom or nursery blind. If you are artistic you can create wonderful pictures, building up layers of fabric appliquéd on top of each other.

Unless your work is very inspired and you can break into the boutique end of the market, concentrate on children's clothes and cushions which are always popular. Sell on stalls in craft markets and through craft shops, and approach shops specialising in children's clothes. You could also sell by mail order, advertising in newspapers and magazines.

Hand and Machine Embroidery Many people with modern sewing machines have never used the wide range of embroidery stitches with which most machines are equipped. Compared to hand embroidery, machine embroidery is very quick and also very versatile – even with only the basic set stitches you can achieve a great variety of decorative effects. Attend one of the many courses run by the adult education institutes or the Embroiderers' Guild, and visit your local sewing machine supplier for a demonstration of what your machine will do.

You cannot compete with cheap, mass-produced embroidery, so try to think of a specialised angle which your customers will be prepared to pay a little extra for: make pretty cot covers embroidered with the baby's name and date of birth, or make framed pictures to hang on the wall. Hand embroidery should be used to maximum effect, rather than attempting to cover a large area: embroider flowers round the neckline of a woollen jersey, or stitch beads and sequins on an evening bag or jacket. Concentrate on small, pretty effects which will transform a simple garment or accessory into something unique.

Traditional techniques are still enjoying a great revival, so you could specialise in modern equivalents of Victorian samplers or shepherds' smocks (to sell to mothers of little girls, rather than shepherds!). Advertise with small ads in newspapers and magazines, as well as taking samples to local shops.

Enamelling

Enamelling is the art of fusing glass to metal, using heat to marry the two materials. The metal normally used is copper; silver and gold can also be used but copper is cheaper and easier to cut and shape. The glass, which forms the enamel, can be purchased in opaque or transparent form and comes in different colours.

Enamelling has been practised since before the birth of Christ. Traditionally it was widely used as a finish on utilitarian articles, and it has become increasingly popular for more sophisticated decoration and ornament. Allegedly difficult, the process, once learnt, is simple and inexpensive. Many colleges have special enamel kilns and adult education institutes run courses.

For cutting the metal, you will need shears, a file, a mallet, a block and plate, a gas torch, a vice and a sandbag. For preparing and grinding the chunks of enamel (unless you buy it ready ground), you need a mortar and pestle, sieves, bowls and sifters. And for firing, you need a kiln, racks, forks and asbestos mittens. Even with the kiln, the workroom need only be a small room with shelves and running water. (Some kilns consume as little electricity as a one-bar heater.)

Attend a course in enamelling and read the relevant craft books. Artist Enamellers and the Guild of Craft Enamellers will also supply you with information.

Enamelling is very creative and one area of craft which isn't too competitive as most people think enamelling is too complicated to try it. It is very flexible and enamel can equally well be applied to small items like earrings, brooches, bowls and boxes, or to large wall hangings and vases. Buyers will pay well for beautiful enamelwork.

Most books on enamelling list suppliers of enamel and equipment, and many suppliers advertise in the magazine *Gem Craft*.

Flower Making

Plastic flowers may be frowned on nowadays, but silk and paper flowers fit in very well with modern furnishings. They appeal to town-dwellers who cannot afford to keep buying expensive flowers from florists, and to hotels and offices which do not have the time or the staff to make arrangements of fresh flowers. Dust them occasionally and keep them away from an open fire. Arrangements can be made to look very stylish indeed.

Paper Flowers These are simply made from crêpe paper or coloured tissue paper, and the only equipment needed is glue, scissors and a pair of pliers. Stems can be made from lengths of wire or bamboo, and you can buy artificial stamens from craft and hobby shops. Once you have found an attractive design, you can build up speed and 'mass-produce' flowers in a range of colours. There are several books on paper flowers and often a section in general craft books.

Feather Flowers These were popular in Victorian England, though they are more rarely seen today. Ordinary chicken feathers can be dyed in exotic colours, or you can collect feathers in the country – pheasants' feathers are very beautiful and some people keep peacocks which, of course, possess the ultimate in feathers. Otherwise approach zoos or shops selling gamebirds, and for mass production go to a poultry farm. Attaching wires to the quills is rather fiddly work, requiring patience and practice.

Silk Flowers These are very luxurious, and you can charge higher prices to allow for the cost of materials. Silk comes in many beautifully subtle colours and textures, and you can create some exquisite works of art which can be sold in exclusive outlets. To cut down the cost, you can also use man-made fabrics with a similar silky texture.

Other materials lend themselves to flowermaking, for example, beads and shells, so look at a few craft books and visit gift shops for ideas and inspiration. Adult education institutes run flower-making courses but this is something you can easily learn from books and your own experiments.

Sell your flowers through gift shops and craft shops, and even to some florists who do not see them as competition but rather an extension of their own trade. You could also make yourself known to party caterers and suggest they use artificial flowers at functions where fresh flowers might not be suitable. Having made the flowers, you could then charge extra to make up a complete arrangement.

Artificial flowers are cheap and quick to make; the market is growing and the returns are good.

Handspinning

Spinning has hardly changed since man first discovered that twisting fibres produces a continuous thread. It is very satisfying work, and the rhythmic motion of the spinning wheel is very soothing at the end of a hard day.

There are no short cuts to spinning. If you practise for six hours a day, you should be able to produce a fairly reasonable yarn after three days, but first you have to know about fibre preparation – what fleece to buy, how to wash it, oil it, card it (optional), and comb it.

Buy a small wheel to begin with, as they are quite an investment, and look in craft magazines for one to purchase second-hand.

Audrey started with one wheel, but as it was too big to take away with the family on holiday she also bought a smaller one. Now she has five and gives spinning lessons at home when not actually spinning herself: *'There are so many nice things you can do with spinning once you've learnt how. I have to admit costs are high while you're learning, but when you become more organised you find remedies and ways of avoiding the problems that beginners always seem to have. I took it up to grow old gracefully but now I spend all my spare time shooting off round the country to buy fleeces! A lot of wool I pick off hedges and fences to save money. I can spin a 5 lb fleece into enough wool to make two large jumpers which, hand-knitted in pure wool, can fetch quite a price in smart shops.'*

Unless you keep your own sheep, buy fleeces through the Wool Marketing Board which acts as a central clearing house and also advises on the kind of wool needed for the end product, whether a coarse rug or much finer work. The Board also publishes educational material. Courses in spinning are run at adult education institutes and private centres such as The Handweavers' Studio. The Association of Guilds of Weavers, Spinners and Dyers will give you information.

Advertise through craft magazines and craft shops, and be prepared to travel to agricultural and county shows to exhibit your products. You can sell the wool or make it up into clothes and furnishings. You can also experiment with vegetable dyes, which look wonderful on natural-textured handspun yarn.

Jewellery

Jewellery can be practised at different levels, involving more or less skill and equipment and using materials ranging from pebbles found on the beach to precious metals like gold and silver.

At the most basic level, you can make earrings, necklaces and bracelets simply by purchasing beads from specialist bead suppliers and threading them in attractive combinations. Experiment with unusual materials, such as plastic-coated wire, feathers and buttons. (Look in magazines like *Crafts* and modern jewellery shops for inspiration; modern jewellery makes use of all kinds of materials, the wittier the better.) The various accessories, such as bead thread and clasps, can be purchased from bead and jewellery suppliers and craft shops. Sell on stalls in craft markets and through modern craft and jewellery shops.

Lapidary, the art of polishing and cutting stones, is not as fashionable as it used to be so check your market before you invest in a tumbling machine. Remember, too, that the machines are noisy so install one well away from the living room.

Machines and other equipment are advertised in *Gemcraft*, the monthly magazine in this field. Prices you can charge depend as much on the kind of mount you use as on the value of the stone, so again check whether your market calls for precious metals like gold and silver before you commit yourself. Mounts can be purchased from craft shops.

Once you get into precious metals like gold and silver, you need much more equipment and you must be prepared to invest money in materials. To operate from home you need a fully equipped workshop, so first take a course at an art college or through the City and Guilds Institute and practise on college equipment. Adult education institutes do courses in silverwork and there are several excellent practical books to learn from. Recently jewellery has branched out into modern materials such as plastics and titanium, so you should think whether you want to make traditional or modern jewellery and choose your outlets accordingly.

For precious metals, it is wise to take out extra insurance and to keep them, and the finished pieces of jewellery, in a safe. This is another craft where it is as well to exclude children from your workroom – they may not appreciate the difference between a marble and a precious stone!

Leatherwork

Hand-tooled leather is always in demand, especially accessories like bags, belts and wallets, and connoisseur items like leather chessboards can command a very high price.

Modern tools have greatly simplified the various procedures involved in leatherwork: carving, punching, stitching and dyeing.

The basic tools are knives, a revolving punch, glue and brushes, scissors and a leather needle. For soft leather, you can use a sewing machine. Buy the leather direct from the tanneries and leather suppliers (see the Yellow Pages and consult the British Leather Carvers' Association); most sell offcuts and rejected skins, which you can use to practise on and to make small items, such as purses and watchstraps. Store it in a cool, dry place, away from the light – and away from your dog, if he has a penchant for chewing leather until it looks like an old rag!

For more decorative effects, dye the leather different colours or print designs into the leather surface, using heated tools (see Decorative Wood Techniques). Use the offcuts from your work to make patchwork or appliqué, for example on clutchbags.

Sell accessories and smaller items on a craft stall or through craft shops. Larger, luxury items should be made to commission, either from individual customers or from shops. Even offcuts of leather are expensive, so you need to be sure of your market before you spend a lot of money on first-class skins.

If you have fashion sense and enjoy dressmaking, you could specialise in leather clothes to sell in boutiques and through advertisements in fashion magazines. Combine leather with other materials, such as tweed, denim or wool.

Shoes are rather more difficult, but there is a great demand for hand-crafted sandals and basic low-heeled shoes. Make up popular sizes for display, and take orders for other sizes and colours.

Saddlery   This is a dying trade but for this very reason you may find yourself in demand in a rural area, and people are now prepared to travel miles to visit a saddler whereas once there would be one in every village. Adult education institutes do courses in saddlery and harness making, as well as in leatherwork generally. Advertise in hunting and country magazines, and contact the Master of the local hunt and local riding schools.

Leather is a lovely material to work with and you should have no difficulty finding a market. But it is quite a competitive field, so your work needs to be good or original to sell. At the upper end of the market, if you can find the outlets, the profits can be very high.

Macramé

Macramé is decorative knotting, based on the simple process of tying lengths of yarn together to make textured patterns. With the recent revival in this craft, macramé has become very much an accepted part of home decoration, ranging from plant holders to curtains and wall hangings. It is also used for clothing and accessories, particularly belts and bags.

Basic macramé calls for no equipment other than flexible fingers. Once the knots are learnt and understood, it is possible to read a pattern from a photograph or drawing, and you can experiment with your own designs. You need a piece of board to pin the foundation threads to, but even this can be excluded if you use the legs of an upturned chair or two clamps fixed on either side of a tabletop.

Yarns (rope, string or finer materials, depending on what you are making) can be purchased at stationers, garden and yacht suppliers, hardware stores and craft shops. They should be non-elastic and not too stiff. Craft shops also sell wooden and glass beads which you can thread onto the yarn for decoration.

Many adult education institutes run courses and macramé can easily be mastered from step-by-step books. Sell to florists and gift shops, and take a market stall at Christmas.

There is almost no investment, and macramé is pleasant and quick to do. It also has the advantage that you can put it down and pick it up again at a moment's notice. (Guard it from children and cats!)

Mosaics

Mosaic work is fiddly but fun to do and very creative, even if you are not naturally artistic. It is the craft of making designs and pictures out of innumerable small stones, pieces of coloured glass, shells, and fragments of plastic or pottery. Traditionally it was used for floors, both indoors and outdoors, but it looks equally effective on tabletops, mirror frames and teapot stands. It has the advantage of being strong and hardwearing. Some Roman mosaic floors look as beautiful today as the day they were created.

The equipment is fairly simple, consisting of tile cutters, tweezers, grouting cement or magnasite, a mixing bowl, adhesives and a spatula, an abrasive stone (for filing rough edges) and a screwdriver for removing mistakes. You should wear goggles in case of accidents.

For your workroom, choose somewhere well lit and well ventilated, as you are working with adhesives. Store the mosaic pieces in clear glass or plastic jars (sweet jars are ideal), grouped according to size and colour. Glass offcuts can be bought from glass merchants (see the Yellow Pages), and pieces of plastic can be cut from old kitchen containers and broken equipment (for example, car brakelight covers). Some stones, among them flint, limestone, felspar, jaspar and quartz, can simply be picked up off the ground or beach; more exotic, semi-precious stones come from craft shops and jewellery suppliers. Pebbles (graded and sold by the sack) can be obtained from gravel pits.

Check with your local evening institute to see if they do a course in mosaics, otherwise you can learn the technique from books. For inspiration, study illustrations of the early Byzantine mosaics and visit places like Westminster Abbey and the Houses of Parliament.

Sell tabletops and larger pieces of indoor mosaics through furniture shops or work to private commission. Smaller items can be sold through craft shops or on a market stall. For outdoor work, try to link up with a landscape gardener and advertise in garden suppliers and nurseries.

Moulding with Polyester Resin

Polyester resin is liquid plastic which solidifies by a chemical reaction when a catalyst is added. It turns from a liquid to a jelly, then to a soft but solid state, and finally it becomes very hard.

There are various types of resin, ranging from a very clear resin suitable for embedding objects (anything from flowers to watch parts) in paperweights, doorknobs and ornaments, to mixes which can be used for laminates and for large items like slabs and blocks. Resin can be tinted with pigment, and it can be cast into flexible or rigid moulds – simple shapes, using plastic cups or bowls for moulds, or complex shapes such as intricate chessmen. Polyester resin kits can be bought from most craft shops.

The equipment needed to work in polyester resin is minimal: the resin and catalyst, moulds, pigments, a measuring jug, a flat wooden spoon and cleaner (polyester resin solvent or concentrated resin detergent). Plastics must be stored in a cool place and work *must* be carried out in a well-ventilated room (resin fumes are toxic) with no open fire and preferably nobody smoking. Always wear protective gloves, or at least a protective cream on your hands, and work on a heat-resistant surface covered by newspaper. The smell of resin is unpleasant, so keep it well away from food – ideally, work in a separate room.

This craft is very simple and can easily be learnt from books. The outlay is small for good returns and it is not very time-consuming.

Ornamental Ironwork

The village blacksmith may be a thing of the past, but ornamental ironwork is making a comeback. Small objects such as candlesticks and plant holders are popular with gift shops, and there is a demand for gates and gardenware. You can also work to commission on larger designs.

You need a suitable workshop, preferably set away from the house, equipped with either a brick hearth or a portable metal one, which you can make yourself. You will definitely have to apply for planning permission, and you should also consult the local authorities about fire regulations and check your insurance policy. Blacksmiths' tools can be bought from specialists dealers, or, better still, try to buy them second-hand from a blacksmith. Rusted steel is easier to forge than new steel for some reason, and you can buy it second-hand from steel merchants (see the Yellow Pages). Try and find a cheap supply. You will need a van or car for transporting it.

The British Artists Blacksmiths' Association will advise on setting up a forge, and on training. Courses are held at CoSIRA (the Council for Small Industries in Rural Areas), at West Dean College, near Chichester, and at Claydon Forge, near Ipswich. A week of concentrated tuition should be enough for you to start working on your own at home.

Advertise your ironwork in home and gardening magazines, and display samples at garden centres and nurseries, offering a made-to-order service. Smaller items can be sold through gift shops. You could also offer a repair service as many people are now restoring old houses, keeping the original fittings such as fireplaces and railings.

This is creative work, requiring muscles and an ability to survive in front of the flames! There are good profits to be made.

Papermaking

Hand-made paper seems to be here to stay. It appeals to our increasing awareness of the need to conserve resources and recycle materials, and the desire for personal goods made by hand rather than machine. There has also been a sudden explosion of upmarket stationery shops, selling beautiful (and expensive) notepaper, wrapping paper, greetings cards, folders, and so on – including hand-made products.

The raw materials for papermaking are widely available and free, and the basic equipment is found in most kitchens. Waste paper can be recycled to make new paper, and we all know how much paper we throw away every day. (Newsprint does not make very good paper, but that still leaves all the supermarket packaging, discarded envelopes, and so on – you could even recycle the gas bill!) Printing inks are washed out in the papermaking process, and if you want to remove their colour you can add a small amount of bleach to the paper pulp. Vegetable fibres are the other source of raw materials, and you can have great fun collecting and experimenting with different plants, each of which will give a different texture, colour and even scent to the finished sheets of paper. (Imagine paper made from nettles, straw or iris leaves.) Coarser stems and leaves will leave particles of fibre in the paper, which add to its natural, 'hand-made' attraction.

Papermaking is a messy procedure, involving a lot of liquid. You need easy access to a sink and also to a stove, so the obvious place to work is in the kitchen. The first stage is to shred the raw material, for which you need an electric blender, preferably one with a large capacity. You will also need scissors and knives for cutting up the plants or paper to fit them into the blender. The shredded material is then boiled with water in a large pan to reduce it to a pulp, at which stage you break up the fibres even further with an electric handmixer. Only when you come to make the actual sheets of paper do you need specialist equipment, a mould and deckle which sift the pulp from the water solution and spread it out to form an even sheet of paper. Moulds can be made by hand or bought from shops which sell papermaking kits. The kits explain the process and there are also practical reference books to learn from.

Hand-made paper is beautiful in itself, particularly if you experiment with different plants, but you can also treat it in a variety of ways. Dyes can be added to the pulp to give coloured paper, and if you want a glazed finish suitable for drawing and calligraphy you press the sheets of paper between two smooth metal plates. Watermarks are made by attaching wire or brass designs to the sieve on the mould, so that a negative image is left on the sheet of paper. Leaves and pressed flowers can be placed between two layers of paper pulp, and you can add all kinds of materials to the pulp, for example, tiny pieces of glitter or tree bark. If you place the wet sheets of paper on a textured surface, such as a coarse towel, and pour the pulp over three-dimensional shapes, such as shells, buttons or rope, you can create paper 'sculptures'. Finally, a craft in its own right, you can marble the paper by floating coloured dyes across the surface in beautiful swirling patterns.

There are many outlets for hand-made paper. Sell sheets of notepaper and envelopes on market stalls and through craft shops and specialist stationers. Make simple books for use as photo albums or recipe books, and make greetings cards decorated with pressed flowers and leaves. Working to commission, you can supply individual watermarked stationery, and once your work is good enough you can supply printmakers, calligraphers and artists, either directly or through their suppliers of other materials. Hand-made paper also makes beautiful lampshades, particularly if you use an interestingly textured paper, and you can sell these through craft shops or interior design shops.

Papier Mâché

With the current emphasis on recycling waste material, papier mâché is an ideal way to make use of all those old newspapers and bits of packaging which are usually put out for the dustmen. Pasted paper is soaked in water to produce a pulp and then moulded into different shapes. When it dries out it is very hard and strong enough to be used for containers, bowls, trays, flowerpots and even small tables, chairs and firescreens. It is also ideal for making masks, puppets and models, and can be painted when dry.

Papier mâché is simple to do and the only equipment is a table with a washable top, and a paste brush, buckets, moulds and scissors. The kitchen is the ideal place to work.

The shredded paper is soaked in a solution of water and glue to form a mashy dough which can be sculpted almost like clay. Alternatively, you can cut the paper into strips, coat it with paste and then stick it onto a mould made of wire, cardboard or wood. Most paper mâché objects will dry overnight, after which they can be sanded and painted. A clear acrylic sealer can be sprayed onto the finished piece to protect and waterproof it.

This is a truly simple craft, using remarkably cheap materials. The art is in creating something attractive, rather than the traditional lumpy offering. Read up on the subject and practise until you are confident enough of your results to be able to sell them. Unusual or useful paper mâché objects sell well in gift shops and the gift sections of department stores. There is plenty of scope too in the children's toy market, and if you are artistic you could experiment with larger-than-life models of animals and children's book characters.

Papier mâché is fun to do and the children will love it!

Patchwork and Quilting

Patchwork is enjoying an enormous revival. Originally it was a 'thrift' craft, particularly associated with the early American settlers who hoarded every precious scrap of fabric to be recycled into warm patchwork quilts and bedcovers. Intricate designs were made by cutting the fabric into different shapes (hexagons, triangles, diamonds, and so on) and stitching them together in various patterns with names like 'Grandmother's Flower Garden', 'Log Cabin' and 'Flying Geese'.

Patchwork can be done either by hand or on a sewing machine, depending on the complexity of the designs. Accuracy is absolutely vital if all the pieces are to fit together, and you need to be very patient and painstaking. A sense of colour and design is also very important, and you should spend some time planning the arrangement of colours and patterns before you start. An unplanned quilt can easily look a mess, whereas a beautiful, vibrant design will be a work of art and become a treasured family heirloom.

The only special equipment needed are the metal or plastic templates used in hand-sewn patchwork, and these can be bought from needlecraft shops or by mail order (see advertisements in craft magazines). Otherwise you need basic sewing equipment, in particular a good pair of scissors for cutting out the fabric. Most important is a supply of fabric: try and buy remnants and bargains in sales, and if you are very lucky you may find a factory which will let you have offcuts free or at nominal cost. Cotton is the easiest fabric for beginners to work with, but patchwork can be made from a wide variety of fabrics as long as you remember to use similar weights of fabric together. Experiment with velvets and corduroys for a sumptuous floor cushion, with silks and satins for an evening waistcoat, and with furnishing fabrics as well as dress fabrics.

The finished patchwork is often quilted, depending on what you are making – obviously a patchwork quilt needs to be quilted!

There are many beautiful traditional quilting designs, or you can simply quilt along the lines of the patchwork. It can be done either by hand or by machine.

Adult education institutes and the Women's Institute do courses in quilting and patchwork, as does the Embroiderers' Guild which has branches all over the country. There is also an organisation devoted exclusively to patchwork and quilting, the Quilters' Guild, which will supply information on courses and suppliers. There are also innumerable books from which you can learn. Neither patchwork nor quilting require any specialist skills except that of being an extremely neat seamstress.

Full-size quilts are popular but they are also very time-consuming and you have to charge a very high price to cover both your time and materials. It may be safer to concentrate on smaller items, such as clothes, cot quilts, cushions, tablelinen and pincushions, to sell in craft shops and on market stalls or through magazines. Approach interior decorators to see if you can offer a complete service for bedroom furnishings, with toning curtains and quilts. Several shops, such as Laura Ashley, now sell co-ordinated ranges of wallpaper and fabric, in small repeat patterns ideal for patchwork.

For inspiration, visit the various museums which house collections of patchwork quilts: the Victoria and Albert Museum in London, the American Museum near Bath, and the Welsh Folk Museum in St Fagans, near Cardiff.

Picture Framing

Picture framing requires plenty of space and is not something you should attempt to do in a small back room. Glass and hardboard come in large sheets and, quite apart from storage, you need space in which to lay them out and cut them to size. Also essential is a good, well-lit work table, storage shelves (including long shelves to hold mouldings), a mitre saw for cutting corners, clamps to hold joins after glueing, a glasscutter, rules and set squares, and a hammer and nails. Optional extras are a vice and a mount cutter. Most important of all is the mitre saw, so do buy a good one. You will need a small van or car in which to transport materials and maybe deliver the frames.

Warning: Keep children out of the way when you are cutting glass, wear goggles and gloves for protection and sweep up carefully afterwards.

Prices are linked to the size of the frame and the moulding (gold, metal, antique style, plain wood, etc), and you should be competitive with the prices charged in the shops. To give a comprehensive service, you will need a good selection of moulding styles, mounts and backing boards for customers to choose from, so your initial outlay may be quite large.

Advertise through local newspapers and also in art galleries, art schools, architects' offices, photographers' studios, colleges and craft, book and map shops. See if you can land a contract with a print shop, and consider revamping old frames (link up with a gilder) or offering a picture cleaning service.

Picture framing is satisfying work and a junk shop picture can be completely transformed by the right frame. Adult education colleges run courses and there are several books to learn from. Frames are expensive in the shops so a fast, reliable framing service should do well.

Pottery

The investment in pottery equipment is comparatively high, so attend a course first if you are a beginner to see if you have flair and are really serious about it.

Second-hand kilns and wheels are advertised in craft magazines and in *Ceramic Review*, the specialist magazine in this field. The minimum you need is a small electric kiln, and a kick wheel if you intend to make pots. Clay can be bought from pottery suppliers or in bulk from brickworks, and you can dig your own in certain parts of the country. Glazes can be bought ready mixed, or you can prepare your own.

A shed or garage would make the most suitable workroom if you are working at home. It must have a sink with running water, electric power points, a cupboard lined with plastic sheeting, and a good, big, solid work surface. Make sure the kiln is correctly installed – it may be necessary to set it in a solid concrete floor, and you may need extra ventilation. The supplier or the Electricity Board should be able to advise you.

Adult education colleges run courses in pottery and ceramics, and there are also concentrated residential courses advertised in crafts magazines. Expect a high failure rate to begin with, but remember that with more experience you will be able to work much faster and have fewer rejects. Once you have got the knack, working with clay is very rewarding.

Pottery sells well on market stalls, and you can take samples to craft shops to sell on a sale-or-return basis. If you are enterprising, you can also work to commission: see if your local health food shop would like to place an order for their china, or suggest to a florist's shop that you supply them with pots to be planted with spring bulbs, for sale at Christmas. Not all pottery has to be for the kitchen or garden, although practical items, such as bowls, mugs, casseroles and ashtrays, are usually the best sellers. You could also make small ornaments, necklaces of clay beads or tiles, to vary your range.

It is worth joining the Craftsmen Potters' Association and the Small Potteries Trade Association, to keep in touch with news on outlets and suppliers as well as for general support and to be kept up to date on new trends and design ideas.

Silkscreen Printing

Silkscreen printing may sound ambitious, but with a little investment you can set up a printing studio at home, and if your designs have flair and originality you can sell them for a high price.

Screenprinting is suitable for both fabric and paper. In both the design is printed by forcing ink or dye through a fine screen, on which the areas not to take the colour have been blocked out by a stencil. The screen can be made of cotton organdie or terylene, which are much less expensive than silk. For the stencils you can use a variety of materials, depending on the sophistication of the technique you are working with. The same design can be printed over and over again, so you can print a continuous length of dress or furnishing fabric, or a set of posters or stationery.

June learnt silkscreening from a book: '*I work at home on a large table covered with a blanket. I have a frame and get screens made up for me by a man a few villages away. My first attempt at silkscreening was on my daughter's shirt and I showed it to somebody in the motor trade who took it to a rally and came back with a hundred orders! Now I specialise in logos on sportswear, mainly sweatshirts. Often I work on spec and print up a nice logo and send it to a company that I think might like it.*'

Your first attempts at silkscreening will probably be rather awkward and messy. Some adult education institutes do courses but it is still a relatively new craft in Britain, although it is very popular in America. There are several books on the subject.

Silkscreen frames can be bought from artists' suppliers or you can make your own (an old picture frame would do). As well as the screen and frame, you need a large, unpadded, work table – lengths of material must be spread out flat – with a washable surface. You must have ready access to a sink. You will also need a squeegee with which to spread the ink or dye evenly across the screen. There are several different fabric dyes and printing inks on the market – choose fabric dyes which are easy to fix, for example by ironing the fabric after printing.

If you are not a dressmaker, sell fabric in dress lengths or in the form of scarves or very simple garments like kimonos. If you can join forces with a dress designer, you can sell to exclusive boutiques as well as through craft shops. Screenprinted fabric makes beautiful soft furnishings – make up cushions and table-linen to sell through craft shops, and print blinds to order. Approach interior decorators and ask them to recommend your service to their clients.

The most remunerative approach to printing on paper is limited editions of prints, which you can sell either framed or unframed through print shops. Your work will need to be good, so you do need artistic talent, too. You can also approach local societies or galleries wanting posters for special events, or produce an exclusive range of beautiful greetings cards and wrapping paper, but remember that screenprinting cannot compete with commercial litho printing in speed and therefore cost. Concentrate on quality rather than quantity.

Soft Toys

Making soft toys is fun to do and can be quite profitable, especially if you already have pieces of fabric left over from dressmaking. It is very competitive, so novel ideas are important as well as good-quality workmanship.

Joanne makes enormous silk clowns to match her clients' bedrooms: *'They are almost as big as eiderdowns and twice the price!'*

Mary makes rag dolls in period dress, which she sells in stately homes.

Gina stocks an entire shop with toy animals, everything from tiny mice to life-sized sheepdogs.

And Jean limits herself to making toy cats, in all sizes and colours. In each case, their main customers are adults buying for themselves, not for their children!

There are several courses on toymaking through the City and Guilds Institute and adult education institutes, as well as many books on the subject. You should work in a childproof room, and for equipment you need a sewing machine (although you can sew toys entirely by hand), scissors and stuffing, plus a supply of artificial eyes, etc. The British Toys and Hobbies Association publishes a directory giving the names and addresses of suppliers of eyes, noses, patterns and so on. Scraps of leather and felt can be used for animals' paws and noses, and factories supply offcuts of fur fabric. Choose hardwearing fabrics to stand up to the rough-and-tumble of children's games, and make sure the seams are very well finished.

Soft toys are subject to stringent safety requirements under the Toys (Safety) Regulations Act of 1974: noses and eyes must be firmly attached so that children cannot swallow them, there should be no metal parts, and the filling and cover should be non-flammable and washable (see HMSO leaflet SI 1974 No.1367). If a customer complains about one of your toys, you could be prosecuted by either the Trading Standards Office or the Environmental Health Department, so it is worth sending a sample of your toys to the British Standards Institute Test House at Hemel Hempstead (they charge a fee for the tests). You also have to be careful if you make toys representing television or book characters, because these are protected by copyright and you can only manufacture under licence. It may be worth taking out extra insurance cover as you, rather than the supplier of the materials, are responsible for any illness or injury caused by the toys.

Sell on craft stalls and through gift shops and toy shops, and be prepared for rush orders just before Christmas.

Stained Glass

Traditional stained glass is created by joining small pieces of coloured glass with strips of lead. The technique is not difficult to learn, and there is a definite demand for ornamental and functional stained glass for windows, lamps, frames, terrariums, boxes and hangings. The glass can be bought already coloured from glass merchants, although you can achieve a similar effect with transparent glass paints. It is sold in sheets, which you cut to size following a paper pattern of the design. Always wear goggles and gloves when you are cutting glass, and brush up the dust and offcuts afterwards. Leading is available single channel (for the outside edges) and double channel (for the inner lines). It is cut into lengths to fit the pieces of glass and then soldered together to form a whole.

You will need a steel wheel glasscutter, a lead-cutting knife, pliers, a small hammer, a soldering iron and a gas cooker or bunsen burner. The workshop *must* be childproof, well ventilated and well lit.

There are short courses in stained glass at craft centres and adult education institutes, and it can also be learnt from step-by-step books.

The number of items which can be enhanced by or made from leaded glass is limited only by your imagination! It is stimulating and creative work to do, and the rewards are high. Sell on market stalls and take samples of your work to craft and gift shops.

Weaving

There are numerous ways of weaving thread to make a fabric, each using different equipment. You can produce complex and beautiful designs using simply a set of cards with holes punched in them, or a backstrap loom which you tie round your waist. But if you intend to make a living from weaving, you will need a treadle loom which can be operated much more quickly than a primitive loom and also be used to make larger pieces such as rugs and wallhangings.

Treadle looms are relatively expensive and take up a lot of space, so you will need to set aside a room as a permanent studio. Second-hand looms are advertised in crafts magazines and in *The Weavers Journal*, published quarterly by the Association of Guilds of Weavers, Spinners and Dyers. (Ask the advice of a professional weaver before buying a second-hand loom.) You will also need the various other pieces of equipment used in weaving, including warping spools, shuttles, bobbins, a skein winder, bobbin winder, warping board and beater. Many different yarns can be used for weaving, with new synthetic yarns rivalling the traditional wool and cotton and creating exciting new design opportunities. Professional weavers often dye their own yarns, using either chemical or vegetable dyes. Weaving suppliers advertise in crafts magazines and you can also buy direct from textile mills. If you make rag rugs, which are now very popular, all you need is a plentiful supply of recycled material to cut up into strips. (Jumble sales are a good source.)

There are many books on weaving, from which you can learn the simpler methods such as card and band weaving, but for loom weaving you should attend a course at an adult education institute or one of the many courses advertised in crafts magazines.

Weaving is a slow process, extremely satisfying to do but difficult to price realistically as the cost of time and materials is usually high. Aim at the top end of the market: sell through craft shops and exhibit in local craft galleries, and work to commission. If you weave in fine threads, make the fabric up into beautiful clothes to sell either direct to private clients or through exclusive boutiques. Smaller work, such as bags, cushions and scarves, can be sold on market stalls as well as to gift and craft shops. Think about weaving curtains and bedcovers as well as floor rugs, and maybe team up with an interior decorator to design furnishing fabrics for particular settings such as hotels and offices.

If your work is good and you find the right outlets, you can command high prices and make a good income from a very creative and absorbing craft.

FOOD

'Hello dear, your sandwich is in the fridge.'

You will need a well-equipped and spacious kitchen, but before your business can begin there are several official channels you will have to venture down.

○ All premises to be used for cooking food for sale to the public have to be inspected by an Environmental Health Officer, who will check that they meet the Food Hygiene Regulations. These regulations relate to cleanliness, equipment, storage, waste disposal and water supply, and they are very stringent. They can be studied in HMSO leaflet SI 1970 No.1172.

○ You might require planning permission from the council if you want to make alterations to your property in order to operate a business involving foodstuffs.

○ You should take out a public liability insurance policy to protect you if your food were to poison a customer.

○ If you are a member of the Women's Institute, they will advise on legal matters and offer courses in catering and cookery. Courses are also available through private and adult education colleges. The City and Guilds schemes cover hotels and catering, food and drink.

O If you are going to transport food, you should have a vehicle with a boot fitted and lined to Department of the Environment specifications.

O The Ministry of Agriculture, Fisheries and Food prints a leaflet on the correct way to make jams and chutneys. Called *Domestic Preservation of Fruit and Vegetables*, it is Bulletin 21

available from HMSO.

O You will need a licence if you are going to supply alcohol but you do not need one if the client buys the alcohol and you serve it in your glasses.

O Just for the record, somewhere along the line you are sure to come up against certain personal restrictions, like cooks not being allowed to wear nail polish, having to have their hair tied back off the face and having to sport special overalls and aprons!

Baking and Cake-making

There is no point trying to compete with the local baker's shop, so concentrate your efforts on providing a specialist, high-quality service. Make wedding and birthday cakes to order, and supply local shops with Christmas and Simnel cakes. (Simnel cakes are the traditional marzipanned cakes made for Easter.) Alternatively you could specialise in quiches, pizzas or unusual breads, to supply wine bars, pubs and restaurants. Tea shops and cake shops may be interested in home-made cakes, cheesecakes and scones, and attractively wrapped packets of home-made biscuits are very popular. Batches of cakes can be sold on market stalls, especially the Women's Institute markets held weekly in many towns.

You will need a large, well-equipped kitchen, with a supply of good-quality baking tins and biscuit cutters, plus an electric cakemixer and whisk. Remember to include the cost of gas or electricity in your prices. Buy ingredients in bulk from catering suppliers (see the Yellow Pages) and cash-and-carry retailers, but take care not to over-order perishable goods unless you are able to store them. Baked food keeps very well in a deep freeze, so you should also invest in a large-capacity freezer – cakes often come out tasting all the better for having been frozen! Cake decorations can be bought in bulk from specialist suppliers, and you may be able to buy other ingredients or materials economically, for instance, if you specialise in quiches and live in the country you may find a local egg farm which will supply you with cracked eggs not suitable for sale to shops.

Baking fits in well with family life as you can be getting on with other things in the kitchen while a batch of cakes is in the oven. There are special courses at adult education institutes and, although much of the knowledge is basic good cooking, you may need instruction in icing cakes, for instance. There are many books available, and ones on traditional recipes will be particularly useful. Learn how to make local specialities too.

Confectionery and Preserves

Confectionery and preserves are both areas where, if you have one good idea, it is worth spending all your time developing it. You will make more money by turning out prettily packed truffles or unusual chutneys in imaginatively-decorated jars than by producing sweets and jams which are mass-produced at prices far lower than you could achieve.

Whatever you produce – marmalades, marzipan animals, glacé cherries, chocolates, fudge, brandy butter – it should look good as well as taste good. Put your name and address on labels so that more orders can be taken. Sell on market stalls, in particular Women's Institute markets, and through tea rooms, gift shops and delicatessens. Advertise your product in sample form! However, you will have to conform to Food Hygiene Regulations and you may not sell home-made yoghurt or ice-cream to the general public (see HMSO leaflet SI 1970 No.1172). Adult education institutes run courses on confectionery, and there are dozens of books to learn from.

Unless you spend a lot on packaging, the outlay is small and you can charge good prices. The work is fun to do, and very creative.

Deep-freeze Cooking Service

Freezer-filling (preparing frozen meals for a client's deep freeze) is a branch of cookery which is on the increase. There are stringent rules to adhere to and a completely different cooking routine to organise. First, it is important to learn how to freeze and package correctly and how to defreeze. The Women's Institute, the Department of the Environment and books on freezer cookery will help, and adult education institutes run courses in deep-freezing. Once the food has been cooked, cooled, put into containers and frozen, you must make sure that you label each container with the name of the dish, the date of freezing, and instructions for thawing. The wrong thawing procedure can cause food poisoning (take out a substantial public liability insurance policy, to cover you even in the eventuality of a customer's death).

Wendy runs a thriving freezer-filling business with two friends: *'We have a large menu for the customer to choose from. It is essential to get orders well in advance so that you can buy in bulk and try to keep the prices down. So many shops stock frozen meals now which forces you to be cheaper* and *better! You really need two large freezers for storage and freezing, one for meat and fish and one for vegetables, desserts and cheese. The law states how quickly food has to be cooled after cooking, how soon it can be frozen after being cooled and so on. You also have to have a fitted travelling freezer chest in the boot of your vehicle for transporting the food. We charge per dish, costing it all up to the last pinch of salt and adding a 50% mark up.'*

Advertise locally in shops and newspapers. It is a very sound business to be in especially during school holidays, Christmas, Easter and in the summer.

Directors' Lunches

You need to be an efficient cook rather than a *cordon bleu* if you want to cater for business lunches. A simple, well-cooked meal is more palatable in the middle of a working day than some fantasy flambé. The preparation and cooking is either done at your home and then transported to the office, where it is served using office crockery and cutlery, or cooked by you in the directors' kitchen. Sometimes a secretary will buy things for you, sometimes not.

Michael has covered the business circuit for years: *'I trained through the Hotel and Catering Industry Training Board and started working through agencies. I have a massive library of recipe books so I never dish up the same meal twice to any client. Charges are for shopping, cooking, delivery, serving and clearing up, with food prices (which change weekly) on top. All my customers provide their own utensils and I transport the meal to them in an endless selection of plastic containers, tinfoil and take-away cartons and reheat it in situ. I always buy food in bulk and store it at home – you can find cash-and-carry places listed in* The Grocer, *which should be in the local library – and often when I find really good bargains I design set menus around them in order to shift my stock quickly.'*

Advertise in business journals and local newspapers, and go round offices with a brochure listing menus and prices. It is also a good idea to put up notices in city clubs frequented by business people.

Business concerns pay well for reliable service. Aim for the security of a couple of regular accounts – occasional work can be very time-consuming, insomuch as you have to find your way round a new kitchen, or lack of, each time!

Fruit Baskets

Fruit makes a perfect gift, especially if it is well arranged in an attractive basket.

Fruit can be bought wholesale in fruit markets (see the National Federation of Fruit and Potato Trades' annual handbook). It is worth finding a cheap source of supply so that you can buy little and often to ensure that the fruit is always fresh. Make a deal with a craft centre or basket shop for high quality baskets, or, for cheaper models, go to importers of mass-produced basketry from the East. The protective wrapping to go over the fruit can be either cellophane or plastic, enhanced with ribbons, dried flowers etc.

Store the fruit in a cool, well-ventilated room, out of direct sunlight – one bruised or over-ripe pear and bang go your profits. Advertise your fruit baskets with posters or samples in gift shops, florists and garden centres. Approach offices as they often need presentation packs and Christmas gifts for staff and customers.

Price is related to contents, and delivery should be included. Remember that prices will increase in winter when fruit is more expensive.

Packed Lunches and Sandwiches

Supplying sandwiches and packed lunches to offices is a service which has become very popular, so make sure you do your market research thoroughly. Most big businesses have subsidised canteens, so canvass the smaller ones, and don't forget the pubs. You can provide either a simple lunchtime service and arrive in the office with a basket of ordered (preferably) or unordered sandwiches, salads, quiches or snacks, all separately wrapped and priced, or a full-day service with morning coffee and afternoon tea included. Try to suit your product to your purchaser – if the market is weight-watching secretaries, provide accordingly.

You must be licensed by the local authority to sell your sandwiches. You will need a sizeable fridge to store the food in, and some form of transport to take you and your basket or trolley to the customers. Buy wholesale containers and wrappings (see the Yellow Pages: Disposable Product Manufacturers) and include the cost in your prices. Make an agreement with your local baker for wholesale bread, and check the prices of similar food in cafés and snack bars. Remember that there is an optimum price for a sandwich, so do not expect to make a profit on ones with extravagant fillings – it is hard to make a crab or quail's egg sandwich pay unless it's in very exclusive surroundings! Well-made, tasty, fresh sandwiches of known fillings usually go down better.

This is a demanding job as you often have to be up very early in the day to butter bread. Try and recruit your children or friends to help out.

Party Catering

All food should be attractively presented, especially party food. What you cook must look 'good enough to eat'. A party caterer who presents the client and his guests with soggy, dull-coloured canapés will not be asked to do so again.

Parties range from cocktails to weddings, children's birthdays to dinner-dances with breakfast. Jenny caters for all of them: *'When you start large-scale catering you have to borrow most of the equipment, because you cannot splash out and buy 250 or 300 sets of crockery, cutlery and glasses until you've built up a solid clientele. Also, you tend not to prepare enough storage space for bulk buying, or to buy large enough mixers, deep freezes or stoves – you can spend more time coping with these problems than actually improving the service offered. And at the start, one buys either too much or too little of everything. The cooking is the easy part: organising, buying, preparing and transporting the food is the bulk of the work. I now hire freelances to cook and wait at table and concentrate on the rest myself – discussing the menu, organising the waitress(es) or waiter(s), arranging the flowers, laying the tables, getting the ice for the drinks (you need a licence to sell alcohol, so I find it simpler to ask clients to buy it and let me ice and serve it for them in my own glasses), and setting up an oven in which to keep the hot snacks hot. Of course, if the client wants a five-course dinner then I have to check that their kitchen can cope, or make alternative arrange-*

ments. *Even though all the cooking is done at my home, certain things need last-minute heating or chilling. I charge per head, depending on whether it's a finger buffet or a sumptuous six-courser. Recommendation can be through the people who rent out marquees, photographers who cover weddings, shops that sell wedding dresses and evening wear and through advertisements in the local shop windows and newspapers.'*

Jenny's word of warning: Never take on too big a job. One 'poor' party can ruin a sparkling reputation and word-of-mouth advertising is vital.

Party catering is hard work, but interesting and rewarding for cooks with imagination, and you meet a good selection of people. If you need special training, take a catering course at an adult education institute or catering college. Once you have built up contacts and established a name for yourself, you should be able to run a very profitable business.

Party Organisation

Many people are terrified at the thought of having to organise a large social event, such as a wedding reception, a twenty-first birthday party, a children's party or a golden wedding anniversary. These people and societies and businesses may prefer to engage a party organiser, someone who will take charge of all the arrangements and leave the participants free to relax and enjoy themselves.

As a party organiser, you handle everything for the client from start to finish, which means liaising with other people to provide flower arrangements, band or discotheque, tables and chairs, glasses, waiters, barmen and maybe a marquee – and, most important, the food! Your function is as a middle-man. Ask the clients to order the liquor (otherwise you will need a licence) and then you take charge of putting the champagne on ice, mixing cocktails, serving the drinks etc.

Your major outlay will therefore be in a van, large enough to transport everything without making too many separate journeys. Ask for funds in advance to cover the cost of the provisions and services, otherwise you could be out of pocket if anything goes wrong and the bride changes her mind at the last minute. Present the customer with a breakdown of your expenses, and estimate the overall price per head, ranging from a wine-and-cheese evening to a six-course banquet. Make sure that you understand what the client wants before you start – some caterers offer clients a 'mini-meal' several weeks before the event so that they know exactly what to expect and can make any changes.

The summer months, Christmas and Easter are the busiest times for parties, although weddings, birthdays and anniversaries happen all year round. Advertise in local newspapers and by word of mouth, and try to establish a reputation for absolute reliability which is almost as important as competitive prices – your clients have hired you to relieve them of the responsibility of organising the event, and they do not expect to be worried by a last-minute panic when the glasses haven't arrived. You need to be prepared for all eventualities and you should choose suppliers and caterers you can rely on. Above all, you need a cool head and a talent for organising and diplomacy, whether it's persuading the caterers to add a vegetarian dish at short notice or simply reassuring the client that everything will be perfect.

With good contacts, you can establish a very profitable business for very little outlay.

Party and Picnic Packs

Cardboard fruit punnets are perfect for packing up snacks and sweets for picnics or children's parties. Picnic packs should contain a snack, sandwich or salad meal plus a beverage and fresh fruit or dessert. For the party packs, concentrate on children's favourites: sweets, biscuits, cupcakes, jellies, soft drinks. In both cases, the food needs to be packed solidly for easy transport and to prevent leakage.

Spread the word through schools and colleges, sports' clubs and tour companies, especially those dealing with younger people. A junior school sports team, for example, could use both! The big selling point is to sell the two together: charm the adults with the party snacks, and then impress them with the high standard of your varied picnic pack! Convenience food is such an accepted part of life nowadays that, with good marketing, your packs could become nice little money earners.

Specialist Cooking

There are so many people who need special food – diabetics, allergics, vegans and heart problem sufferers to name but a few.

Many cannot be bothered to experiment with different foods themselves and tend to eat the same meals day in and day out.

If you are prepared to put a little time into studying the requirements and special ingredients needed for certain complaints, for example cooking for diabetics, there is a virtually untapped market for deep-frozen or delivered meals.

Advertise with notices in hospitals, health farms, medical journals, agencies and places where old people and invalids congregate. Expect customers to want to see where the food is coming from – let them visit your home and see the kitchen. Remember to include the cost of delivery in the price. In such an uncatered-for field, profits could soar.

Tea Room

If you have the space, a tea room or small café can be a very profitable business to run from home. To attract custom you need to be in a city or town, particularly one visited by tourists, or in a village or near a beauty spot which attracts people out for the day.

Forget about fast-food hamburgers and 'chips with everything', as this side of the trade is already very well catered for. Concentrate instead on good, home-made food which people will be prepared to pay a little extra for. Cream teas are always popular, especially if you enjoy making your own scones and jam, and you can do a brisk trade in mid-morning coffee and cakes. Unless you really want to get into restaurant catering, serve light salads and snacks at lunchtime. Presentation is very important, so put flowers on each table and make pretty tablecloths – as well as paying attention to the food.

There are several regulations you have to comply with, including the provision of toilets, and you will need to invest in tables, cutlery and crockery as well as maybe adapting your kitchen to take the extra load (for instance, you will probably need a coffee machine). You must also be prepared for a substantial loss of privacy, so you should make sure the family are behind you before you start. Weekends and public holidays will be your busiest times, which may conflict with your normal social and family routine.

If you decide to take the plunge, consult the Planning Department and the Environmental Health Department. You will need planning permission to build toilets and for change-of-use of the property. You should also have a car park. A pretty garden is a great asset and means that you can accommodate extra tables and chairs, and therefore extra custom, especially in the summer when trade is at its peak.

It is worth taking out insurance to cover yourself for accidents related to your business. You should also make sure you understand the duties of an employer, for example, paying national insurance, as you will almost certainly need waitresses, even if you do all the cooking yourself. This is a popular holiday and weekend job for students, but make sure you have adequate help before you start as this could be a problem later. Maybe you could join forces with other people in the area, to supply cakes and also to help out part-time when you are busy.

One of the main problems is supply and demand, knowing how much milk and bread to order each day and how many cakes you will need. A deep-freeze is a great asset and it is wise not to offer too varied a menu, at least to begin with. People have an irritating habit of ordering what other customers are eating (if it looks good, of course!) so it helps to have a trolley or counter where you can display a selection of cakes and pastries, otherwise you find yourself with no scones and stuck with a batch of cream cakes which will not keep.

If you put up a sign, this will be advertisement enough in itself and there is not much point advertising locally as most of your trade will be from farther afield. It is worth, however, putting a notice in local gift shops or places where tourists and visitors will see it. If you can get yourself listed in one of the good food guides you will find people travelling miles out of their way to visit you.

Once you have got going, a tea room is an ideal place to sell other things: pots of home-made jam and preserves, potpourri from the garden, local pottery and the like. You can also sell mass-produced confectionery and cigarettes, supplied by companies which send travelling salesman to deliver and take orders.

People do not go out for tea nearly as much as they used to – Sunday tea in the country used to be quite an institution before petrol prices increased – but you can charge high enough prices for good quality to be able to make a reasonable profit. It is a busy (often hectic), sociable life and ideal if you feel stuck at home without being able to meet people. In this respect, it will appeal to some people more than many other home-based jobs, which are often very solitary for a greater part of the time.

Weekend Cooking

Many people who live in cities spend their weekends and holidays at their 'second homes' in the country and like to hire somebody who lives locally to cook their main meals for them.

Roland lives in a wealthy part of the country where he provides Friday and Saturday night dinners and Sunday lunches for houseparties throughout most of the year, with a fuller service over Christmas, Easter and summer holidays: *'If you are catering for the top end of the market, you are expected to be able to serve a perfectly suckled pig or stuffed pheasant, so you should take a high-class cookery course and read up on period cooking. My customers alert me to numbers etc in advance and I buy the provisions for them. Usually they give me a key and I open up the house, clean up the kitchen, and cook their first meal. I charge a fee per "banquet", which works out at about half a day's work for me in their home, plus expenses. For an exclusive service such as this, the fees are high, but then expectations are limitless!'*

You need to be an excellent cook, and to be mobile. It is important to have your family 100% behind you as it usually means that you are not home at the weekends to cook for them! Advertise in smart magazines and at places where the rich and famous gather.

FURNITURE AND SOFT FURNISHINGS

'Have you seen the budgie?'

○ The soft furnishings business includes cushions, curtains, loose covers and upholstery. For those without much time, doing just one branch of the trade makes sense.

○ There are an enormous number of reference books available on making furniture and furnishings, explained in ways easily digested by the ordinary person.

○ Most adult education colleges and technical schools have several courses in furnishing subjects, and small workshops teaching woodcraft and upholstery have sprung up countrywide. There are also courses at the London College of Furniture and at the Association of Master Upholsterers. The City and Guilds of London Institute also runs a furniture scheme.

○ If you are working with furniture or furnishings belonging to a customer, you will need public liability insurance to cover you against damage to property or injury to person when handling the furniture or delivering it to the customer.

○ Your local authority might require you to apply for planning permission if you intend to shift large pieces of furniture in and out of your house or garage. Enquire at the local Town Hall to discover your position.

○ See Contacts for addresses and reference books.

Caning

Between the 1920s and the 1960s the market for caning and rushwork slumped and only recently has that type of furniture come back into favour. The traditional craftsmen who used to travel around caning people's chairs on the pavement disappeared, and for years it was almost impossible to find somebody to recane grandfather's old armchair. Now there is a new band of enthusiasts who find old, broken cane chairs and settees on skips and rubbish dumps and try to repair them.

Liz bought six such chairs for a song and taught herself how to cane them by reading a couple of books from the library: *'It's not easy to work fast but it is interesting work. It takes me ages to do a settee but I can cane the seat of a small Victorian chair in about four hours, which I reckon is average. I buy lengths of ready-made cane. You do have considerable expenses to bear from time to time – materials are cheaper in the country and you have to drive to, say, East Anglia and buy in bulk to cover the cost of the petrol. One doesn't need a lot of equipment – pegs to hold the cane in position, a hammer, stanley knife, blunt instrument, stiletto, hand drills, wood stain and French polish. You will need a van, and a dry room in which to store both furniture and materials. It is well worth taking a course in wood care so that you can restore the whole piece of furniture and not just the seat.'*

There are classes at evening institutes and craft workshops around the country. Caning is in ever-increasing demand. Advertise in magazines, sell to shops and persuade antique furniture shops to have an example of your work on display. The profits are good, particularly if you restore furniture too.

Curtains

Made-to-order curtain services in shops are both expensive and slow, with the added disadvantage that you have to buy the material from the shop before they will make up your curtains for you.

Jill, who lives with her family in a small bungalow, arranged for a workroom to be added to their home: *'When I started 13 years ago I knew nothing whatever about curtain-making so I borrowed a couple of books from the library and put an advertisement in the local newspaper. Now I employ up to three helpers to cope with the continuous stream of work. Provided you remember a few obvious things like allowing double the width of the window for the fabric measurements, washing the material and lining first when making washable curtains and, when working with patterned materials or velvet, making sure the pattern or pile runs together, you can't go wrong. Anybody who is reasonably good at sewing can do it.'*

There are courses in curtain-making and pelmet-making at adult education colleges throughout the country. Shops which make up curtains for customers normally send them out to freelances, so attempt to tie up a contract with a large concern.

The workroom should be large enough to spread out fabric in. You can manage with an ordinary sewing machine and a cupboard in which to store lining, curtain tape and other sewing materials. Put in a bit of practice on the different types of curtain headings and make sure every curtain in your home looks marvellous. Expect to deliver the finished product.

This can be very quick work to do and the profits are good.

Cushions

Most people who have sewing machines can run up simple cushions, but there is a demand for more extravagant, unusual and professionally finished cushions.

The price of cushions depends on the fabric, the filling and your time. Obviously hand-made patchwork covers, or an elborate silk collage worked on a heart-shaped satin cushion, would take much longer to make than pretty little scatter cushions. Feathers are more expensive than an inflammable terylene filling, and pot-pourri for scented cushions takes time to prepare. When business builds up, buy fabrics in bulk from a wholesaler.

Here are some ideas for cushions that not everybody (but you) could produce: large corduroy-covered square cushions filled with foam rubber, for piling on the floor in lieu of chairs; pillow-sized cushions with tough hessian or canvas covers and cheaper terylene

Furniture and soft furnishings

filling, for offices, games rooms etc; traditional embroidered or lace-covered cushions to scatter on beds; outrageously bright satin cushions in the shapes of lips, hearts, fruit and vegetables; cotton-covered cushions stuffed with potpourri (a good potpourri should last two years); bouncy, soft, patchwork-covered cushions; velvet-covered cushions with crocheted frills.

Advertise in 'home' magazines, take samples of your cushions to shops and sell them in markets. Include a colour print with the advertisement if you are displaying it in a newsagent's window. It is creative work, with no limits to the design possibilities. It is also a job you can pick up and put down at will to fit in with your home routine.

French Polishing

French polishing is a messy job (your hands will always be brown with stain), but it is the kind of work that can transform a neglected piece of wooden furniture into something that looks almost new. Beech and mahogany react best to French polishing, and the process involves stripping the wood, sandpapering and polishing.

Equipment is minimal (inflammable spirit and French polish) but it is important to have premises which are dry, light and spacious enough to store several pieces of furniture in various stages of polishing. There is a high fire risk with French polishing so check the safety of the premises and consider extra insurance.

The art of French polishing is taught at adult education institutes, but the skill can also be learnt from books. Make yourself known to local antique dealers and upholstery workshops and advertise in newspapers and shop windows.

There is now a demand for good French polishers, because for some time it has been a dying trade. It is time-consuming work – one tabletop can take all week – and you should give the customer an estimate of the cost before taking on the job.

Warning: French polishing is not suitable work for smokers as so much of it involves inflammable liquids and, for the same reason, children should be kept away.

Gilding

Gilding on furniture has rather fallen out of favour since the nineteenth century, but you could find that there is a demand in your area for restoration work which no-one else is able to undertake.

Gilding is done with gold powder or gold leaf, and applying it is not difficult to master provided you have patience and like meticulous work. Restoration usually means cleaning the item to be gilded and filling in cracks with woodfiller before you can start work, so as well as gilder's tools such as knives and brushes you will need basic wood repair equipment. The size of your workroom depends on the pieces you work on, ranging from large pieces of furniture to small ornaments. Equipment is not expensive but gold leaf is, so your prices will need to reflect the outlay on materials.

As well as restoration work, there is also a demand for gilded signs and fairground-style decoration for mirror frames, rocking horses, and so on, combining gilding with painting and airbrush spraying. If you do a sign for a shop or pub, this will be advertisement in itself, and you can take examples of your work to expensive craft shops and picture framers. Advertise in antiques magazines and approach antiques shops direct.

There is no specific organisation for gilding but the Crafts Council and the Guild of Master Craftsmen can advise you.

This is specialist work so you can charge relatively high prices and operate quite a profitable business.

Lampshades

There are soft and hard lampshades, and soft ones are the easy ones. These are fine to start on, but most people can make them so, for profitable lampshade-making you will have to aim at the more complicated types – hard, swirled, gathered, pleated, shaped from polyester resin, cane, stained glass, metal and even wood.

Wire frames can be bought from craft shops or big stores, other materials depend on your choice. For soft lampshades, a sewing machine is needed. Other equipment includes glue, scissors, a stanley knife, and formica or hardboard templates to cut out shapes against.

Aim to have several lampshades on the go at once, so that you can spend a day cutting (on the floor, but cover the carpet first), a day stitching and glueing, and so on. It's heavy work on the fingers, but easy once you've got the knack.

Lampshade-making is a job often done by homeworkers for factories, in which case somebody is sent round to train you, but it is easy to learn from books or from adult education classes. If you do work for a factory make sure you are paid the correct hourly rate – the Low Pay Unit will advise. Otherwise go it alone with an advertisement in the paper and take samples round to suitable shops. Keep a keen eye on fashion trends – people can still afford to be fashion-conscious and stylish about their lampshades.

Invest in a selection of lamp bases to show off your shades when customers visit you. Obviously making lampshades to order is the sensible way to work but take time off to experiment. It is often the flash-of-inspiration shades that bring in the big profits.

Loose Covers

Loose covers are covers for chairs and sofas, and can include bedspreads and dressing table skirts.

Furnishing fabrics can be difficult to work with and tough on the hands – and knees, as Molly, a 61-year-old grandmother who is never short of work, points out: *'It is 31 years since I had my last child and I started making loose covers, and I've never been out of work. The cutting out is difficult, but the worst part of the job is the time you spend on your knees while cutting. It can be up to four hours a day! And often you're dealing with fabrics you really don't like even to touch! But otherwise it's good work. You meet people in their homes when you go to measure up the furniture in order to make the pattern, and gradually one learns how to deal with customers and talk them round to something better suited to the chair or sofa. People have such funny ideas about things like covers.'*

You will need a sewing machine (with piping foot), plenty of floor space for cutting out, a large table to work on, and a good back. It is useful to have a selection of fabric samples to show clients, but usually they will have already chosen material to fit in with their colour scheme.

There are classes in loose cover cutting at adult education colleges, and various courses in soft furnishings are available through the London College of Furniture, technical colleges and the Women's Institute.

Advertise your service in local newspapers and newsagents' windows. There is a good demand for loose covers. It is strenuous work, but it is very satisfying to see an old armchair given a new lease of life.

Making Wooden Furniture

Moving on from renovating something old to creating something new, there is always a market for good hand-made furniture. Saleability naturally depends on the design and the quality of workmanship. If you think you've hit upon something potentially successful, expect a period of trial and error before you make the perfect prototype.

For equipment, start with a basic woodworking tool set available from specialist shops and gradually add to it. Tools are expensive but you must have a basic saw, hammer, drill, chisels, set square, screwdriver, plane and sander. (There is no point in buying a lathe unless you are going to make chairs or tables with fancy legs. Start with straight legs and take it from there!)

You will need a lot of space to make large items like beds, tables, benches and kitchen units, but a shed or small room is big enough for making chairs, stools, chests, coffee tables, bookshelves and smaller household items such as wine racks, salad bowls, breadboards and plaques. Wood must be stored somewhere dry.

Wood is expensive. To keep the price down, buy in bulk from local timber merchants (see the Yellow Pages). Learn how to tell if wood is twisted or warped, otherwise you will end up spending more time straightening it than working with it.

Adult education colleges run courses in furniture design and carpentry and several workshops around the country teach furniture-making, often combined with recycling old furniture.

Advertise your furniture in local newspapers and relevant magazines. It is worth producing an illustrated brochure, and also displaying examples of your furniture in appropriate shops (if you make wine racks you could approach local wine merchants).

A high degree of skill is required in furniture-making and, as you expand, the equipment needed becomes increasingly expensive. The more you work with wood, the more you will want to know about different woods and to work with them – and the more equipment you will need. Enjoyable as it is to work in wood, your profits lie in the speed at which you produce.

Marquetry

Marquetry is the ancient craft of inlaid wood, a design of different wood veneers used to decorate the surface of tables and small items such as boxes. For anyone who already enjoys working with wood and has an eye for design, this is a lovely craft. You learn to appreciate and exploit the natural properties of wood and the different grains and colours.

Training can be obtained from the Marquetry Society, which runs courses and publishes a quarterly journal, *The Marquetarian*, available free to members of the society. There are several local marquetry groups throughout the country and the larger adult education institutes also offer training courses. This craft is rapidly gaining in popularity.

For equipment, you will need a veneering press and a veneer hammer as well as the normal tools used in woodwork. The finished piece of work needs to be sanded down and French polished (see French Polishing). Your workroom should have a good source of natural daylight so that you can see the colours of the wood.

Marquetry is popular for chess sets, coffee tables, boxes and picture frames. It sells well in the more expensive furniture and gift shops and commands a high price. Approach antique shops and offer to restore damaged or incomplete pieces of original work, or to add new marquetry surfaces to antique tables and desks. Traditionally mother of pearl was frequently incorporated into marquetry designs but, as marquetry enthusiasts point out, it is difficult to get hold of shells unless you find them on the beach yourself!

When you have fully mastered the technique, you may also be able to do restoration work for museums.

Mirrors

Mirrors emphasise space and add atmosphere to a room and different frames fit in with different styles of furnishing. Making mirrors is creative work, and gives plenty of opportunity for using the imagination.

Glass merchants (see the Yellow Pages) sell and cut sheet mirror glass, and will bevel the edges for you if the mirror is not to be framed. Do not buy mirror glass thinner than ⅛ inch unless it is already mounted on a solid backing.

Frames can be new, restored or dispensed with altogether. Old wooden frames should be stripped and then varnished or re-painted, and gilded frames can be rebuilt with plaster of Paris and then regilded. New frames can be made of virtually any material, including leaded glass (as in stained glass), cane, ceramic, mosaic, plastic, metal and glass fibre. Cheap plastic frames can be revamped with aerosol spray paint, using masking tape and cut outs to make a pattern – the more unusual the better. There are several books on the subject.

Mirror glass is fairly cheap but having it cut adds to the price. Learn how to cut it yourself with a glasscutter – it is quite a skill and you must wear gloves and goggles. Always cut glass on a flat worktop and sweep up the chips and slivers immediately. Finish off the edges with silicon carbide sandpaper.

Take examples of your mirrors to gift shops, furniture shops and interior design shops. It is also worth renting a market stall as people often buy attractive mirrors on impulse.

Working with mirrors is interesting as it is a form of art. Fashions and tastes change, so make sure you keep up to date by looking at mirrors and frames in shops and interior design magazines.

Restoring Wooden Furniture

Restoring and repairing old wooden furniture and selling it is a field wide open for exploitation. For the enthusiastic amateur with a keen eye and an understanding of how to treat wood, there are thousands of people wanting to buy stripped pine dressers, chairs and tables, restored mirror frames and mahogany chests. To find a decrepit piece of furniture, to clean it, repair it and sand it down for finishing is a very satisfying way of making money.

Paul works from his basement: *'You need to know how to restore wood. It's messy but very therapeutic and involves stripping off all the old paint or varnish with a blowtorch or wood stripper, bleaching or rubbing down the wood with liquid caustic (be sure to wash it off), mending the parts that need repair and filling in the holes with wood stopping, then sanding, staining and finally finishing with wax, varnish or paint. There are literally dozens of effective aids for wood restoring on the market.'*

There are several courses in furniture restoration at adult education institutes, colleges and workshops. There are also numerous books on the subject – which also give details of the types of furniture not worth restoring.

Sell the restored furniture on a market stall (rent one for the day) or sell to individual customers and period furniture shops. To buy the original furniture, visit country markets. If the area is affluent, you may be able to sell the restored piece at the same market. Junk shops are always worth investigating but 'finds' are few and far between. Never buy an item that you do not like – you will find it hard to convince somebody else to buy it when it has been repaired. Once you become known, people will bring you their old furniture to work on. You will need a garage or shed in which to store the furniture, a car or van and a well-ventilated workroom.

Excellent profits can be made restoring furniture and the work can take up as much time as you want it to. It is a very flexible pastime, and anybody can do it.

Antique Dealing   To deal in antiques on a more serious level is very different to simply finding and restoring nice old pieces. The British Antique Dealers' Association has all the details. As a guideline, a registered antique dealer in Britain should not deal in items less than 100 years old. Initial outlay can be high.

Upholstery

By tradition, upholstering is an apprentice trade, and it takes quite a bit of practice for the DIY enthusiast to upholster an antique chair to a standard worthy of payment. For beginners, the best advice is to concentrate on one type of furniture, and start small – sofas and armchairs can come later.

You will need a workroom equipped with a heavy-duty sewing machine, upholstering needles, shears (or very sharp scissors), springs, a web stretcher, a tack hammer and tacks (unless you plan to use a staple gun instead). Some of this equipment can be bought second-hand. Allow space to store bulky materials, linings, canvas, webbing, hair and other under-cover and stuffing items, and a good selection of braids, fringes, buttons and other finishing items.

Check with neighbours that the sound of hammering and the industrial sewing machine will not disturb them. As the initial outlay is quite considerable, sound out your market very thoroughly and bear in mind that collecting and delivering large pieces of furniture requires strength (yours) and an estate car or van. Try to link up with a furniture repair person, as repairs are often needed to the frame and must be done before reupholstering.

For advice on learning how to upholster, contact the Association of Master Upholsterers and the London College of Furniture. Adult education colleges, Women's Institutes and technical colleges run courses, as do several schools of upholstery.

If you intend to specialise in priceless antique furniture, you should take out public liability insurance – if anything happens to your client's Louis XV chair while it is under your roof, it is your responsibility. You should also have a working knowledge of period braids and materials.

Reasonably priced upholsterers are in tremendous demand and income can be high to very high for top-quality work. Advertise in local newspapers, shop windows, junk shops, fabric shops and sale rooms.

HEALTH AND BEAUTY

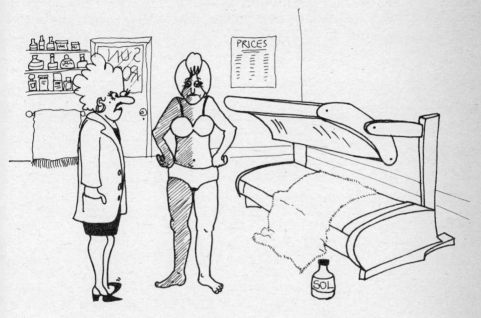

'Can't help feeling we should have turned you over earlier, Mrs. Jones!'

○ To do beauty work at home on a professional basis, you may need planning permission from the local authority. This covers granting consent or a licence to run such a business in your home and the obvious essentials such as toilet facilities, running water and power. The room you plan to practise in will probably have to be converted to accommodate the equipment you need and it should be well heated and stylishly decorated. If necessary, make provision for a waiting room.

○ You do not need a licence to prac-tise if you work freelance and visit people in their homes, but you some-times need one to practise in your own home. Check with the authorities. In all cases, subscribe to a public liability insurance policy covering you from liability if customers are injured during treatment.

○ Unlike working in a high-street salon, it will be you who has to clean up after each client, launder the gowns and towels and keep the place looking smart and clean.

○ A beautician or beauty therapist

must be qualified. Training for any area of beauty can be done at state colleges: a full beautician's course takes three years, and a course without hairdressing two years. A course at a private college takes much less time, but you pay higher fees. Specialised skills, like manicuring and electrolysis, take two to five weeks to learn, and can be studied at many colleges which will award you with a recognised diploma.

○ See Contacts for addresses and reference books.

Beauty Salon

A beautician (or beauty therapist) must be qualified before going solo, but you need not necessarily offer the full service – there is a good living to be made following a short course in manicure, electrolysis, facials, bust treatment or whatever aspect interests you most. Your activities will largely depend on your speciality, how much space you have and how much money you can afford to invest in equipment. You will need one smart room, equipped with a hand basin, an adjoining toilet, and probably a waiting room. Equipment will depend on your chosen line of beauty work – to save money, buy second-hand, and order materials wholesale.

There are numerous courses in beauty therapy at colleges and adult education institutes. They vary in length and award certificates or diplomas (don't forget to display them!) The Confederation of Beauty Therapy and the British Association of Beauty Therapy and Cosmetology list colleges and courses, and the Society of Beauticians will also advise. Because of the need for training and qualifications, this would be ideal work for someone who has beauty salon experience.

If you specialise in beauty treatments involving cosmetics, approach one of the larger cosmetic houses and ask to be their representative and thereby get a good rate on their products. You could also run a retail sideline from your salon. A beauty counsellor, in contrast, is trained (usually free by a major cosmetic manufacturer) to advise clients on cosmetics and to perform simple beauty treatments relevant to those products, such as a manicure if you are selling nail polish.

Take out a special insurance to cover you against any injury to the customer. Remember that some people are allergic to certain ingredients used in cosmetics; if in doubt test the product on a small area of skin which will not show if the customer does come out in a rash.

Advertise locally and in women's magazines, stating what services you offer. Prices will depend on your qualifications and the service. If you have transport, you may get more business by giving treatments in customers' homes, using a foldaway portable couch if necessary.

Chiropody

Before you work as a chiropodist, you need a training from a school of chiropody – there are eleven in Britain. Courses for state registration take three years and require candidates to be over 18, with five O levels. There are also short evening refresher courses. More details can be obtained from the Society of Chiropodists and the London Foot Hospital.

If you are trained and you intend to operate from home, you have to register with the local authority. New equipment is quite a considerable outlay but you can buy it second-hand. You will need a room, with a hand basin, in which to practise and also a waiting room. There are very few chiropodists in Britain, so you can expect a sizeable clientele. Advertise by leaving cards in hospitals, clinics, shoe shops and libraries, and put an entry in the Yellow Pages.

Hairdressing

You must be an experienced hairdresser to set up a salon at home, so, again, this job would be most suitable if you have already trained and are now at home looking after children.

Apply for planning permission to convert a large room to take basins, driers, mirrors and hairdressing chairs. Choose a room in your home which is close to the existing plumbing in order to keep down conversion costs. You will probably have to add more power points. A second room could be turned into a storeroom and laundry (hairdressing means a vast number of towels to wash). Equipment can be bought second-hand through such publications as *Exchange and Mart* and *Hairdressers Journal*, and materials can be bought wholesale (see the Yellow Pages: Hairdressers Supplies).

A proper training usually consists of a two-year course at a college followed by another two years as an apprentice in a salon. There are shorter courses at adult education colleges and through the City and Guilds Institute. Check details with the Hairdressing Council. The Council does insist that freelance hairdressers are properly trained, so it is not enough to leap in with enthusiasm and some shampoo!

To protect yourself against negligence, a special insurance policy can be obtained from the Hairdressers' Insurance Bureau.

Your prices can easily undercut those at the local salon as your overheads will be much lower. Once business has built up (and many people prefer individual treatment), consider selling shampoos and cosmetics as a sideline. If you are mobile, you can, of course, visit clients in their homes. Your overheads will be very low as the client foots the bill for electricity and towels. The only extra piece of equipment you will need is a portable hairdryer.

Keep Fit Classes

Many people prefer to exercise in a group; they need the incentive and encouragement, and keeping fit is much more fun if it is a social activity.

To run classes, you need first to train yourself in one of the many different 'movement' methods – gymnastics, slimnastics, yoga or pure 'keep fit'. The Keep Fit Association runs evening courses which train you to teach, and more informal courses are available through adult education institutes. There is a wide range of informative literature available. You are dealing with other people's bodies and it is important to acquire the correct training and knowledge.

You need a large heated room with a non-slip, splinter-free floor cleared of furniture. You also need a place for students to change and wash. It helps to exercise to music, and a tape recorder and a collection of suitable tapes will make the classes much more enjoyable.

Advertise locally, particularly in beauty and hairdressing salons, clinics, clubs and colleges. Charge for individual lessons with a reduction for a course of classes.

It is lovely work to do as you keep yourself in shape and get paid for it at the same time! It's ideal work for former dancers, gymnasts and games teachers.

Massage

You must have a diploma to do massage professionally and a three-month course is the minimum training recommended; longer courses are preferred. An unskilled masseur or masseuse can do more harm than good. Training courses can be found in the advertisement section of magazines allied to beauty practice.

You should apply for a a licence from the local authority. This is subject to a clause in the Massage and Special Treatments Act which states that a beauty clinic (or similar) for women may not include massage for men.

You will need a very warm room, big enough for a couch and a hand basin. You also need oils to work with, but beware of aromatic oils as it takes a chemist to blend them and many of those available on the market are not the genuine article.

This is ideal work for former physiotherapists and beauticians, but anyone with an interest in how the body works can train without too much effort. People are prepared to pay high rates for first-class massage.

Natural Beauty Products

Herbal cosmetics have suddenly become very popular, and making wonderful concoctions out of plants, leaves and fruit can be terrific fun. It is quite easy to teach yourself from the dozens of excellent books on the subject of herbs and herbal products. As yet there are no specific courses but the Herb Society supplies information.

Jane keeps a garden full of herbs: *'You need fresh herbs and natural products, which are expensive to buy and sometimes difficult to find because they're seasonal. I find that this is a perfect job to do at home because it is time-consuming, but unless you have good outlets it is not commercially viable. When your materials are expensive (you tend to use only the best), you have to sell the products to a particular kind of shop, rather than depend on craft markets. Basic equipment is simple: a mortar and pestle, double saucepan, sieves and general kitchen utensils. The main danger is lack of hygiene – if a fungus develops on one of your products, it could easily blind the user. Everything has to be sterilised and products used must be fresh.'*

Try herbal soaps, shampoos, creams, moisturisers, balms, conditioners, and package your products elegantly. Advertise in health and beauty magazines and aim at the top end of the market.

145

Slimming Treatments and Sunbeds

Anybody can buy a slimming treatment kit or an ultra-violet sunbed and install it in their home for their own use or for renting out to friends. At the moment there are no legal restrictions on this equipment, but legislation will be passed in the near future, making it necessary for owners to have a licence if they wish to offer a service. As with most beauty treatment, damage can be done if you are not properly trained.

Courses are available, mainly through private beauty therapy colleges (contact the British Association of Beauty Therapy and Cosmetology for information) which issue diplomas. Unless you are trained, you cannot get public liability insurance covering you if a customer is injured while using your equipment. The courses range from two days for the sunbed course to a month for slimming treatment courses.

The initial outlay is high, although these machines are becoming less expensive every day, but the returns will be good. Budget for overheads such as electricity. Check the prices charged at the local beauty salon and undercut.

PLANTS

'A little too much fertilizer again, dear?'

○ There is no need to apply for planning permission if you want to grow fruit, vegetables and flowers in your garden, unless you intend to re-organise the whole property and turn it into a mini-farm. If this is the case, let the local council know.

○ Certain plants are protected by plant breeders' rights and cannot be propagated for sale without a licence. Check with the local Ministry of Agriculture, Fisheries and Food office.

○ If you are going to sell your produce from a roadside stall, you will need a licence from the local authority.

○ The County Horticultural Adviser will give advice to small-scale producers on the soil, pests and allied topics relevant to your area.

○ If you intend to take your produce to market, the Women's Institute booklet *Markets: Pleasure and Profit* gives the rules on packaging and labelling. Under the Trade Descriptions Act, plants have to be labelled correctly.

○ See Contacts for addresses and reference books.

Compost

Few people in towns have gardens large enough to make even a small compost heap, and most urban soils have to be supplemented with fertiliser, manure or compost to reinforce their lack of natural organic richness. Keen gardeners will travel miles to buy good, country compost.

If you live on a farm or near a fruit and vegetable market, it is a simple matter to make compost. There are various methods, but all of them require good aeration, free drainage, adequate moisture and a balance between dry material and soft green plant tissues. Consult a gardening book for full details.

Compost is ready to be bagged and used in four to six months, so it is quite a long-term project. It involves little effort and it is very rewarding to know that you are recycling waste materials and making a small profit at the same time.

Advertise your compost in town gardening shops and centres and put a sign outside your gate. If you live on a farm you could also sell manure in bags. Advertise manure in gardening magazines, and maybe offer a delivery service, although your price would have to rise to cover transport costs.

Profits are good as this is a labour-based occupation.

Dried Flowers

Dried and pressed flowers are a booming industry, understandably so as they are convenient, everlasting and delicately pretty. They can be used for huge floral arrangements or small bouquets and posies, presented in glass jars and baskets, and used to decorate an endless list of items, including pictures, lampshades, paperweights, fingerplates, cards, bookmarks and brooches.

You need a spare room, attic or shed with racks or lines on which to dry your flowers, and a source of dry heat. Cut your flowers in the evening, just before they reach maturity, and start the drying process immediately. The art of drying, pressing and arranging can easily be learnt from books or from your local flower club. Contact the National Association of Flower Arrangement Societies or the Society of Floristry for details of clubs and courses.

It is very pleasant, light work to do, and dried flowers can be marketed through numerous outlets. Drying flowers involves time rather than money. Grow your own flowers and use seedheads, grasses, berries and leaves found free in the countryside.

Farm Cropwork

Consider farm cropwork if you live in a farming area or near a market garden and have time on your hands. You can usually take your children with you, but you must be prepared to work long hours picking a crop once it is ripe. It is hard physical work.

Enquire at your local market or job centre, or write to the Women's Farm and Garden Association for assistance. The pay is low, however.

Growing Decorative Plants

There is a constant market for pot plants, bedding plants and more mature plants. You need a medium-sized garden and, ideally, a greenhouse in order to keep the supply constant. You will also need basic gardening tools (see Market Gardening), and a small van in which to transport your plants. There are plenty of books on the subject and the Flowers and Plants Advisory Council is very helpful.

Ken started cultivating plants in his urban back garden to supply a landscaping project a friend had taken on. Soon he found the general demand for flowering shrubs and bushes so large that he rented an allotment as well: *'Once I was over the initial outlay on equipment and perennial plants, my costs dropped considerably. For every plant bought, I took cuttings and was able to propagate the species indefinitely. I quickly learnt how to thin out my seeds properly so that almost every one would grow into a healthy plant. Now I specialise in ornamental and exotic shrubs – they get a very high price when nicely presented in a fancy vase, bamboo tub or hand-painted pot (buy a clay pot and paint it with a felt-tip pen). Luckily I've struck a deal with my local garden centre and they supply me with inexpensive containers.'* Ken's main market is windowboxes for banks, estate agents, property developers, offices and pubs.

There is money to be made from potted plants, especially from unusual varieties, interesting grasses and brightly coloured flowering shrubs. But the rarer the plant, the more care it needs. Any sort of specialist growing (for example, lawn turf, gladioli, watercress, roses, carnations or holly) is profitable provided you find the right market. Take your plants to garden centres, markets and offices or rent a stall at your local market.

Herbs

There are still comparatively few shops where one can buy a wide range of fresh herbs. There are about 65 different varieties which can be grown in Britain. As well as the market for fresh and dried culinary herbs there is an increasing demand for herbs for use in potpourri, lavender bags, herb pillows and so on.

The plants do not take up much space in the garden, and once they are established they need little attention: weeding, watering, and pulling out annuals or cutting back perennials at the end of the season, unless you are cultivating them under cover during the winter. Most of the popular herbs can be grown from seed in gardens, and even on window-sills. If you know what you are looking for, you will find plenty of herbs growing wild – like the dill which thrives beside London's North Circular Road! There are courses on herbs at adult education colleges and the Herb Society is very helpful. There are also numerous reference books on all aspects of growing and using herbs.

Sue lives outside a village and recently graduated from selling herbs direct to a greengrocer to marketing six-herb gift packs: *'The most expensive item is the packaging, because people are not going to pay a "bijou" price unless the containers and gift box look like a "bijou" present. I now work in conjunction with a neighbour who makes terracotta containers in the shape of animals, but with the backs open for me to fill with herb plants. In very good seasons I dry my herbs (hung in bags in dark places or spread out on muslin "trays" in the airing cupboard) and sell them in little jars with airtight stoppers and handwritten labels. But you must do a little research to find out which are the best methods of packaging dried herbs in order to preserve their oils and flavours. A "faded" herb is useless.'*

This need not be a full-time job, and good profits can be made for relatively little work.

Indoor Plants

If you love plants but do not have a garden, this is the job for you. Choose plants which are likely to flourish under the available conditions, whether in a warm spare room or an artificially lit cellar, a cool porch or a heated shed. There is a huge variety of indoor plants to choose from – ferns and aspidistras which can be sold to banks and offices, begonias and African violets for hotels and restaurants, and bottle gardens, cacti and bonsai trees for very small spaces. Indoor plants sell all year round, and seem to be in ever-growing demand. City-dwellers, in particular, are filling their homes with plants in order to maintain their links with nature.

The equipment is minimal: flowerpots (plastic ones are cheaper and easier to store), a large bench or table to propagate on, a dibber, trowel, pebbles (for drainage), and compost and/or sterilised soil. Concentrate on the plants which commercial growers find too labour-intensive to bother with, and on rare plants and exotic and tropical species (like ginger bushes, banana plants, coffee bushes and pineapple trees) which, with care, grow very well indoors. Mail-order cuttings of rare plants are becoming big business. Each cutting is packed in damp moss and then put in a plastic bag, wrapped and sent by first-class letter post.

Home producers are not allowed, by law, to sell bulbs, seeds, rhizomes, corms and tubers as they cannot treat them against pests or diseases. They may only sell *growing* plants.

The Flowers and Plants Advisory Council will help with advice on houseplants. Always use seed from reputable firms, make sure your plants are well rooted and grow them in sterile compost. Your initial outlay on seeds and cuttings may seem high at the time, but you will recover it very quickly.

Advertise in magazines for the home and in office journals. Try to set up a display of your plants in the foyer of large offices, with your name and details alongside.

Jobbing Gardening

This is all-weather work, and you need to be both strong and healthy. Digging, planting, pruning, hoeing, weeding and mowing with perhaps an antiquated lawnmower is heavy work.

Your employer should supply the tools and you work on an hourly rate. Although general gardening experience certainly helps, it is quite possible to find all the information you are ever likely to need in the vast selection of gardening books available. Gardening is a continuous occupation: unless a very deep frost strikes, there is always something to do, if only clearance work.

Buy a comfortable, waterproof, set of clothes including a hat and wellington boots, plus a pair of sharp secateurs and shears. People do not realise how much extra effort is needed to prune with blunt, rusty implements.

There is a good profit to be made on top of your hourly rate if you cultivate plants at home to put in your employers' gardens. The cost of a packet of seeds is almost the same as the amount you can charge for each single healthy plant. Advertise in local newspapers and shopwindows, but expect to get most of your business by word-of-mouth recommendation.

Adult eduction colleges run an elementary gardening course and City and Guilds has a horticulture certificate scheme.

Landscape Gardening

If you like gardens as well as gardening, planning them could be the start of a new career. Make a start with your own!

Many home-owners are either too busy or too unimaginative to use their gardens to the best advantage. So often they cram too many ill-assorted plants into too small an area when a few choice climbers and long-flowering bushes would look far better and require far less care. The key to successful landscape gardening is simplicity of design. The smaller the plot, the more essential proper landscaping becomes. Landscape gardening is stimulating and creative work and there is great satisfaction to be gained in transforming a dreary backyard into a beautiful garden.

The garden should be an extension of the home. Start by drawing up a list of priorities and, working on a scale plan, see if the existing space could be better used. You will need a measuring tape, a big table to work on and graph paper. There is no lack of books for ideas and inspiration on landscaping.

This sort of enterprise operates best in areas where people are sufficiently prosperous to pay for advice on their garden and patio planning (even if they do not want you to do the manual work). There is a growing demand for specialist gardens: stylish Tao landscapes, Japanese, Chinese or Persian gardens, and gardens which incorporate a children's play area or paved paths for the disabled.

TOPS do a course in landscape gardening, and the Institute of Landscape Architects and the Royal Horticultural Society will provide details on college courses. There are numerous reference books giving information on the plants most suitable for different soil types, sunny or shady gardens, and small or large gardens.

Advertise through *local* newspapers and appropriate shops and centres as you will have to transport the plants and turf to the site, unless you can arrange for them to be delivered. Fees can be either estimated for the individual project or charged by the hour.

Market Gardening

You will need a garden of two or three acres or an allotment, to make market gardening pay. Profit is directly related to the scale on which you operate. You should buy a heated greenhouse so that you can cultivate bedding plants and seedlings during the winter. You also need basic gardening tools (try for second-hand ones): a spade, fork, rake, hoe, secateurs, hoses and sprays, and insecticides, canes, nets, fertilisers and seeds.

To begin with, specialise in one aspect of market gardening, such as raspberry or strawberry growing. Out-of-season produce is always in demand, but for this you will need a greenhouse, and a deep freeze if you wish to store the summer surplus until winter. Market gardens need constant attention and the produce has to be sold instantly before it loses its bloom.

Local and Women's Institute markets, nearby shops and a roadside stall are all good outlets, and prices should be linked to those in the shops. If you are selling from a roadside stall, choose a route used by city-dwellers at weekends, and remember that you will need a licence from the local authority. Check with the Citizens' Advice Bureau to find out whether selling your produce contravenes EEC regulations on the sale of farm produce. Unless you have obtained a Ministry of Agriculture certificate to the effect that your soft fruit plants are free from disease, you cannot sell them, and you must never sell seed potatoes. Ask your local council whether putting your property under cultivation will change the rating on your house under the change-of-use ruling. Spend a little time investigating precautions against pests, slugs, blight, and, if you live in a rural area, take preventative measures against wildlife *before* you start.

The County Horticultural Adviser helps small-scale growers with local problems, and the National Farmers' Union and the Agricultural Development Advisory Service can give more general advice. The Royal Horticultural Society will give you the addresses of horticultural colleges for part-time or full-time courses, and elementary evening classes in gardening are run by adult education colleges.

Expect a lot of physical hard work and be prepared for the weather to ruin crops overnight, but as jobs go gardening is very satisfying and can prove very profitable. It is a full-time job, for even when you are not planting or cropping you have to prepare the ground. Children can help with keeping down the weeds and picking fruit.

Mushroom Growing

Mushroom growing is a very popular money-earner. Mushrooms are considered a delicacy and usually hold their price. They also have the additional advantage of being in season all year round. But be warned, while it may be simple to grow mushrooms on a small scale in the garden shed, it takes good organisation to make a large-scale mushroom farm work smoothly.

You have to start growing your mushrooms afresh at the end of each season (six to eight weeks). A good compost (either bought or made yourself) is essential, but it will only do for one crop. (It is, however, still full of nutrients and can be put on the garden.) The mushroom spore, grown on compost in trays or boxes, needs to be kept at a steady temperature of 50–55°F. Put the trays somewhere dimly lit and well ventilated, such as an empty cellar or a farm building, or even a spare room indoors.

Georgie uses five old stables on her farm to cultivate a good-sized crop: *'It's a really convenient pastime because it's not labour intensive. My only outlay is on spore, which is cheap, and sometimes compost when I can't make my own on the farm. I water the mushrooms daily and pick twice a week – it takes about ten minutes – and then parcel them up to sell at the local markets. The yield is about 2 pounds per square foot. It's marvellous! And profitable!'*

The Mushroom Growers' Association (a branch of the National Farmers' Union) gives lectures on mushroom growing, and advises on insurance, legal matters and advertising. It also supports planning applications. The spores are virtually indestructible and can be bought all year round. Mature mushrooms do not keep, however, so you must sell them quickly after picking, or freeze or can them. If you do have to store the mushrooms for a day or two, keep them in a cool place. Sell to vegetable shops and on a stall at your local market. You could also arrange to supply direct to local restaurants.

Office Windowbox Service

If you decide to grow plants specifically for offices, why not offer a full service and look after the plants on a regular basis?

Hilary has been servicing office plants for years. She rents her plants to companies on a monthly basis: *'You have to charge enough for a service like this to cover replacing the plants when they are destroyed – which is pretty often. Plants never get enough fresh air if they are in a smoke-filled office, people stub out their cigarettes in their tubs and even water them with iced water. I water my plants weekly and, when necessary, wash and polish the leaves and feed them liquid manure. There's a lot of theft, too – you go back and the plants are gone. There is plenty of work to be found on the patio-tending front. Many offices have patios, and most tubs. Again there's a high proportion of theft, particularly with pub patio plants. You have to chain them to the wall! Windowboxes are not so bad – people normally confine themselves to picking the flowers.'*

For this service you need a car or van to carry your plants and equipment, and it is advisable to find work locally or you will find most of your profits go on petrol. Try to get the plant contract for a whole building by applying to the management company in charge. If you are renting out your plants, you should draw up an agreement to cover you against loss or theft and to cover the offices against replacement due to natural causes. Discourage the office-workers from 'tending' the plants themselves, and try to place the plants where they will not be in the way.

Include growing time (if you cultivate your own plants), your own time, transport costs, plant food etc in the price you charge. Advertise in office journals and approach local offices direct.

— REPAIR WORK —

'Are you sure you had the arms when you brought it here?'

○ Repair work is notorious for customers failing to collect their possessions. If you cannot extract a deposit from them when they bring the item to you, note down their name and address or telephone number. It is a good policy to tell customers how much you think the repair will cost, to avoid a difficult confrontation when they find out it will cost more to repair than it did to buy.

○ Because you are housing other people's goods, make sure you have adequate insurance against loss or damage to items in your care.

○ Any kind of repair work which is going to involve you and your equipment spreading beyond a room in your home should be mentioned to the Council. For example, if you intend to run a motor repair shop beside a quiet residential house it is unlikely that either the Planning Department or the neighbours will approve.

○ Make sure that the room you are working from is childproof.

○ See Contacts for addresses and reference books.

Bicycle Repairs

Bicycle repair work is on the increase. Bicycles are becoming a more and more popular form of transport as fares and petrol prices continue to rise. The recent 'health boom' has also promoted cycling as one of the best ways to get fresh air and exercise, without polluting the atmosphere.

André runs a bicycle repair business and supplies bicycle parts and accessories: *'You don't need a large area to work in, but you have to have a place where people can bring their bikes. Your workshop needs a bench, a small vice and a selection of good metric tools. Good tools last for ever so don't invest in cheap ones. A bike is a very simple piece of machinery and you should make a note of how you dismantle it and use your common sense. Richard's Bicycle Book covers all aspects of bike repair. Contact your local dealer to find out the name of your nearest wholesaler and get in a stock of the most popular components: cables, brake blocks, tyres, tubes and patches – because people will buy them to do their own running repairs. I'd get insurance cover against a client having an accident on his bike after I'd fixed it, even though if one's work is good it shouldn't happen! It is important, too, to try to rebuild old bikes for resale. It's a lucrative sideline. The police pound is always a good place to look for them.'*

Advertise in *Cycle World* and through cycling clubs and colleges in the area, as well as in the local newspaper and local newsagents. No-one will want to peddle far on a broken bike. You could always go as far as stopping and chatting to people on bicycles, and dropping your card in their baskets.

Hard work for fair returns – if you don't mind getting your hands dirty.

Wheel Building   Bicycle repair shops often send buckled wheels out to freelance wheel builders, who are much in demand. The best way to learn is by experience. There is a book on the subject, *Building Bicycle Wheels* by Robert Wright (Selpress Books), but there are several other ways to lace and true a wheel (the process of dropping spokes into hubs and fixing them). Equipment is merely a jig (use an old bicycle frame) and a spoke key.

Advertise in cycling magazines and cycling clubs as well as in local bicycle shops. Charge per set of wheels, and consider offering a mail order wheel building service.

Car Repairs

All cars need regular servicing as well as repairs when something goes wrong. If you are already able to service your own car satisfactorily, you should be able to service other people's and undertake minor repairs. If you are going to get dirty, you may as well get very dirty and make some money out of it! Don't take on anything you cannot handle, or you will find that the owners keep bringing the car back for you to repair, at your time and expense.

A garage training is the best but, failing that, you can take a course in motor car maintenance at adult education institutes and read up the subject in reference books and car manuals.

You will need a garage or large shed to work in, and you will need to dig a pit so that you can work underneath the vehicles. Councils do not allow cars to be repaired in the street in residential areas. You may also need planning permission if you intend to repair cars full-time, so enquire about this before you start.

There is quite an outlay in equipment, so try to buy as much as possible second-hand. You need a hydraulic jack, a ramp, an air pump, a battery charger and a workbench with a good selection of car repair tools. You will also need access to spare parts for different makes of car, and a collection of car manuals. You may find it simpler to specialise in one particular model, in which case advertise your service through that particular car dealer – you could even put cards under the windscreen wipers of each of these cars you see in your area! Elbow grease and a certain amount of guile is needed for this sort of work.

For a more general service, advertise in local newspapers and in motor accessory shops. Check your prices against those of local garages, and make sure you offer a fast, reliable service. You could also offer a car-washing and cleaning service at the same time, especially if you have children who are willing to help.

Clock and Watch Repairs

If you are the sort of person who proceeds on the theory that if it doesn't work, oil it, then reassess whether clocks and watches are for you. Cleaning and repairing them takes aptitude and patience, combined with proper tools and quite extensive knowledge. It is not a job for those who take things apart and cannot put them back together again – but it would appeal to those fascinated by cogs and springs and wheels and things.

There are six-month graded correspondence courses in technical horology from the British Horological Institute, as well as evening courses at adult education centres.

Clock and watch repairing is very pleasant work to do, and needs only a clean corner with good light. The list of essential tools (screwdrivers, pliers, tweezers, punches, files, soldering iron, etc) is within most budgets but it can become quite extensive when you branch out into, say, antique clocks. Some suppliers will only deal with the trade, so look in *Exchange and Mart, Horological Journal* and *Clocks* for second-hand tools. A stroll around the Clerkenwell area of London will also turn up as many suppliers as you will need. Otherwise look in the Yellow Pages: Clock & Watch Importers, Wholesalers/Spare Parts. Pick up old clocks and watches for spares.

Dave started working on clocks when he was made redundant at the age of 45: '*I learnt from books and have accumulated enough bits and pieces to be able to work on virtually any type of clock. It is very important to be able to recognise the different types before you begin.*'

Offer your services to jewellers and advertise in local newspapers. You can also buy old clocks in antique markets, do them up and resell them for much more than you paid.

Price is linked to the time it takes. Because this can be rather specialist work, proving your skill will be very much a case of demonstration.

General Repairs

Working on the premise that more and more of us prefer to have an old commodity repaired than to buy a new one with a life expectancy of four or five years, there is a good future in repairing things like washing machines, television sets, hoovers, hi-fi equipment, hairdryers, radios, typewriters, electric blankets – in fact, anything electrical or mechanical. Anybody with a basic set of tools and a rough working knowledge of repair work can bump up their know-how by reading the many do-it-yourself books available and by taking a selection of adult education courses, such as radio maintenance and electrics. You can also apply to the Manpower Services Commission or the Youth Opportunities Programme for training.

This is messy work, so put a room aside if you have no garage or shed to work from. Ideally you should be mobile enough to visit clients if necessary.

Equipment depends on the service you provide. Buy second-hand (remember you're the one who can repair and overhaul!).

Advertise in shop windows, social centres, Citizens' Advice Bureaux and libraries, as well as in local newspapers.

Prices are geared to time and parts. Be prepared to give estimates, and give guarantees where possible. Considering that most people can never find a handyman when something breaks down, you should be able to build up quite a business, and you could also run a second-hand shop on the side. Apart from the financial rewards, there is also a great deal of satisfaction to be gained from restoring things to working order.

Restoring Antique Dolls

Antique dolls are very highly prized by collectors, many of whom visit this country from Europe and America in search of original Victorian examples. Dolls in good condition are particularly valuable, as time has often caused the fabrics to deteriorate, even if small hands have not been allowed to play with them. Restoring the dolls can prove a lucrative business; on the Continent it's already a thriving one.

This is a fascinating occupation, involving several different skills, mainly china restoration and costume making. The first step is to research the subject (there are several specialist books) and to learn as much as you can about period costume by visiting museums and reading books on costume. The Costume Society arranges visits to public and private collections, and publishes the journal *Costume*.

To do the job properly, you should take a course in china restoration, for restoring the bisque (or china) dolls, and also a course in soft toy making, for repairing rag dolls. Courses in both subjects are held at adult education institutes and the Women's Institute also covers soft toy making. It is also worth visiting toy museums and doll collections, and making notes of the various ways in which the dolls are dressed and decorated, for example their 'make-up'.

Set aside a separate workroom as many of the dolls are both valuable and fragile, and children will probably not understand that they are not to be played with! The equipment and materials are the same as those already covered under Soft Toys and Restoring China and Ceramics, but you should try to find dress fabrics as similar as possible to the original Victorian designs.

There should be no difficulty finding a market with antique dealers, and there are several who specialise in dolls. You could also buy old dolls in a dilapidated state from street markets and junk shops and resell them later at a profit. Advertise in antiques magazines and attend antiques fairs to make yourself known to dealers.

It is time-consuming and delicate work, which is hard on the eyes but hugely gratifying on completion.

Restoring China and Ceramics

Restoring old pieces of china and ceramics is a skill which can be acquired quite quickly. Many restorers keep their methods and materials a closely guarded secret, but there are private courses (for example, at West Dean College, Chichester, and at London's Robin Hood's Workshop) and courses at adult education institutes.

Your workroom should be dust-free, well ventilated and well lit, including natural light. If you decide to offer a complete service from the initial cleaning right through to final retouching, then you will need to buy an airbrush, compressor and drill as well as a selection of inexpensive tools and materials. These include a palette knife, spatulas, tweezers, boxwood modelling tools (availble from artists' materials shops), a scalpel, a pair of pliers and a medium-sized vice, and cleaning agents, solvents, adhesives, fillings, paints and glazes.

Advertise in shops which sell china and inform antique shops, museums and art dealers of your service. This is detailed work and to make any money from it the results must be perfect: the breaks have to be aligned, the replaced hands accurately fitted onto the shattered arms and the retouching absolutely undetectable! Patience and an eye for detail are essential. For skilled work, the pay is good to very good.

Sharpening Shop

It can often be difficult to find somewhere to repair or sharpen scissors, knives and garden tools, and then when you do the price charged is almost as much as the cost of replacing the blunt tools with new ones. Do some market research to see if people in your area would appreciate and use such a service, and you may find there is scope for you to run a small but thriving business.

You need a well-lit workshop, which may require planning permission, and it is as well to check that the neighbours will give their blessing to the project because the machinery can be noisy. Initial outlay can be high: you need a powered grindstone which, with the addition of a small generator, could be fitted into the back of a van to provide a mobile service (the modern equivalent of the knife-grinders who used to offer a door-to-door service, grinding knives and scissors on machines powered by their bicycle wheels!). For a mobile, sharpening shop you will need a pedlar's licence from the police.

Think about investing in a key-cutting and/or a shoe-heeling machine. These services are allied to sharpening. Consult *Handyman WHICH?* for product reliability and prices. Put up a sign outside your workshop to attract local attention, and advertise in local newspapers and hardware shops.

For those with good eyesight and steady hands there could be an excellent living to be made.

SERVICES

'Doreen, have you been taking in lodgers again?'

◌ This section deals with work which is done as a service to others.

○ As you are working from home, however small the scale of your activities, you should adjust your householder's insurance policy to cover you against any liability to customers. Check also that your fire and burglary policies are adequate.

○ Certain services are subject to planning legislation and you should ask the local authority for planning permission or for a licence to run your business from your home.

○ You should check whether there is a covenant on your house excluding the use of machines or, indeed, excluding the use of the premises for business purposes.

○ If you are going to trade under your own name you may do so, but if you want to use a trading name for your business you must display a notice visible to your clients stating your own name, and also put your own name and address on business stationery.

○ If your car or van is used in connection with your work, you should extend the policy to include business usage. Discuss this carefully with your insurance broker – if you are involved in an accident carrying goods for business reasons without adequate insurance you will not be compensated for the damaged goods.

O See Contacts for addresses and reference books.

Accountancy

There are no restrictions on unqualified and semi-qualified accountants working from home.

You can offer a comprehensive service or specialise in one aspect, such as tax, auditing or cost accounting, in which case you only need train or study in that particular area. Polytechnics and private colleges offer full- and part-time courses. There are evening courses at adult education institutes, and the School of Accountancy and Business Studies does home study courses. Hatfield Polytechnic in Hertfordshire recently started accountancy courses for women. There are also numerous books you can learn from dealing with various aspects of accountancy.

Chartered accountants are now allowed to advertise discreetly in local newspapers, and unqualified accountants can put advertisements in too. There are several accountancy agencies (see the Yellow Pages: Accountants) and you can also approach local businesses direct, especially those just starting up. If you specialise in one kind of business, for example builders and decorators, you will probably find that your clients recommend you to others in the same trade.

All you need is a quiet room with reference books and a calculator, so this kind of work involves no disturbance of home and family life. Charge per hour or per project and, if you have plenty of time to spare, you can make a good income.

Address Service

A surprising number of individuals and businesses need a special address for mail. It may sound rather underhand but there are perfectly legitimate reasons: mail-order firms must have a fixed address, people who live abroad may need a permanent address in this country, or simply small country companies may want a town address. This service is not terribly lucrative, but then the effort needed is by no means taxing. But it does mean that you cannot move house...!

Payment is agreed on a weekly or monthly fee basis, with a set amount added on top for each item forwarded. You can check your fees with firms listed in the Yellow Pages (see Accommodation Address Agents). Advertise in magazines and newspapers that are read abroad and in *Dalton's Weekly* and *Exchange and Mart*.

Astrology

There is an amazing amount of interest in astrology, the study of the occult influence on human affairs, and it is beginning to be taken seriously. Many people want a detailed interpretation of their individual birth date rather than to read a phoney or generalised forecast in the newspapers.

It takes several years to reach the top of the astrology tree and to become well-known enough to be able to charge high fees. There is a great deal involved in each study, so it is quite hard work and many astrologers supplement their income by giving talks on the subject.

Courses in astrology are held by the Faculty of Astrological Studies and the Mayo School, and there are also correspondence courses. Most astrologers work by post, so all you need are the reference books (the ephemerides) and charts and you can work when you choose. You have to take astrology seriously of course and be aware that you are dealing with people's lives, so it is very much a job that involves responsibility and dedication. For the astrologer there are rewards of self-knowledge to be acquired through interpreting the lives of others, but it can be emotionally exhausting.

Tarot and I Ching   Other similar studies are Tarot cards and the I Ching. These are less developed commercially and there are no college courses, but there are plenty of private classes advertised in the alternative press and numerous books on both subjects.

Bed and Breakfast

If you live near a holiday area and have a couple of spare bedrooms (maybe the children have grown up and left home), why not slap a 'vacancies' sign on the gatepost and earn some extra money (see also Taking in Lodgers). It is a natural extension of running an ordinary home, so involves no special skills or training, and the income can be quite good, especially if you live in an area where accommodation is at a premium. Bed and breakfast trade will be seasonal, but some people combine holiday trade with letting rooms to students who leave the rooms free in the summer.

To display a 'B & B' or any sign outside your house, you need to comply with the Town and Country Planning Control of Advertisements Regulations (1969), a copy of which is available from your Town Hall. With short-term letting there is nothing to stop you putting a 'No Vacancies' sign in your window when you do not feel like welcoming strangers into your home.

Be prepared for people knocking on your door late at night, and remember that you will need to provide clean linen for each overnight visitor so you will have to do laundry regularly unless you have a plentiful supply of (non-iron) sheets. A washbasin in the room is an advantage, but not essential if there are adequate bathroom and toilet facilities close by for visitors. Keep the bathroom clean and tidy. To cause less disturbance to family life, you can serve breakfast in the room, though a good cooked breakfast is usually much appreciated and will ensure that visitors come back regularly and recommend you to their friends. Use of a sitting room and television is optional and rather depends on how much space you have and how sociable you want to be.

Advertise in local shops and garages, and let the local police station know of your existence as travellers often call on them if they are stranded. If there is a tourist information centre in the area, make sure you are on their list of accommodation. If you are really proud of the service you give, try to get included in one of the annual guides to holiday accommodation by writing direct to the publishers.

This is a nice, flexible, way to earn money at home.

Book-keeping

If accuracy is your forte and you like figures, learning how to keep books should not be difficult. A book-keeper records all transactions (trading between two people) in books specially designed for the purpose, copes with VAT, salaries, etc. An experienced book-keeper produces a set of accounts and knows the mechanics of stock-taking figures and annual returns.

You will need a desk, a typewriter, a calculator, files, ledgers and a telephone. The people whose books you keep should provide the stationery. Payment is by the hour, and remember to include extra expenses like petrol, postage and telephone, and also charge for travelling time if you collect and deliver the work.

It might help to spend some time at the client's office sorting out their accounting system before you take the books home to work on them. Businesses, particularly small ones, often have very strange methods of book-keeping!

Approach businesses by letter or in person. It is worth the investment to advertise in professional business publications as well as in local newspapers.

Simple book-keeping is something you can teach yourself from books. However, if you lack the confidence to set yourself up as a fully-fledged book-keeper when you have not taken a training course, see what is available at your local polytechnic or adult education college. You will have to keep abreast with the latest tax requirements, but otherwise the procedures are constant.

It can be repetitive work but ideal if you are housebound, as you can operate successfully from the kitchen table. Most firms need their books done on a weekly or monthly basis so the work is regular – once you have the clients. A good book-keeper is an asset to any small company.

Car Washing

Canvass the market carefully before you start. Few people who live in towns have sufficient parking space outside or even near their homes to operate a car washing service. If you do have plenty of space ask clients to bring their cars to you, otherwise walk or cycle to them. Collect the car keys (and payment) the night before and drop the keys back through the letterbox when you have finished. Undoubtedly customers will want references if you are to operate this way.

The outlay on equipment is small: a bucket, several good rags, sponges, chamois leathers, windscreen scrapers, cleaners, polishes, a reasonable-length hose with an adjustable connection so that it can be attached to the nearest tap, a small vacuum cleaner for the inside of the car, window cleaner and chrome polish.

Prices depend on the size of the car and whether the owner wants a simple wash or a complete clean and polish inside and out. As a guideline, see what the automatic car wash costs at a garage and add 25% for your services, plus pre-set amounts for additional requests (such as polishing a tarnished old bumper and cleaning mud from the undercarriage).

It is worth asking car wax and polish manufacturers to sponsor you: they could advertise by providing you with monogrammed overalls and special containers bearing their products. It is also worth putting your own name and details on your bucket, overall or T-shirt for self-promotion. Make your service known to car-owners by dropping leaflets into neighbouring homes and putting notices up in garages not already equipped with an automatic car wash service.

Car washing is hard work for not a great deal of money, but in good weather it is a nice way to work out of doors and the children can always lend a hand. It's not an all-weather occupation, but it is very simple and anyone can do it.

Compiling Crosswords

Most crosswords are compiled by journalists already employed on the newspaper in question, but at the same time there is a shortage of crosswords in Britain and many have to be imported from America. (There is a knack to compiling crosswords; it does not follow that a person who can solve one will be able to compile one.)

To make a reasonable income, you need to be taken on as a regular contributor. Take your crosswords to press agencies or, better still, send them direct to the features editor of the newspaper you think they are most suited to. Read a few books on the subject, start a filing system of clues, and keep a notebook on you wherever you go and jot down clues whenever they come to mind. This is something you can do anywhere and anytime, requiring no workroom, only a fertile mind!

Computers

In the past few years computers have shed their 'space age' image and become an accepted part of the everyday business world. Now there is increasing talk of home-based computer equipment linked to central offices, which means that many more people will be able to work at home, either full- or part-time. Of all the ways in which you can earn money at home, this is undoubtedly the new growth area and well worth getting into.

Like calculators, computers are becoming more and more accessible to the general public and, contrary to what you may think, you do not need a degree in mathematics in order to operate one! Micro-computers are small and simple to use, but they do represent quite a large investment so you should consider this as a full-time occupation in order to cover your initial costs.

Frances and Liz shared the cost of a micro-computer and bought one with a data-based programme. They provide a service which caters for small businesses, societies and people working from home: *'A micro-computer is terrifically flexible. It'll store information like an enormous card index (anything from reports to recipes), do repetitive things like mailing lists and then tell you who's buying what from them, and, on command, find some remote detail you fed into it at some time. There are plenty of different programmes written for different aspects – the National Computing Centre advises on programmes and what computer would suit you best. Every computer comes with a manual written, literally, for idiots! The mystique of a computer evaporates quickly enough after you've spent a few days "playing" with it to build up your confidence.*

Our computer is in the sitting room on a little desk. It takes up about 2½ feet and is rather an attractive machine! We have three power points – one for the printer, one for the video and one for the computer. When we're not using it, the kids are making lists of their spelling homework or playing games on it.'

Rates for computer work are good, higher than typing or word processing. When you are pricing individual jobs, bear in mind that micro-computers can do very uncomplicated as well as quite complex work and can be used by a wide selection of businesses, so charge accordingly. You can learn from books and manuals and general information on all branches of the computer world is obtainable from the British Computer Society, which also operates an advisory service for the disabled.

Advertise in the local business press, and approach small businesses, shops and organisations you think would benefit from this service. They may well be ignorant and rather shy of computing methods, so take some time to explain exactly how the system works and in particular how it could simplify their own business transactions.

Duplicating

Photocopying has rather taken over from duplicating in the last few years as it is both quick and clean, but duplicating is still used, particularly by small business and in rural areas. It is cheaper than photocopying and printing. Reasonably priced second-hand machines are often advertised (see *Exchange and Mart*), but you should check that they are in good condition. Otherwise you may end up spending even more money on servicing, and you cannot afford to lose business if your one machine is frequently out of action. To find the correct machine for your purposes, go round duplicator showrooms, study the office machinery booklets and ask advice.

You will need a good typewriter (preferably electric) for cutting the stencils, a long-armed stapler and a guillotine. Duplicating machines are noisy, so work in a room as far away from your family as possible, and check that you will not disturb your neighbours. Have an area were people can wait, and consider offering a 24-hour express service.

Joan duplicates six church magazines every month, as well as individual projects: *'I like typing and I particularly like seeing the job through from a scribbled handful of papers to a neat, well-designed little magazine. It's not work you can do with the constant interruptions of small children because once you've started duplicating it's quite a time-consuming process which you shouldn't really break off from and then start up again.'*

Offer a choice of inks and attractive layouts, and display interesting examples of your work in clubs, schools and local shops advertising the service. You could also approach small business direct.

The days of carbon copies are over. If your prices undercut others in the area, then business is bound to come your way.

Graphic Design

Many graphic designers work freelance from home, designing books, catalogues, record sleeves, brochures, leaflets and so on. Publishers like to have designers they can call on to supplement their own (often very busy) in-house design team. Companies and businesses which only produce occasional printed matter do not usually employ full-time designers but instead put the work out to design groups and freelances. This is creative and well-paid work, with plenty of outlets if you can build up the right contacts.

Courses in typography and book design are held at adult education institutes, art schools and through City and Guilds schemes. The London College of Printing and most art schools have a variety of courses to choose from. As well as the actual techniques of graphic design, you also need to understand printing and production methods and this is usually included in a basic course. There are several reference books on different aspects of the subject. If you have no formal training you will need to gain experience working in a design studio before you can offer your services as a designer.

You do not need a special workroom, although you will find you need plenty of space when it comes to pasting up a lengthy book. The main requirements are a drawing board, equipped with parallel motion, and a type scale. You can also buy special parallel motion boards, but these are more expensive and not necessary to begin with. There are specialist graphics suppliers and equipment can also be bought from artists' suppliers and good stationers.

Approach publishers direct and show them samples of your work, and also look in *The Bookseller* and *Campaign* magazines for advertisements. Introduce yourself to local printers as they are often asked to design as well as print brochures, posters, letter headings and so on.

Rates of pay are usually by the hour and are relatively high, but you may also be offered a set fee for a particular piece of work. Remember to include in your estimate the cost of materials, which are often expensive.

Graphology

Graphology, the ancient art of studying handwriting (the Americans call it graphonomy) is finally gaining respectability in Britain. In America graphologists work with the police and psychiatrists and are highly skilled and highly paid, but here they have until recently been employed only as pseudo fortune tellers, appearing at village fêtes. Now the Bell House Study Centre in Norfolk has started weekend courses and adult education institutes have also begun to offer courses in handwriting.

Much of a person's psychological make-up, aptitudes, neuroses, health and emotional patterns can be uncovered by graphology, and frequently your handwriting tells more about you than the words you write. Anyone with a keen sense of observation can become an enthusiastic amateur, but it takes a great deal of study and experience to become a professional graphologist.

Patricia, one of the country's leading graphologists, explains: *'It is a very complicated subject which really has to be studied to the full to do properly, and because it has only recently become accepted as something serious it takes a long while to become established. If you work in the women's field you tend to get landed with all their problems which can be very demanding, but increasingly it is being used by people like businessmen, criminologists and sex therapists for advice and guidance.'*

The only equipment you need is a magnifying glass and you can work anywhere, so this is a very simple occupation to take up at home. Advertise in women's magazines and the personal columns of newspapers, and also approach official bodies likely to use this increasingly popular and respectable service.

Home Economics

Home economics is a relatively new profession and it is concerned with the study of food, nutrition, clothing, community services and products for the home. Work in this field involves testing products, researching, preparing diets and advising on consumer affairs.

To qualify as a home economist, there are two- to four-year courses at colleges throughout Britain. Details can be obtained from the Association of Home Economists (you need four O levels to apply). As a member of the Association you can be included on their list of freelance economists, to work either in or from the home.

It is a well-paid and interesting job, so it is worth the time spent on qualifying if this sort of work appeals to you. The Association describes the people they are looking for as 'lively-minded, articulate, literate, numerate and capable of inspiring trust'. You need to keep right up to date with new products and processes.

Jobs are advertised in the Association's journals and also in trade magazines and the business section of newspapers.

Home Laundry

Do not consider taking in laundry unless you have, or plan to have, a *good* automatic washing machine and adequate drying facilities.

Many people do not have the time or inclination to do their own washing and either take it to a laundry or leave if for a service wash at a launderette. Find out what your local laundry charges and also what the launderette would cost (including the time spent sitting there) and compare those figures with what the same service would cost you in washing powder, electricity and time. If you find your profit margin is not very big, offer an additional service such as ironing, darning or button-replacement. Once you have established a small satisfied clientele, the news will travel and prices can be gradually increased as your business expands.

Provided you know your machine and are familiar with softeners, bleaches and starches, the only danger is the possible ruination of a garment designed for a specific type of laundering. Learn to recognise different fabrics and always observe the washing instructions on garments.

This is a service well-used by professional people, particularly businessmen who need clean ironed shirts daily, so advertise accordingly.

House Guardian

For most of us our home is our castle, and many people are prepared to pay to have their house looked after while they are away.

Being a house guardian means that *you* run the risk of disturbing the burglars on the job! You are responsible for turning lights on and off while the occupants are away, checking that the mail and milk isn't accumulating on the front doorstep, feeding the goldfish, watering the plants, picking the fruit, and calling in the right person if a pipe bursts, a window is broken or a fire breaks out. You should compile a register of local tradesmen prepared to do emergency services, and alert the local police station to what you are doing. If you feel nervous in a strange house on your own, you could always work in partnership with a friend. Before the owners leave, list the items you are caring for and note the state in which you find them – if you are left tending a dying rubber plant, you do not want to end up paying for a replacement! Impress people with your efficiency and help them to feel they are leaving their belongings in good hands. Undoubtedly references will be requested for this sort of service.

> Dick has been a house guardian for some time: *'I always carry a walking stick with me, and have lately taken out special insurance cover against anything happening to me while on the job. Nothing ever has – yet! I visit my clients' houses daily, at different times, and offer them the additional service of looking after their valuables in my home. A solicitor draws up an agreement between myself and the client, exonerating me from any responsibility if their house is vandalised or damaged while I'm looking after it and protecting them should their valuables be stolen while in my safekeeping.'*

Advertise in local travel agencies, in places where people going away board their pets and in local newspapers. You should include expenses, overtime and risk money in your fee, as well as charging an hourly rate for time spent visiting the house. This sort of work usually pays very well, especially if you aim at the upper end of the market.

Household Help

Charring Cleaning for money is not nearly as bad as cleaning your own home! Somehow keeping other people's homes clean presents a challenge, while cleaning one's own does not. In private houses you can often take your child with you, and it is quite accepted that he or she sits and watches television or plays in the garden whle you sweep and dust. Office cleaning is normally done early in the morning or after 6 p.m., as is school and college cleaning. These jobs are not demanding and can be found through job centres or in local newspapers. Charring work is always done on an hourly rate.

Home Help This is a scheme run by the local Social Services Department and they expect more than just cleaning from you. The job involves working in the homes of people who are unable to look after them for themselves, so you might be expected to shop, cook and care for the family while, say, the mother is ill or away in hospital. A home help is paid by the hour.

Mother's Help This is a service for mothers (and fathers) who need an extra hand to help with the domestic chores, looking after the children, or just running errands. Night work particularly is in great demand, to help cook the evening meal or to look after a sick member of the family. Rates are hourly and high, and you will probably be asked for references. Advertise in shop windows, health centres and newspapers or work through an agency.

The advantage of this sort of work is that there is nearly always a demand for it, the hours are flexible and can fit in with your family routine. Being prepared to work at short notice is valued: help in a hurry is worth twice as much as help too late! Many people doing domestic work organise themselves into cooperative groups, so that they can net all the jobs in a certain area and guarantee a reliable service – when one is unable to work, another will step in.

Househunting Service

This job aims to take the slog out of househunting and is a service for people who live abroad or simply do not have the time to do their own legwork – or are too rich, famous or lazy! You are paid a set fee (based on time) to go and see all the houses for sale which conform to the specifications laid down by the client.

Sarah Jane started looking for homes for others after spending seven months looking for one for herself: *'I found that estate agents are more interested in selling you the property than in finding you the right one. The service I offer is based on descriptions given to me by my clients. I try to meet them in their own surroundings to get a feel of their taste in decor, furniture and style and am happy to go out and find them what they're looking for. I will get all the estate agents' lists and ask to be taken round the ones that look suitable. I charge an hourly rate and ask for a small lump sum in advance. I guarantee not to exceed ½% of the value of the property.'*

Outlay is fairly basic and comprises business stationery, a desk, a telephone, a typewriter and a car. Advertising should be pitched at those who would be unwilling to trudge around houses after a day's work, such as tired executives, celebrities, people who live in the country and, of course, people who live abroad. Older people who are looking for somewhere smaller to live and young couples looking for somewhere larger are two categories well worth approaching. Advertise in national newspapers and journals that are read abroad, and in glossy magazines. Tell estate agents about your service (it does not conflict with their business, merely eases their work) and publicise your activities at the local building centre, design centre and home owners' exhibitions.

This is interesting work that takes you out of the house, but you should learn to tell if houses are structurally sound, etc. Even though the house market rises and falls, people will always need homes.

Indexing

The function of an index is to enable the reader to find the information held within a book. You have to be able to think vertically and laterally, and to work out cross references to do this sort of work. Above all, you need a very organised mind which can put things neatly into compartments.

Liz works, like most indexers, at home: *'It helps to be familiar with the subject of the book you are indexing if it's technical or academic, but it doesn't matter if you have no knowledge of the subject if it's a book on, say, craftwork or recipes. If the subject interests you, the work is very enjoyable! My only moan about indexing is that, as a profession, you have little status and publishers undervalue you. They never give you enough time so you're always under pressure when you work – you need white-hot nerves!'*

Indexing is one of those jobs you learn by doing it. The Rapid Results College do a correspondence course on indexing, and you can make enquiries to the Society of Indexers which publishes the only journal in this field, *The Indexer*.

You will need a large table, indexing cards, index boxes, a typewriter and stationery. Most indexing work is with London-based publishers. Let them know of your service by sending a circular letter, and advertise in the publishing trade magazine, *The Bookseller*.

The work is interesting and varied, and the pay is medium to good on an hourly rate.

Kits

Kits, which customers assemble themselves, are becoming increasingly popular; they avoid the middle-man and the retailer and therefore keep down costs. People are beginning to acquire a taste for this method of shopping.

However, it is one thing to make up a kit, but quite another to sell it, and the success of the business lies as much in the selling as in the initial idea. You need to know what the customer wants and also be a bit of a wheeler-dealer. Kits are usually sold mail order, so the first step is to decide on your market and advertise in a newspaper or magazine which your potential customers are likely to read. Give some thought to your advertisement and make the kit sound simple to assemble as well as being a practical or attractive end-product. If you can, include a simple drawing (it helps if people can actually visualise what you are offering).

Kits can be anything from children's clothes to garden sheds. Allow for business to be slow at first, which means you need some capital to cover the cost of materials in the meantime. However good you think your idea is, don't prepare too many kits until you start getting orders even if that means a slight delay in sending them out.

John made up a burglar deterrent kit which he sold mail order: '*I bought doorspies from a hardwear wholesaler and packed them in one container with the correct sized hand-drill for the doorspy, also bought wholesale. Then I bought up a consignment of disused metal boxes to make the "This house is protected by an XYZ burglar alarm system" burglar alarm box that is fixed to an external wall, and stuck two screws and rawlplugs in with it. Finally I had sticky labels made up with the "This house is . . ." wording, stuck one on to each box, packaged the lot and sent them off.*'

As you can see, inventiveness is a great asset when it comes to designing kits!

You will need a large, dry room in which to store the materials, and later the kits. Make sure they are well wrapped, otherwise you might lose a lot of your profits in replacing damaged goods. If you cannot face the thought of packaging each individual kit (and your market justifies it), you could consider selling the kits through a major mail order company. Remember, too, that people are more likely to order through the post if you offer them the chance of returning the kit within a specified time limit for a refund.

For your own sake as well as that of your customers, give clear instructions for assembly and supply absolutely everything that will be needed, down to glue and screws or zips and buttons. Otherwise you may find yourself involved in correspondence and telephone calls with customers who are not natural handymen or dressmakers.

Letter Writing/Typing Service

Many people are totally unable to write formal or official letters, and most people loathe doing it anyway. In areas where foreigners live, a letter writing service is much-needed.

You must possess a mind which can decipher bureaucratic or legal jargon and reply accordingly. You also need a decent typewriter and a supply of stationery. Rates vary, depending on whether you are asked to type a client's handwritten letter or to compose a tough letter on his behalf to make a claim for damaged goods. For a straightforward letter charge per page, and add on extra for special stationery. Charge more if you have to compose the letter yourself.

Advertise in factories and schools where there are foreigners, and in newsagents and stationery shops. You could also approach your local newspaper for editorial coverage.

Minicab Driving

If you are free to leave the house and you enjoy driving, then this is a good way to make the maximum use of your car. There is no governing body for minicabs, but good agencies will only take on neatly dressed drivers with clean licences and well-maintained cars.

You need to take out a special hire-and-reward insurance to cover you in case of any accident involving passengers. Before you start working as a driver you must have a good knowledge of the area, including places like hotels and restaurants. You will be expected to give an estimate of the cost of the journey in advance. Charges are based on mileage.

Find work by approaching the agencies in your area (see Minicab Agency). They will equip you with a two-way radio, and you pay them a regular weekly fee for providing you with work. You will be self-employed, contracted to the agency, so you can choose your hours of work. As a driver/owner, you are responsible for your car, petrol and regular servicing.

Driving can be a good source of income, especially if you are prepared to work in the evenings and at weekends when rates are higher.

Taxi Driving   To become a taxi driver is much more complicated, and in London it takes up to two years to qualify by passing a

178

rigorous knowledge test. Taxi drivers operate as individuals, approved by the Public Carriage Office, or work for central agencies which own the vehicles.

Model Making

There is quite a demand for scale models, from architects, developers, theatrical stage managers, people organising exhibition stands and the like. Good fees are paid for neat, accurate work. It is fun to do but don't underestimate the time models can take to make.

Outlay on equipment is reasonable and you will not need a large work space. Tools include knives, tweezers, scissors, a hammer, a pair of pliers, a hand drill, a small fret saw and a tri-square. Many different materials can be used, including cardboard, polystyrene and plaster of Paris, and you may need accessories such as model trees. If you work small, a little goes a long way!

There are courses in model making at art colleges and adult education institutes, and it is quite possible to learn the technique from books.

Advertise in design magazines and approach potential clients direct. Have some of your models available (or photographs) to show as examples of your work.

Nursing

No formal training is needed to become a nursing auxiliary, working either in a hospital ward or assisting a local district nurse visiting patients in their homes. There is a growing demand for hospital auxiliaries, who bathe, feed and generally care for patients without getting involved in any technical or medical duties. Some hospitals give training and hours are usually flexible, so that you can fit them in with your home routine.

If you are a qualified nurse but unable to work full-time because of family commitments, there is plenty of scope for part-time and evening nursing. Nursing agencies are always looking for more trained nurses, and many hospitals have 'nurse banks' of temporary staff they can call on.

If you cannot work away from home, you could always take an elderly, handicapped or infirm lodger who needs some nursing care (contact the local Health Department and organisations for the elderly). The Red Cross and St John's Ambulance Brigade both hold courses in home nursing.

Nurses are not allowed to advertise so apply for vacancies and make enquiries to your local Health Department, the British Nursing Association, the National Council of Nurses, the Nursing and Health Service Careers Centre or the Royal College of Nursing.

Nursing is notoriously badly paid but the work is extremely rewarding.

'On View' Advertising Service

Some businesses will pay for space in your home which they can use as a showroom for their goods. These are usually mail order companies (maybe specialising in only one item, such as a 'revolutionary' new kettle, 'unique' car-seat covers, or a 'cosy' duvet) or businesses which do not have an office or retailer in that area. Many customers like to see the products before buying them, and you receive a commission on each item sold through you.

You can advertise locally at the company's expense and maybe distribute their leaflets locally when you are expecting a new delivery. The more effort you put into this service, the more commission you are likely to earn. In some cases, you also demonstrate the product working, which involves a higher fee.

Contact mail order firms and make enquiries through the Mail Order Traders' Association. You should inform the local Planning Department as in their eyes this constitutes running a shop.

If you like meeting different people, this would be an ideal way to act as a salesman from home.

Packaging

Unglamorous as this sounds, it can be quite remunerative. It all depends on how quickly you acquire the knack of getting awkward shapes speedily bound and sealed!

You supply the stationery, which comprises boxes, corrugated paper, cardboard, wrapping paper, tape, string, polystyrene pellets for packing around delicate and fragile objects. Buy the packaging wholesale (see the Yellow Pages: Packaging Materials) and, if you have storage space, it is obviously cheaper to buy in bulk.

If you have a car or preferably a van, you can collect the parcels;

otherwise arrange for local companies to drop their parcels off on your doorstep for collection later that day or, if you are prepared to invest in a franking machine (or they are prepared to supply you with one), for you to post.

George started his packaging service when he retired: *'The factory gave me the work to keep me active but now several companies from the same industrial estate are bringing their parcels to me. I charge per package depending on the size, from a few pence upwards.'* He is now branching out and wrapping products for display purposes and he would like to capture the Christmas gift end of the market on the department store circuit.

Approach nearby concerns which mail a varied assortment of items that cannot be packed by machine, and advertise locally. Adult education colleges run courses in carton and box making, and packaging.

The outlay is not exorbitant and the returns are good.

Painting and Illustrating

Like writing, painting for a living is rather precarious – you can make a fortune or earn nothing at all. Unless you are really talented or your work fits in with the latest trends in art, it is safest to operate as a commercial illustrator.

There are several outlets for illustrators, including books and magazines, cartoons, advertising and packaging. You can find work through agents (see *The Writers' and Artists' Yearbook*) or by taking your portfolio round to potential employers. Contacts are all-important, so cultivate the ones you have and attend book fairs and the relevant trade fairs to meet new clients. Most professional illustrators have art school training and you need to be good, the field is so competitive.

You can also work in the crafts field, producing hand-painted tiles, pottery, wallhangings, greeting cards and so on. If you live in the country, there may be a tourist demand for drawings and paintings of local beauty spots (even woodland scenes painted on stones or old tobacco tins seem to sell well), and if you have the right social contacts you could specialise in portrait painting. Limitations are linked to the imagination, and there is no accounting for taste! Display your work where people will see it, for example in a tea shop or on a market stall.

There are many courses in different painting and drawing

techniques, at art schools and adult education institutes and private colleges. The Arts Council and the National Society for Art Education can advise on art colleges and courses. There are also numerous practical books on different techniques, available at art suppliers as well as in bookshops. Materials can be expensive, depending on what medium you work in, and you will probably need a drawing board and a studio of some kind.

You may find it best to operate in more than one area, doing more creative work when you have the opportunity and subsidising it with more routine 'bread-and-butter' fare. Visit galleries for inspiration – and street markets for ideas!

Photographic Processing

This can be a very profitable business, always provided you can find the clients. Darkroom work has become almost as popular a hobby as photography itself! Businesses and newspapers often need a fast, efficient local service and you may be able to find a regular contract if you can operate cheaply.

Black and white processing is still very much a manual operation so the outlay on equipment is reasonable, but to offer a professional colour processing service you will have to invest quite a lot of money. Buy equipment second-hand (look in *Exchange and Mart*, or small ads in photography magazines) but make sure it is in good condition. The darkroom will fit into a small space, but it should contain a sink and needs to be kept at a constant temperature.

There are many books on photographic processing and courses are held at adult education institutes. The Institute of Incorporated Photographers can advise on all aspects of photography.

Advertise in local newspapers and approach local businesses. You can make good profits if you offer a speedy service, but the work is quite gruelling as you are cooped up in a dark, airless studio.

Photography

First, decide exactly what kind of photography you want to do and what your circumstances will permit. The requirements for black and white photography and advanced technical colour work can be very different (see Photographic Processing). In both cases, though, you will need reliable equipment and talent.

You should have a camera, two lenses, a light meter and a flash gun – and more expensive equipment can follow once you have mastered the basic skills. Whether or not you have a studio in your home depends on the kind of work you do, but you will need a darkroom for processing black and white photography. It often works out cheaper to send colour film away for developing. Darkroom equipment will include an enlarger, a marking frame, safelight, developing tanks, chemicals and paper.

If you want to work close to home, there is a wide field to explore. Either work in your own studio concentrating on portraits and passport pictures or work away from the house photographing weddings, pets, parties, shows and items to be included in brochures for auctioneers and estate agents. Approach people direct, advertise in local shops and newspapers and generally be seen with a camera round your neck.

If you decide to work freelance for magazines and newspapers, begin by visiting the picture editor with a portfolio of your photographs. Remember there is a surfeit of photographers looking for work in journalism so try to find a new angle or specialise in an area like cookery or animals. Expect rejections. Always make sure your work is accurately captioned and that it bears your name and address, and never sell the copyright. Artlaw Services will advise on that side of photography and the Photographic Information Centre offers a good cross-section of relevant information.

For training, join the local camera club. Most adult education centres run courses and the Photographic Training Centre will train students in television and video photography. The Institute of Incorporated Photographers advises on specialist training, the Bureau of Freelance Photographers runs a free advisory service and the Arts Council may offer financial encouragement.

The Writers' and Artists' Yearbook has full details on the market for photographers, including names of photographic agencies with whom you can place your work.

Fees can range from very high to very, very low, and it can take months before you are paid.

Printing

The investment involved in setting up as a small local printer is quite high, but there is often a good market for business stationery, posters, leaflets, tickets, invitations and so on. Do some market research before you start as there may be sufficient printers already established in your area.

Small hand-operated printing presses are now only made by one company, Adana Ltd, but you can buy second-hand ones through *Exchange and Mart*. If you graduate to an automatic press, this entails much more serious capital outlay. You need a good range of typefaces and a guillotine, plus a selection of different papers. Printing is classified as a light industry so check with the Council to see if you need planning permission.

Printing is considered an apprenticeship trade and it is difficult to train part-time, so this is something that is best undertaken after working for a time with a commercial printer. The British Printing Society can advise on all aspects of printing, and it runs a postal library of reference books.

As well as understanding the technicalities of printing, clients will often expect you to lay out the text for them, so you need to know about typography and graphic design (see Graphic Design). The London College of Printing holds various courses and so do colleges throughout the country.

Valerie bought herself a small hand machine which she operates six days a week: *'I started by making leaflets to advertise my service and sent them to all the professionals in the local Kelly directory. Now I'm printing everything from posters to visiting cards. I reckon I spend 25% of my turnover on materials and the rest is straight profit.*

'Your major overhead is in paper, and if you're a small outfit it can be hard to avoid having to buy in bulk from paper merchants. I'd advise ringing around and approaching one that sounds sympathetic to your endeavour and open an account there.'

Printing is both creative and practical work. The more experience you can gather the more you will reap. It is not a job gauged by how hard you work – quality is all important. The rewards are worth waiting for.

Proofreading

When printed proofs of a manuscript come back from the type-setters, they are proofread for mistakes or omissions and marked accordingly. It does not take long to master proofreading but it does call for good eyesight and an eye for detail (spotting mistakes doesn't come naturally), good grammar and spelling, and a great deal of concentration and accuracy. This is a job best done at home in a quiet corner.

The signs used in proof correction are a language of their own and have to be learnt. Because of the nature of the work, it helps to have an understanding of how a book is put together, from manuscript to final volume.

Publishing is a fairly closed shop, so try to find proofreading work through somebody already in the business. If a certain subject interests you, approach publishers who specialise in that area. Advertise and look for work in *The Bookseller*, the chief magazine of the book trade. There are also a few agencies handling part-time proofreading work (see *The Writers' and Artists' Yearbook*).

Public Relations/Promotions

Public relations work is ideal for people who have worked in a firm's publicity or PR department and understand the ins and outs of promoting a product, how to create an image for a person or company and how to communicate facts and ideas to the right people. As a considerable amount of PR is concerned with getting stories in newspapers and magazines or on radio and television, you have to know how to approach the media outlets (features editors, press officers, contacts in your specific field) and what to offer them in the way of promotional material. Work, a lot of which can be done at home, ranges from writing and handling straightforward press releases (mailed out to selected people) to organising launch parties with product samples, and press conferences and interviews.

Cathy runs her own business specialising in restaurants and records, two subjects she knows about: *'It is vital to stick to areas you are familiar with and expand within them rather than taking on new and exciting projects, which will take you twice as long to promote because you are not au fait with them. You should limit the number of clients you take on because when you're actively promoting one client and maybe spending time away from home you simply aren't available to handle several others at the same time. This sort of work is geared to contacts, recommendation and word of mouth, so it's important to be seen and to go out and about rather than stay tucked away in your little office at home, if you can'.*

Equipment includes a telephone, answering machine, typewriter and, if possible, a duplicator as so much of PR and promotion is the writing and sending out of mail shots. Helpful handbooks include the *Creative Handbook* and *Marketing Handbook* (from Creative Handbook Publications) and the *Hollis Press and Public Relations Annual*. The Institute of Public Relations offers advice. Try to get your name in the Yellow Pages.

Fees vary depending on the job and can be negotiated per job, or worked out on a retainer basis.

Publishing

Publishing from home is best suited to small projects, such as magazines, newsletters, brochures, guides, hand-printed books and limited editions. You could offer an editing and design service or go a stage further and handle the printing, sales and distribution too. Books, brochures, etc can be produced for a client, sold privately, through local shops or through a distributor or large publisher. Costs are high so make sure of your market before you print thousands of copies!

The publishing process begins with accepting or commissioning a manuscript, and is followed by editing, designing, typesetting, proof-reading, picture selecting and paste-up. You could handle most of these stages yourself, or put them out to freelance people also working from home. The book or brochure is then printed and bound.

There is a lot to know about publishing and printing and much of it can be read up in books (start with *The Writers' and Artists' Yearbook*). There are a couple of libraries specialising in books on publishing, the Mark Longman Library at the National Book League and St Bride Printing Library. The Publishers Association and the Independent Publishers Guild can advise.

To become a small, independent (probably specialist) publisher you need good ideas and initiative, experience in origination and in marketing, and reliable contacts.

Advertise in trade journals if you want to attract the attention of companies needing brochures and glossy reports, and approach tour companies, clubs and hotel chains.

Reading to the Blind

Registered blind students who are following prescribed full-time courses are given a small grant for the payment of readers' fees. The work includes reading onto tape, reading over the telephone and reading to the student in person, either at your home if you are in his vicinity or at a mutually convenient place. A good reading voice helps.

The fee, per hour, is negotiable. It is usually small as the allocated monies for this service are limited. It is best not to make a commitment until you have met the blind person and know exactly what is required.

To become a reader, have your name and details put on local college and university lists.

Research

Research can be for yourself, for somebody else, for publishers, television, businesses and numerous other outlets. It calls for an interested and clear mind, and is very stimulating work to do. There are no specific qualifications, but it helps to know one or more subjects in detail and you must be familiar with information sources. (Librarians make marvellous researchers as they understand library and cataloguing systems.) You are expected to work quickly and neatly, and to type up your findings in coherent language. Much reseach work is done over the telephone and a lot of time is taken up collating the results.

The Association of Special Libraries and Information Bureaux runs an information service and training programme, and the Library Association (and your local library) can point you in the direction of specialist knowledge. HMSO publishes two booklets, No 4 *Library Information and Archive Work* and No 100 *The Scientist*. Jobs are advertised in business publications (for example, a battery company might want somebody to investigate the battery market) and newspapers like *The Times* or *The Guardian*. Rates of pay vary enormously.

Picture Research Picture research involves more travel, visiting photographic libraries to look through their collections, though much of it can be done by post. The Publishers' Association runs a course in picture research, but it is only open to publishing employees from firms who are members of the PA. There are several reference books, including *The Picture Researchers' Handbook* by Hilary and Mary Evans, an international guide to picture sources and how to use them. See *The Writers' and Artists' Yearbook* for more details.

Abstracting Abstracting is also work carried out by researchers. It involves selecting the main points in reports and studies so that others can immediately see what is in the source material. It is ideal work to do at home.

Information Consultancy This can be an extremely interesting occupation, particularly if you enjoy spending hours in reference libraries and searching through reference books. Information consultants can be highly specialised, dealing only with, say, business studies, nuclear physics or alternative systems, or very general providing all kinds of information. Work can stretch from improving a small business's filing system to producing a complex report for a group of industries. It helps to have an academic qualification and experience in some field of specialist work, and to have charm and self-confidence to inspire confidence in your sources in order to persuade them to part with their information, particularly if you do not belong to a recognised company. Contacts are very important, though you will build these up as you gain experience.

Rose is an information consultant working from home: *'Nobody expects you to have a huge library at home, but you must know your way round the specialist libraries and their cataloguing systems like the back of your hand. Also you need the obvious – like desk, typewriter, filing cabinets, a telephone and, if you can run to it, a photocopying machine. When business picks up you have to budget to pay researchers a fee, but you time-cost all that in. An information scientist should be familiar with the potential of on-line systems (computer-assisted searches) which, although they can be expensive, are sometimes the only sensible way to research. Find out about them through public library centres and commercial information brokers.'*

All kinds of people need information scientists: businesses, foreign companies, academics, authors, television and film companies, and societies – people who either do not have access to information sources or do not have time to look out the information they need. The scope of individual projects is equally varied, and the work may take a couple of days or six months. Present the information clearly and concisely in a typed report, or in folders, filing systems, indexes, as appropriate, and keep a record of your sources. A good filing system is essential.

Look in national newspapers and business journals for advertisements, and advertise your research service in the same publications. The Institute of Information Scientists will give advice on research generally.

Genealogy Another specialist area of research is genealogy – researching people's family histories. This is much in demand from Americans, Australians, Canadians etc, whose ancestors lived in England. It is also used by adoption agencies and in detective work.

It is fascinating work but often time-consuming, and also expensive as fees and certificates are often involved as well as travelling expenses. Most records are kept in London, but you also often need to consult local parish registers and county archives. St Catherine's House keeps records of births, marriages and deaths (they accept postal enquiries) and the Public Records Office handles census returns. Other sources are Burke's *Peerage* and the College of Arms.

Some adult education institutes do courses on genealogy and heraldry, and the Women's Institute holds a course on heraldry and family records. The Society of Genealogists can offer advice and there are several reference books available.

Shopping on Order

If you have a large car and a spacious house, go out and buy big. Buying in bulk and bargain buys work out much cheaper than buying at the corner shop, but few people are able to buy this way because they do not have storage space. People who are housebound or short of time are often very happy to pay somebody else to shop for them.

A well-organised shopping service can be very successful. Bargain buys are pre-publicised by the big stores so get on their mailing lists. Alternatively, buy in bulk direct from the supplier or from a cash-and-carry warehouse, and divide up and package your purchases. Shopping for others can often be fitted in with your own shopping programme.

Circulate a duplicated list each week giving items you could buy and the price: bargain buys of electrical goods, records, tableware or garden equipment, and bulk buys of staple foods, wines, fresh fruit or vegetables. You can also include special offers such as Christmas gifts, car parts or exotic foods.

The prices you ask should be slightly less than the shop price. To make a profit you have to add commission to cover petrol, parking, wear and tear of the vehicle, delivery and your time. A reasonable commission would be 10–15% of the price of the purchase. Do not accept responsibility for any fault in the merchandise, which is a matter for the customer to take up with the supplier. In the case of perishables such as fruit, make sure you have the orders in advance. If you cannot afford to buy first and sell later, ask for deposits from your customers.

Try to interest the local newspaper in your service, talk about it and drop leaflets describing your service at houses, businesses and clubs. Once you have a regular group of customers, see if shops would be prepared to give discounts to the group. To ensure the group stays constant, each member should pay an annual fee.

Sign Writing

Sign writing has traditionally been a job where you start as an apprentice with a big company, and it is therefore a very hard trade to break into. There is, however, a shortage of trained sign writers, so if you think you have the necessary talent it is well worth trying.

There are part-time and evening courses in sign writing but only in the London area, at the School of Building in Lime Grove and the Vauxhall College of Building and Further Education. Sign writing is usually included in more general courses taken by painters and decorators, so it might be possible to attend those classes. Although there are reference books on subjects related to sign writing, such as calligraphy, typography and lettering, there are as yet no practical books on sign writing itself.

Most sign writing is done outdoors *in situ*, on shopfronts, pub windows and the sides of vans, but there is also a demand for beautifully painted small signs which can be done from home.

The equipment consists of a palette and knife, brushes, a mould stick, the material on which you are going to work (if not already *in situ*) and ladder(s) for outside work.

James, a traditionally trained sign writer advises: *'Because sign writing changes as fashions change, there's always something to do that you've never tackled before. You learn all the time and you have to keep in touch with the trade to find out what is going on. If you're good you get good money. You have to be patient and good at detail.'*

Get to know different typefaces, paints and styles and practice hard before showing samples of your work to shops that sell house and garden items, shopfitters and office suppliers. Advertise in DIY magazines and local newspapers.

Singing Telegrams

A recent import from America, singing telegrams is catching on as a novel way to surprise friends on birthdays, anniversaries and other celebrations.

Julie explains: *'It is by no means easy to start up because unless you're fabulously punctual, efficient and talented the whole exercise becomes very cowboy. You need to be able to write songs suitable for a person you have only been given a description of over the telephone by their friend or a member of their family. Then you have to choose the right performer to deliver it. We have "resting" actors and singers on our books who are prepared to sing, often make fools of themselves and essentially look good. We now have dozens of costumes but have to keep a check so that the same costume never goes to the same client twice. That means thinking up new, inexpensive ones all the time – girls in corsets and suspenders aren't good enough! We charge per telegram with an additional fee if more than one performer has to go or if the client wants, for example, a girl jumping out of a cake. Advertising is through word of mouth, free publicity by wooing newspapers and moving in media circles where we make contact with the type of person likely to want a singing telegram.'*

There is work here either for an organiser or a performer – but you must be a bit of a showman. It is tremendously satisfying and great fun when the message hits the right note! Current 'Singing Telegram' people say that they hope to build up a network of performers and organisers around the country so that they can all interact.

Spray Painting Cars

If you can turn out really professional work, there are excellent profits to be made here. Car spraying requires plenty of practice and experience, so start with your own car before spraying someone else's! Your car will also be one of your best advertisements.

Professionals use a special spray booth, but you can work in your own garage provided it is well-lit, well-ventilated and as dust-free as is humanly possible. A speck of dust will ruin the finish, and you have to keep the spray gun scrupulously clean or it will not work properly.

There are adult education courses in spray painting and step-by-step books on the technique. The consumer magazine *Which?* has published an issue on paint sprayers. For small jobs, use a suction-feed spray gun; for larger jobs you need a pressure-feed gun which is connected to a container holding up to 40 gallons of paint. You will also need an orbital sander and a polishing machine (an electric hand drill with a buffing attachment is fine), so there is quite a large investment involved.

Before spraying the car, you have to prepare it by washing and sanding the paintwork and removing as much of the chrome as possible. You then mask off the glass, chrome and other areas not to be sprayed, and apply two coats of paint. Each coat takes four to six hours to dry. You could also offer a more comprehensive service, including bodywork repairs. (Nobody wants a respray if the car is scratched or dented.)

Advertise in the motoring services columns of local newspapers, and in local garages and car accessory shops.

Still Life Modelling

Art schools are always looking for models, and modelling is one way to earn a little bit of extra money if you have only a limited, but regular, amount of time you can spend away from home – and there's an art school nearby.

Approach art schools and adult evening colleges direct, but beware of advertising as you may not get quite the response you intended! Still life modelling often means being prepared to model nude, but once you get over the initial embarrassment you quickly get used to it. It doesn't matter what sex or shape you are, so don't worry if your figure is less than perfect. You may also find work modelling privately for artists and sculptors, probably as a result of contacts made through the art school classes.

Modelling is not very highly paid, but it is undemanding work and can made quite a relaxing break from a busy family life.

Taking in Lodgers

If you have a large house with spare bedrooms (for instance, if your family has grown up and left home) you could take in a lodger (see also Bed and Breakfast). Board is by agreement, and lodgers can be asked to leave, given 'reasonable notice'.

First check that you are not infringing any building society regulations or, if you are a tenant, that your landlord does not object. Council tenants should consult their local Housing Department. It is always worth speaking to the local Citizens' Advice Bureau or Housing Aid Centre because different boroughs have different rules.

The Department of the Environment publishes advisory leaflets (*Rooms to Let* and *Landlords and the Law*) for landlords. If you are an owner/occupier, letting a room in your own home, you need not worry about the danger of sitting tenants.

When you take a lodger, make sure that the terms are fully understood from the outset so that there is no unpleasantness later. Rent is usually paid weekly (you must issue a rent book, which can be bought from most stationers) in advance so that lodgers cannot do a 'moonlight flit', leaving the rent unpaid. Many landlords ask for a deposit, which covers you in the event of any damage to the property and also gives you some assurance of the lodger's financial stability. You can also ask for references, including a reference from the lodger's bank manager. Legally lodgers are allowed to have visitors and the landlord or landlady cannot enter the room without 'reasonable notice'. In practice, it is far more satisfactory to get on good terms with your lodger as he or she will be living in your home. You may need to alter your householder's insurance policy to cover you in case of injury or damage to the lodger's property caused by your negligence, for instance a burst pipe or a leaking roof.

The Dennises decided to take student lodgers from the local university: '*We let the three rooms our children once had to students, rather than leave our house. We provide bed and breakfast and all meals on Sunday at a rate set by the university. This is included in the tax return, indicating that it breaks even and that details will be provided if required. The details would be a percentage of the rates, heating, electricity, maintenance, decorating, food and laundry bills.*'

Advertise in local colleges, universities and EFL schools in the area, the 'Rooms to Let' section of newspapers and shop windows. Rents and profits depend very much on the area in which you live and how much accommodation is in demand, as well as the facilities you have to offer.

Sharing your home with a stranger can be difficult and can prove stressful, but often the lodger becomes a part of the family. Try to find out as much as you can about the person in the initial interview, and be prepared for a little 'give-and-take' during the first few weeks while they settle in.

Telephone Message Service

Operating a telephone message service can prove to be a lifeline for someone who is unable to leave the house. As well as bringing in extra income, it will make life much more interesting. Called Subscriber's Control Transfer, your telephone is connected to a subscriber in the same exchange area who has a switch on his (or her) telephone enabling him to put calls through to yours while he is out. When the person returns, he rings you for the messages and then switches the telephone back to normal.

Anne was bored when her children left home and, being supremely diplomatic herself, discovered that she really enjoyed 'kindling' business for others. She soon found that she could handle more than one person's messages and built up a group of five subscribers.

If you offer additional office services, such as keeping a diary for each subscriber, you can charge extra. This system generally works out cheaper for the client than the GPO's operator referral service, and is much more personal than an answering machine.

The GPO charges a connection fee plus quarterly rental (which the client subscriber pays). The wiring is complicated so expect a fairly long delay. Contact the telephone sales department in your area for details.

Advertise through channels in which the self-employed operate (look through the Yellow Pages for professions and trades which take people out of their place of work and contact those in your exchange area). Telephone them rather than writing so that they can hear your voice. It is also worth canvassing local offices rented by small concerns.

Tourist Guide

Guiding is not for those who dislike history, old buildings, foreigners and breaking into informed bursts of monologue. If it gives you pleasure to show strangers around your town, telling them all the interesting facts and enjoying visits to museums, monuments and mausoleums, then being a tourist guide is the perfect job for you. The work tends to be seasonal, so would suit someone who is not looking for a full-time commitment.

Tours can be on particular buildings and sites in your area (if you live near a canal, why not organise an 'Industrial Revolution Canal

Walk', for example) or in the form of coach tours of a whole city or area. In both cases, you have to read up on dates, kings, wars, and all the local background. Your local library should have a good stock of reference books, and museums and churches often publish their own leaflets. The London Tourist Board runs a part-time course for guides, at the end of which you take an examination which qualifies you as a Blue Badge tourist guide. Some tour firms also give training. Go on a few tours to see how other guides operate and brush up on your foreign languages.

Rates of pay are set by the Guild of Guides and Lecturers and they will also advise on legal matters. You can expect to get tips on top of the fixed fee, especially if you put a little extra effort into your talk and welcome questions.

Advertise in local travel agents, travel magazines, local hotels and local tourist or information centres. In London there is the London Tourist Board, and you should also recommend your service to the British Tourist Authority.

The pay can be very good (especially the tips!) but being a guide is hard work!

Transcribing Braille

The Royal National Institute for the Blind periodically recruits sighted people to learn braille. Training lasts for three to six months (in London), and once qualified the braillists are given books to transcribe. You need A Level qualifications to be taken on as a transcriber. In Scotland, the Scottish Braille Press employs only the registered disabled for this work, and the National Library for the Blind employs blind people to proofread braille and work as braille copyists. Some local authorities are now starting braille transcribing schemes for homeworkers.

Braille is not easy to learn and the rates of pay are only modest, but the work is extremely rewarding. Recruiting advertisements are published in national papers like *The Guardian* and *New Scientist*, or you can apply direct to the above organisations.

Translating

There are no official qualifications for a translator but, apart from knowing your own language exceptionally well, you must have a perfect knowledge, both written and spoken, of the other language. The demand for translations is increasing in specialist work, so expect to expand your vocabulary even if you are already fluent in the language.

The largest field for translation is technical books, brochures, text books and business letters; literary translation of foreign fiction is less common. Look in *The Writers' and Artists' Yearbook* for suitable publishers and send them a sample of your translation work, remembering that they will expect it to be well-written as well as a good translation. If you have any specialist knowledge, for example tractors, aerodynamics, music or fashion, approach companies operating in those fields (see the Yellow Pages). There are several agencies for this kind of work, but you will earn more by working direct for a client.

Jerry translates from Russian: *'I did a Linguaphone refresher course as my Russian had become rusty, put my details on file at the reference library and the local Chamber of Commerce and worked my way through the Yellow Pages: Translating and Interpreting section. There were literally no overheads to consider as I already had a desk, typewriter and dozens of dictionaries! Later I joined the Institute of Linguists as a Fellow and found that they were a great help when it came to setting fees – it's either per 1,000 words or per hour. The Institute also publish a journal which advertises jobs.'*

The Institute of Linguists incorporates the Translators' Guild, which runs an intermediate exam available for anybody with the appropriate academic or language qualifications. The Translators Association gives advice on more literary work and, like the Institute, publishes leaflets to help translators. The Linguists Club has both clients and translators on their books.

Typing

Typing is one of the easiest jobs to do at home – and consequently one of the most competitive! You need a decent machine (preferably electric with all the modern symbols), a good speed and a high accuracy rate. You must also be able to offer a quick service. Remember speeds don't ever go, they just slow down. Even if you haven't typed since before the children were born, you'll quickly pick it up again. If you need the discipline, take a refresher course at night school or a commercial college.

Advertise in local newspapers to attract the attention of small businesses in the area, and also in magazines like *The Bookseller*

New Statesman in the hope of finding work typing authors' manuscripts. If you live near a university or college, put an advertisement on their notice boards as many students need theses professionally typed. Rates are usually per page or per 1,000 words as the time spent depends on the efficiency of the typist, and no-one wants to pay extra for slow work. If you can offer a 24-hour or overnight service, you can charge really good rates.

Open an account with a stationer and ask for trade discounts as you will be buying in bulk. Remember to include stationery and postage on your invoices.

You can work anywhere in the house, but you will probably want to avoid disturbing other members of the household, especially if you sometimes work late into the night on urgent jobs. Don't take on more work than you can handle as rushed work usually results in bad work and you may lose a client.

Jennifer, a North London typist, comments: *'If you are able to choose who you work for, choose rich people who can afford to pay for good work. If you're known for quality work, don't be tempted to delegate to friends who type – one messy manuscript can lose you your good reputation.'*

You could well combine a typing and duplicating service (see Duplicating), as stencils for duplicating must be typed.

Washing Windows

Washing windows is not as complicated as washing cars, but you do need a ladder and a head for heights. You will also need a bicycle or van on which to carry your ladder, and a rag, a window wiper, a chamois leather and a bucket.

It is easy work, punctuated by cups of tea, and you can take the children with you. Work tends to be seasonal: lovely in summer, cold and less remunerative in winter.

Fees are per window, negotiable with the client. Offices generally pay well, householders are less generous. To raise business, do some door-to-door canvassing. It is worth trying to link up with a glazier, or a carpenter who makes window frames and mends broken sash cords, and between you offering a comprehensive window service – or learn how to do it yourself.

Make sure you are properly insured to cover yourself if you fall and also for damage to the window and the customer's belongings should you have an accident.

Word Processing

Word processing is fast taking over from typing. It is quicker, neater and more reliable – and some say even easier than typing. Word processing is still very lucrative work, and worth getting into while it is still comparatively new.

Secretarial colleges offer training as part of their courses, and you also receive short training when you buy a word processor. Private agencies give tuition.

Chantal persuaded her husband, a computer programmer, to teach her the basic principles: *'If you learn on one kind of processor you can't necessarily work on another without additional training and plenty of practice, but the principles remain constant. It should take about two days to absorb the basic knowledge and then quite a few more of trial and error! It's great to work on a word processor because the final result is something which is completely perfect. It's ideal for typing books or theses because the author can come along two or three weeks after the work has started and make massive changes without it showing.'*

Word processors are still very expensive, though the market is getting more competitive. However, you can offset the initial outlay by charging higher fees than you could if you were just using a typewriter. Be sure that you have access to enough work to justify it. Advertise in business magazines and approach local businesses direct, particularly those which produce lengthy reports. (See also Typing for other sources of work.)

Memory Typewriters These are cheaper than word processors and simpler to operate. They are sold with an instruction manual and some firms offer a two-day training course when you buy their machines. As you do not need to retype pages with corrections and alterations, you can work much faster than on an ordinary typewriter so, again, this would be worth the extra investment if you have a plentiful supply of work. Memory typewriters are particularly suitable for routine letters – letters can be recalled at the push of a button.

Writing

Some authors *do* write a bestseller and spend the rest of their lives as tax exiles in the South of France, but for the vast majority writing is a much less glamorous occupation. It is very solitary, often very frustrating, and, particularly if you want to write fiction, you can spend years working on a book only to find that no-one will publish it.

If you think you have a good idea for a book, do some research and then send a short synopsis to publishers in that field (see *The Writers' and Artists' Yearbook*) before embarking on any detailed writing. If they are interested, they will probably then ask to see a sample of your writing. Be prepared for long delays which mostly end in rejection, and even if your book is accepted do not expect to earn a great deal of money; unless they become bestsellers, most books do not make a big profit, and some even make a loss.

Short stories and articles should be photocopied and sent round to suitable magazines – specialist magazines for highly informed features, women's magazines for certain kinds of romantic short stories, the right newspaper for topical stories. Your ideas have to be new, newsy and just what an editor is looking for! Your style of writing might be better suited to writing ditties for advertisements, mottos or rhymes for greeting cards. Never send the only copy and always type the manuscript (or have it typed for you – presentation is important). Send a covering letter addressed to the right person, *by name*. Again remember this is an extremely competitive field, so be prepared for disappointing rejections.

If you are really determined and sure of your work, persevere as sometimes a manuscript is turned down by several publishers before finding a home. If you find it difficult to sell yourself, take your work to a literary agent (see *The Writers' and Artists' Yearbook*) who will also advise you on whether your writing is good enough to get into print.

There are several other fields open to writers, for example radio and television, but again only the very best is accepted. You may do better to think small to begin with and write articles for local magazines or the magazines published by various societies. Writing for newspapers is difficult unless you are a professional journalist. There are fixed union rates per thousand words (enquire from the National Union of Journalists) but rates of pay do vary, depending both on the publisher and the kind of writing.

The best approach is to write to commission, and here it helps if you have specialist knowledge of a particular subject so that editors will refer to you for articles, or even books, on that subject. Writers do not advertise, so to get known first approach a specialist magazine and, if you are good, work your way up from there.

There are courses on writing, both fiction and non-fiction, and you can join your local branch of the Writers' Circle. Ask for details at your local reference library.

The tools of the writing trade are a typewriter and desk where you can work in peace. Build up a good reference library of dictionaries, a thesaurus and books on your particular subject.

Writing involves talent, vivid imagination and the ability to write fluently, with great wit and/or wisdom – and luck.

TEACHING

'I think we could have worded it better, Cedric!'

○ Check with your insurance company in case they think it advisable to extend your policy to cover extra risk or liability.

○ Inform the local authority if you intend to teach children.

○ Consult the Council before putting up a notice in your front window advertising classes.

○ Remember that you are allowed tax relief on light, heat, rates and rent.

○ Some of the jobs mentioned here are suitable for people who are already trained as teachers, and others are suitable for those with experience. Qualifications for private tuition are not needed unless you are working in conjunction with a State school.

○ See Contacts for addresses and reference books.

Dancing Classes

Modern dance and movement classes are suddenly very popular, and the demand is likely to grow. There is also the more traditional field of ballroom dancing, jazz, tap and Latin American, and little girls are always wanting to become ballet dancers!

You do not have to be a qualified teacher, but you should know what you are doing as working with other people's bodies can be dangerous. The main requirement is premises: a large room with a good, hard-wearing wooden floor, showers and toilets and a changing room. You will also need a source of music (either a tape recorder or a piano), and for ballet exercises you will need bars.

Jean runs a ballet class for ladies in her nearby church hall: *'The great advantage for the teacher is that once you're in the swing of the classes the lessons become more simple to devise. And, of course, as you teach you get a work-out too! It's quite important to look good in the dance business. Because the hall isn't centrally heated we have to take care about warming up gradually. You should never leap into a class, and it's the teacher's responsibility to be careful with the students because you're dealing with the body and it's terribly easy to strain or twist something.'*

The Royal Academy of Dancing do a three-month teachers' course for professional ballet dancers, otherwise you can consult the Dance Teachers' Association or the Council for Dance Education and Training. The magazine *Dance Teacher* has details of courses.

Advertise in local newspapers (try to get an editorial feature when you open), schools and sports centres.

Marvellous work for both the qualified dance teacher and the amateur enthusiast. There is good money to be made if you can build up a lively clientele.

Driving Instruction

To be a driving instructor, it definitely isn't enough just to be a good driver – you have to be a very good driver and pass a written and practical examination set by the Department of Transport.

Once you have been approved, your name goes on the Register of Approved Driving Instructors, and you can display a certificate in your car.

Some clients will bring their own cars, but you also need to provide a car for others to learn on. It should be a saloon or estate car, with right-hand steering and non-automatic transmission, and you need to be insured for all third-party and damage risks and for liability to passengers, which can be expensive. Your car should be in good condition, regularly serviced and well looked after generally.

A word of warning from Dave, who has been instructing from home for a couple of years: *'Make sure you get 24-hours' cancellation notice. Learners know you work from home so they will ring you up at 9.30 p.m. the night before a 9.30 a.m. lesson to cancel, and you can be left with an empty car earning nothing for you.'*

Advertise in local newspapers, in newsagents' windows and car showrooms, and also in colleges as many of your clients will be young people. Base your charges on those of the local driving school, allowing enough to cover all the running and depreciation costs of your car. Rates of pay for driving instructors can be very good, and you should try to build up a good reputation as much of your work will be from personal recommendation.

Foreign-language Conversation

With chartered air travel, more and more people are going abroad for their holidays, and joining the EEC has meant increased international business. Consequently there is an increasing demand for learning and practising languages conversationally, so this is a good field to enter if you speak a foreign language fluently. It can be very nice work to do.

Grade your classes for beginners, intermediate and advanced students, and maybe offer special one-to-one classes for businessmen if there is likely to be a demand for this in your area.

You can hold the classes informally in your living room, in which case you need adequate seating and a blackboard. Some students may prefer to pay extra for individual tuition. Charge for a course of lessons, and ask for a deposit or full payment in advance. It is a good idea to have a small library of books and magazines which students can borrow to read between classes, and you could also sell some language-learning cassettes on commission from the manufacturer.

You may well need to brush up your own vocabulary, especially in business subjects. The Centre for Information on Language Teaching and Research (CILT) provides research facilities and reference books.

Advertise in colleges, libraries, travel agencies, embassies and visitors' clubs, and approach any local companies that do business overseas.

Music Teaching

To enter pupils for the Royal Schools of Music examinations you need to be a qualified music teacher, but if you are a good musician without a diploma you can still teach adults and children who are not concerned about passing examinations. You can earn quite a lot of money, but make sure that the continual noise (not always tuneful!) will not interfere too much with your family or the neighbours.

Pupils bring their own instruments, except for piano players. They also supply the sheet music and music books. Many of the classes will need to be held in the evening, after work or school, and you need a quiet, warm room to teach in.

Susan has 20 pupils learning to play the piano, and another 16 on her waiting list: *'It is the perfect way to earn. It costs me nothing apart from tuning the piano three times a year instead of twice. I charge more per hour for people studying the higher grades and working for exams than I do for children starting out. So that my work doesn't disturb my baby, I teach adults when my husband is home to look after him, and the mothers who bring their children to lessons are always willing to keep an eye on him while their children learn. I feel many more people who learnt up to Grade 8 but dropped out before taking their diploma could teach from home. Most of them have lost their confidence because they think that the students are going to want to study for exams. Most people give up at about Grade 3 or Grade 5 and, frankly, anybody who is a goodish player can teach up to those levels.'*

The Royal College of Music will supply details of examinations, and you can consult the Incorporated Society of Musicians about fees. They will also know about summer schools and refresher courses. The Rural Music Schools Association can help teachers living in the country.

Advertise in music magazines, schools, colleges and musical instrument and record shops.

Teaching English: EFL and ESL

Teaching English as a foreign language (EFL) was a good source of work until about 1980 when the demand suddenly dropped, putting many small (often fly-by-night) EFL schools out of business. The need for EFL teachers still exists but it is more competitive, so it does help to have some training. To be of real value to students, you should be able to construct lessons and know how to present them properly. There are various short courses in teaching EFL, and you can check their reputation with ARELS (the Association of Recognised English Language Schools). Interntional House, the leader in this field, does an excellent four-week course.

English as a second language (ESL) is aimed at immigrants. It covers more basic everyday language than EFL, such as going shopping, catching a train or reporting a theft. Pupils are mainly Asian housewives and they have the added disadvantage of a different alphabet, which makes reading English very difficult. The National Association for the Teaching of English as a Second Language to Adults works in conjunction with local education authorities to provide training for ESL teachers.

In both cases teaching experience is an asset, but patience, humour and a genuine desire to help are equally important. Teaching can be done privately at home, in which case you need a blackboard, table and suitable books, as well as visual aids which you can make yourself. You can also teach students in small groups, in school classrooms in the evenings or in a room in a library or youth club. Local education authorities can help you find premises and they also give guidelines on fees for ESL.

Advertise both services in local newspapers, libraries and in places where foreigners and immigrants work and meet socially. The work is hard but very rewarding and you in turn will learn about other cultures. You will probably earn more teaching EFL than ESL, and it is up to you and the response whether you make this a full- or part-time occupation.

Teaching Lipreading

Lipreading is taught to people who lose their hearing as adults, rather than people who are born deaf. It is a difficult skill to both teach and learn, but very rewarding work.

To teach lipreading you need to be 'lipreadable', and you should have a clear speaking voice and a good knowledge of English. The City Literary Institute in London and Manchester Polytechnic run courses.

Teaching can be done at home, or in classes organised by education authorities at the local adult education institute. Private tuition is very much in demand, but you should check with the local authorities before you start to make sure this service is not already covered. Rates of pay are usually good, but you should remember this is very intense, demanding work and you need to be extremely patient.

Advertise in health clinics, old people's clubs and centres for the deaf, as well as working through the local authorities.

Teaching Literacy and Numeracy

It has been calculated that the reading age required to understand a supplementary benefit form is 17, an income tax form is 15 and the Highway Code and *Daily Mirror* is 13. It is further estimated that one in ten pupils leave school virtually illiterate, and that 4% of the British population is totally illiterate. The figures may well be higher as many people who cannot read or write are experts at concealing the fact. These people are at a great disadvantage when it comes to form-filling etc.

Even more people have hardly any knowledge of mathematics, as was shown in a recent Government report, and this has not been helped by the changeover to the metric system. Basic calculations are needed in everyday life, for shopping and paying bills.

Classes in literacy and numeracy are held at adult education colleges. However, one of the characteristics of these people, especially the illiterate, is a great feeling of shame and inadequacy and they would often prefer to pay for private tuition. A student must trust you not to spread the word about his or her illiteracy. Contact your local education authority for details of available training schemes, and write to the Adult Literacy Unit or Cambridge House for a list of books on the subject. The BBC ran an excellent television series called *On The Move* with an accompanying teaching book, which is a good one to work from.

Advertise by word-of-mouth. Check that your pupils' problems are not to do with poor eyesight or hearing, and that they are not suffering from dyslexia, or word blindness, which will require specialist attention.

There is no outlay on equipment other than a few suitable books for pupils to read, and you can hold the classes in your living room. Tact, sympathy and perseverance are important, and the work is extremely rewarding.

Teaching Self-defence

With the much-publicised increase in violent crime, many people are turning to self-defence as a means of protection, as well as appreciating the martial arts for their own sake as exercise and disciplinary skills.

There are several techniques, including judo, karate, aikido and kendo. You can learn these yourself at private colleges or adult education institutes, and you must be quite highly skilled to be able to set yourself up as a teacher. You have to be particularly careful that students do not injure themselves, and you should take out adequate insurance cover.

The room or hall in which you work needs to be fairly large, so you may have to hire a local hall if you do not have the premises. Showers, toilets and a changing room should also be provided.

As a self-defence instructor, you will be expected to advise on safety and the law, so make sure you are fully briefed. The most common fears are mugging, rape and burglary.

Charge for a course of lessons, rather than for individual lessons, so you keep a regular set of students. A six-week course of two or three hours once a week should be sufficient for self-defence techniques, though some students may want to go on to develop a particular technique.

Advertise in local newspapers and shopwindows, and in schools and colleges. You could also run special classes for the elderly, in which case advertise in local centres and in doctors' surgeries.

Teaching Sports

If you already have a heated swimming pool or a tennis court, this is an ideal way to make the most of it. To teach children doesn't call for Olympic or Wimbledon standards, and it is far more important that you know enough about the sport to be able to coach others. The safety angle is particularly important, especially if you are working with young children.

Mary has a heated indoor pool which she uses for water therapy sessions for very young children: *'My water babies come from 10 weeks onwards so it's hardly a matter of teaching them – the swimming part of it comes spontaneously when they're older. My job is really to bully mothers into getting their children into the water younger and make them realise that children aren't made of glass. They're just like little fishes.'* She does, however, have very good insurance cover in case of accidents.

If you live in the country and own a couple of riding horses, you could give riding lessons. To open a riding school properly you need a British Horse Society certificate, but for basic lessons and escorted outings you need not go this far. If you do decide to expand and do it properly there is a marvellous six-month TOPS course for teachers at the BHS Riding School.

Before you embark on sports teaching, check with the Council in case you need planning permission or special training and facilities. The Citizens' Advice Bureaux can also advise you.

Teaching Typing

If you are an ex-secretary or copy typist now working (or wanting to work) from home, you could consider teaching as well as freelance typing. It will certainly be more companionable than solitary typing, and you can alternate the two.

Some people learn to touch-type in a few hours, others grapple with it for months. You could also include lessons in laying out and writing business letters as well as the actual typing. Shorthand or speedwriting would be another obvious extension of the classes. Try to provide extra personal tuition, as you will be competing with adult education institutes.

Charge a set fee for each course of lessons, with payment in advance, and remember to include the cost of stationery. You will need to supply the typewriters, desks and chairs, but you can keep the costs down by buying them second-hand. It is still best to learn on a manual machine, even if you end up using an electric typewriter. Make sure your machines are serviced regularly.

There are courses in teaching typing at colleges of further education, but experience is the main qualification and you can learn the basic teaching techniques from books.

Remember that several people typing all at once makes quite a noise, so consider the family and neighbours before you start.

Teaching Yoga

Of the many relaxation techniques now practised by more and more people, yoga is one of the most popular. Mastering the physical positions takes considerable practice; mastering the mind even more.

Yoga is taught at adult evening institutes, so check in your area to see if there is a demand for private classes. To train as a teacher, contact one of the many yoga organisations or your local yoga centre. Make sure you fully understand what you are doing, as many of the exercises involve stretching the body into different positions which can be harmful if not done properly.

You need a large, warm and quiet room, and somewhere for students to change. The size of the classes will depend on the number you can attend to – this is not production-line teaching. If there are enough students, you could hold classes at different levels. Charge fees for a course of lessons to ensure regular attendance. It is difficult to get students to leave the house when you teach at home. If you have just spent an hour trying to de-stress the class, the last thing you feel like doing is forcing them out to make way for the next session.

Advertise in local newspapers (try to get them to write a feature when you start), libraries, sports centres, health clinics and beauty salons.

Enjoyable work with loads of feedback.

Tutoring

If you are a retired teacher, or have the right qualifications, you can earn a good income as a private tutor. Schoolchildren often need coaching for examinations in their weak subjects, particularly mathematics and the sciences, but you may find it difficult to get enough regular work to make it a full-time occupation.

You must be up to date with examination requirements, so obtain the relevant information from the GCE examinations boards or university curricula. You will need a good library of reference books and a quiet room to teach in.

Payment is by the hour, and you can advertise in libraries, schools, colleges and local newspapers. There are national education agencies (see *The Times Educational Supplement*), and you could also approach the staff of schools and colleges direct to see if they have any students who need coaching.

If you prefer not to have a string of students visiting you at home, tutors are also required for correspondence courses and the Open University. The Council for the Accreditation of Correspondence Colleges has a list of correspondence courses.

CONTACTS

Enclose a stamped addressed envelope with all letters requesting information or details of courses.

General

Action Resource Centre, 9 Henrietta Place, London W1

Alliance of Small Firms and Self-Employed People (ASP), 42 Vine Road, East Moseley, Surrey

Association of Certified Accountants, 29 Lincoln's Inn Fields, London WC2

Association of Independent Businesses, Europe House, World Trade Centre, St Katherine's Way, London E1

British Institute of Management, Management House, Parker Street, London WC2

Business Publications Limited, 109 Waterloo Road, London SE1

Church Action with the Unemployed, PO Box 576, Aston, Birmingham B6 5QL

Companies House (for limited companies), Crown Way, Maindy, Cardiff DF4

Companies Registration Office (for partnerships and businesses), 55 City Road, London EC1

Cooperative Development Agency (CDA), 20 Albert Embankment, London SE1

Council for Small Industries in Rural Areas (CoSIRA), 141 Castle Street, Salisbury, Wilts

Department of the Environment, 2 Marsham, Street, London SW1

Department of Industry Small Firms Information Service, Abell House, John Islip Street, London SW1P 4LN

Health and Safety Executive, Regina House, Old Marylebone Road, London NW1

HMSO, Atlantic House, Holborn Viaduct, London EC4

Industrial and Commercial Finance Corporation Limited, 91 Waterloo Road, London SE1

Industrial Common Ownership Movement (ICOM) (for advice on cooperatives), 7–8 The Corn Exchange, Leeds LE1 7BP

Institute of Chartered Accountants (England and Wales), Moorgate Place, London EC2

Institute of Chartered Accountants (Scotland), 24 Holborn, London EC1

Institute of Marketing, Moor Hall, Cookham, Berkshire

Institute of Small Businesses, 13 London Road, Bromley, Kent BR1 1TD

The Law Society, 113 Chancery Lane, London WC2

London Enterprise Agency, 69

Cannon Street, London EC4N 5AB

Low Pay Unit, 9 Poland Street, London W1

Mail Order Secretariat, Newspaper Publishers' Association Ltd, 6 Bouverie Street, London EC4Y 8AY

Mail Order Traders' Association, 507 Corn Exchange Building, Fenwick Street, Liverpool L2 7RA

Manpower Services Commission (for Community Enterprise Projects and Training Opportunity Schemes): write to your local Employment Service Agency or Job Centre

Market Research Society, 15 Belgrave Square, London SW1 8PF

Marketing Society, Derwent House, 35 South Park Road, London SW19 8RR

Ministry of Agriculture, Fisheries and Food, Whitehall Place, London SW1

National Advisory Centre on Careers for Women, Drayton House, 30 Gordon Street, London WC1H 0AX

National Federation of Self-Employed and Small Businesses (head office), 32 St Anne's Road West, Lytham St Annes, Lancs FY8 1NY

National Federation of Women's Institutes, 39 Eccleston Street, London SW1W 9NT

Office of Wages Councils, 12 St James's Square, London SW1

The Patent Office, 25 Southampton Buildings, London WC2

Registrar of Business Names (England and Wales), Business Registrar, London Chamber of Commerce, 69 Cannon Street, London EC4N 5AB

Rural Crafts Association, Brook Road, Wormley, Surrey

Small Firms Information Service, 8 Bulstrode Street, London W1

Teledata Ltd, Imperial House, The Hyde, Colindale, London NW9 5AL

Telegraph Information Service, The *Daily Telegraph*, 135 Fleet Street, London EC4

Reading

Creating Your Own Work, Michelle Mason, Gresham Books

Croner's Reference Book for the Self-Employed and Smaller Business, Croner Publications

Going Solo, Jones and Perry, BBC Publications

Guardian Guide to Running a Small Business, Clive Woodcock, Kogan Page

Markets Year Book, World's Fair Ltd

Starting In Business, Department of Inland Revenue

WHICH? issues on *Self-Employment* and *Starting a Business*

Working For Yourself, Godfrey Golzen, Kogan Page

Working For Yourself, Parsons and Neustatter, Pan

General Courses and Training

City and Guilds of London Institute, 76 Portland Place, London W1N 4AA

Committee of Directors of Polytechnics, 309 Regent Street, London W1R 7PE

Crafts Council Information Service, 12 Waterloo Place, London SW1

Department of Education and Science Advisory Council, Elizabeth House, York Road, London SE1

Manpower Services Commission (for Community Enterprise Projects and Training Opportunity Schemes): write to your local Employment Service Agency or Job Centre

National Federation of Women's Institutes, 39 Eccleston Street, London SW1W 9NT

National Institute of Adult Education, De Montfort House, 19b De Montfort Street, Leicester LE1 7GH

Open University, P.O. Box 48, Milton Keynes, Bucks MK7 6AB

Second Chance to Learn, Harrison Jones School, West Derby Street, Liverpool 7

Workers' Educational Association (head office), 9 Upper Berkeley Street, London W1. See also local telephone book for regional offices.

Working for others

Homework
Office of Wages Councils (*see* General)

Homework and the Disabled
REMPLOY, 415 Edgware Road, London NW2 6LR

Direct Sales
Direct Selling Association, 44 Russell Square, London WC1B 4JP

Mail Order
Mail Order Secretariat (*see* General)
Mail Order Traders' Association, (*see* General)

Selling over the 'phone
Sales Force Ltd, 1–2 Berners Street, London W1P 3AG

Computer Work
British Computer Society, 19 Mansfield Street, London W1N 0BP

Corsets
Corsetry Manufacturers' Association, 14 Cockspur Street, London SW1

Invigilating
Open University, PO Box 48, Milton Keynes, Bucks MK7 6AB

Market Research
Market Research Society (*see* General)
Office of Population Censuses and Surveys, St Catherine's House, 10 Kingsway, London WC2B 6JP

Agencies

Department of Employment, Caxton House, Tothill Street, London SW1

Au Pairs Agency
Au Pair Bureau, 87 Regent Street, London W1
En Famille Agency, Westbury House, Queens Lane, Arundel, Essex

Building Repairs Agency
Federation of Master Builders, 33 John Street, London WC1N 2BB

Business Services Agency
London Tourist Board, 26 Grosvenor Gardens, London SW1

Employment Agency
Federation of Personnel Services, 120 Baker Street, London W1

Foreign Student Accommodation
ARELS (*see* Teaching: English)

British Council, 10 Spring Gardens, London SW1
London Tourist Board (*see* Services: Tourist Guide)

Marriage Bureau
National Council for Marriage Guidance, Herbert Gray College, Little Church Street, Rugby, Warwickshire

Minicab Agency
National Federation of Taxicab Associations, PO Box 2BL, Percy Street, Haymarket, Newcastle-on-Tyne

Speakers Agency
Commonwealth Institute, Kensington High Street, London W8
Guild of Professional After Dinner Speakers, 12 Little Bornes, London SE21

Animals

Equine and Livestock Insurance Company, Marlow House, 610–616 Chiswick High Road, London W4
Ministry of Agriculture, Fisheries and Food, Whitehall Place, London SW1
RSPCA, Causeway, Horsham, Sussex RH12 1HG

Beekeeping
British Beekeepers' Association, 35 Fishers Road, Staplehurst, Kent

reading:
Beekeeping, Ministry of Agriculture Bulletin No.9
Complete Guide to Bee Keeping, R. A. Morse, Pelham

Dogs and Cats
Feline Advisory Bureau, 6 Woodthorpe Road, London SW15
Kennel Club, 1 Clarges Street, London W1Y 8AD

reading:
A–Z of Dogs and Puppies, Barbara Woodhouse
The Cat Owner's Encyclopaedia, Brian Vesy-Fitzgerald, Pelham
Dog News, 92 High Street, Lee-on-Solent
Dogs, Their Care, Training and Health, H. E. Bywater, Blandford
How to Have a Well-Mannered Dog, White & Evans, Paperfronts
video:
Training Dogs the Woodhouse Way, BBC

Free-range Eggs
British Poultry Federation, 52 High Holborn, London WC1V 6SX
reading:
Modern Poultry Keeping, J. Portsmouth, Teach Yourself Books

Goatkeeping
British Goat Society, Rougham, Bury St Edmunds, Suffolk IP30 9LJ
reading:
An Introduction to the Goat, British Goat Society
Goat Husbandry, David Mackenzie, Faber

Children

Child Escorts
Universal Aunts, 36 Walpole Street, London SW3

Childminding
National Childminding Association, 236a High Street, Bromley, Kent BR1 1PQ
National Foster Care Association, Francis House, Francis Street, London SW1

Playgroups and Nursery Schools
British Association for Early Childhood Education, Montgomery Hall, Kennington Oval, London SE11 5SW
Pre-School Playgroups Association, Alford House, Aveline Street, London SE11 5DH

Clothes and Accessories

City and Guilds of London Institute (*see* General Courses and Training)
Mail Order Traders Association (*see* General)

Alterations and Mending
reading:
Mend It, Maureen Goldsworthy, Mills & Boon

Sewing Short Cuts from A to Z, Elizabeth Musheno, Granada

Dressmaking

College of Fashion and Design, 20 John Princes Street, London W1M 9HE

School of Dressmaking and Design, 69 Wells Street, London W1P 3RB

suppliers:

J. W. Coates & Co Ltd, Croft Mill, Foulridge, Colne, Lancs

Celic Ltd, PO Box 7, Ashburnham Road, Bedford ML40 1DL

R. D. Franks Ltd, Market Place, London W1N 8EJ

Handbags

Cordwainers Technical College, 182 Mare Street, London E8

reading:

The Design and Construction of Handbags, W. C. Double, OUP

Hatmaking

David Shilling, 36 Marylebone High Street, London W1

reading:

Make Your Own Hat, Jennifer Stuart, Bell & Hyman

Making Hats, Peter Morgan, Batsford

Knitting

British Hand Knitting Association, 60 Toller Lane, Bradford, West Yorks BD8 9BZ

Green Umbrella Enterprises, Nottingham Community Project, Barker Gate House, Belward St, Nottingham NG1 1JZ

Knitmaster Ltd, 30–40 Elcho Street, London SW11

Knitting and Crochet Guild, 6 Crooklands View, Clifton, Penrith, Cumbria

Wool Secretariat, Wool House, Carlton House Gardens, London SW1

Worldwide Machine Knitters' Club, Unit 22, Spring Vale Estate, Cwmbran, Gwent NP4 5YQ

reading:

A Complete Guide to Knitting, Pam Dawson, Marshall Cavendish

Machine Knitting, Hazel Ratcliffe, Pan

suppliers:

Direct Wool Group, PO Box 46, Wheatley Works, Ilkley LS29 9PY

Jamieson & Smith, 90 North Road, Lerwick, Shetland ZE1 0PQ

The Yarn Store, 6 Ganton Street, London W1

Pattern Cutting Classes

reading:

Pattern Cutting and Making, Shoben and Ward, Batsford

Silk Lingerie

reading:

Lingerie, ed. Jack Angell, David & Charles

suppliers:

I. C. Davis & Co Ltd, 94 Seymour Place, London W1

Pongees Ltd, 184–186 Old Street, London EC1V 9BP

Theatrical Costumes

The Costume Society, 6 Buckingham Avenue, Liverpool L17 3BB

suppliers:

(*see* Dressmaking)

Borovick Fabrics Ltd, 16 Berwick Street, London W1

Crafts

British Crafts Centre, 42 Earlham Street, London WC2H 9LD

Crafts Council, 12 Waterloo Place, London SW1Y 4AU

Design Council, 28 Haymarket, London SW1

Federation of British Craft Societies, 8 High Street, Ditchling, Essex

Field Studies Council, Preston Montford, Montford Bridge, Shrewsbury

Hand Crafts Advisory Association for the Disabled, 103 Brighton Road, Purley, Surrey

Homebound Craftsmen Trust, 29 Holland Street, London W8

Scottish Craft Centre, Acheson House, 140 Canongate, Edinburgh EH8 8DD

courses:

CoSIRA, 141 Castle Street, Salisbury, Wilts

Dartington College of Arts, Dartington, Totnes, Devon

Denman College, Marcham, Abingdon, Oxon

Dillington, House, Ilminster, Somerset

The Earnley Concourse, Nr Chichester, Sussex PO20 7JL

National Federation of Women's Institutes, 39 Eccleston Street, London SW1W 9NT

National Union of Townswomen's Guilds, 2 Cromwell Place, London SW7 2JG

The Orton Trust, 82 The Walk, Potters Bar, Herts

West Dean College, West Dean, Chichester, West Sussex PO18 DQZ

Styal Workshop, Quarry Bank Mill, Styal, Cheshire SK9 4LA

Basketry

Basketmakers Association, Millfield Cottage, Little Hadham, Ware, Herts SG11 2ED

reading:

Contemporary Basketry, Sharon Robinson, Davis Publications

suppliers:

The Cane Centre, Bridge Road, Haywards Heath, Sussex

The Cane Store, 377 Seven Sisters Road, London N15

Millfield Cottage, Little Hadham, Ware, Herts SG11 2ED

Swinnertons, Ambercote, Stourbridge, Birmingham

Batik

The Bevere Vivis Group, Bevere Knoll, Bevere, Worcester WR3 7RQ

Southwark College, The Cut, London SE1 8LE

reading:

ABC of Batik, Bernadette Hersk, Hilton Book Co

Bookbinding

Designer Bookbinders, 9 Queen Street, London WC1N 3AR

Society of Bookbinders and Book Restorers, 5 Chiltern Close, Ramsbottom, Lancs

reading:

Basic Bookbinding, A. W. Lewis, Dover

Bookbinding At Home, Riberholt and Drastrup, Thorsons

Manual of Bookbinding, Arthur W. Johnson, Thames and Hudson

Calligraphy

Slapton Ley Field Centre, Slapton, Kingsbridge, Devon

The Society of Scribes and Il-luminators, c/o British Crafts Centre, 43 Earlham Street, London WC2H 9LD

The Society for Italic Handwriting, 69 Arlington Road, London NW1

reading:
  Calligraphic Styles, Tom Gourdie, Studio Vista
  Italic Handwriting, Tom Gourdie, Studio Vista

suppliers:
Falkiner Fine Papers Ltd, 4 Mart Street, London WC2

Philip Poole & Co Ltd, 182 Drury Lane, London WC2

Candlemaking

reading:
  Candlecrafting, William Nussle, Barnes
  Candlemaking, Terence McLaughlan, Pelham

suppliers:
British Wax Refiners, Redhill, Surrey

The Candle Centre, 89 Parkway, London NW1

Candlemakers' Suppliers, 28 Blythe Road, London W14

Poth Hille & Co Ltd, 37 High Street, London E15

Christmas Decorations

reading:
  The Christmas Crafts Book, Search Press
  Christmas Decorations, Alison Liley, Mills & Boon

Crochet

Knitting and Crochet Guild, 6 Crook-lands View, Clifton, Penrith, Cumbria

reading:
  Batsford Book of Crochet, Ann Stearns, Batsford
  Crochet Design from Simple Motifs, Maggi Jo Norton, Batsford
  Crochet, Pretty and Practical, Caroline Horne, Mills & Boon

suppliers:
Needlework Shop, 68 Welbeck Street, London W1

Silken Strands, 33 Linksway, Gatley, Cheadle, Cheshire SK8 4LA

Decorating Glass

British Artists in Glass, 19 Chetwynd End, Newport, Shropshire

The Glasshouse, 65 Long Acre, London WC2

Guild of Glass Engravers, 19 Portland Street, London W1N 4BH

London Glassblowing Workshop, 109 Rotherhithe Street, London SE16

reading:
  Engraving and Decorating Glass, Barbara Norman, David & Charles
  The Techniques of Glass Engraving, Peter Dreiser and Jonothan Matcham, Batsford

Decorative Wood Techniques

Society of Decorative Crafts, 119 Allington Drive, Strood, Rochester, Kent ME2 3TA

reading:
  Book of Tole and Decorative Painting, Priscilla Hauser, Studio Vista
  Paint Magic, Jocasta Innes, Windward
  Victorian Cut-and-Use Stencils, C. B. Grafton, Dover

Embroidery

Embroiders' Guild, Apartment 41A,

Hampton Court Palace, East Moseley, Surrey KT8 9AN

Royal School of Needlework, 25 Princes Gate, London SW7 1QE

suppliers:

Art Needlework Industries Ltd, Ship Street, Oxford

Mace and Nairn, 89 Crane Street, Salisbury, Wilts SP1 2PY

Yarncraft, 112A Westbourne Grove, London W2 5RU

Enamelling

Artist Enamellers, 60 Wellhouse Road, Beech, Alton, Hants

Guild of Craft Enamellers, Renarden, Lyth Hill, Shrewsbury, Shropshire SY3 0BS

reading:

Enamelling, Del Fairfield, Teach Yourself Books

The Technique of Enamelling, Clarke and Fehr, Batsford

suppliers:

Crafts and Kilns, 376 Finchley Road, London NW3

W. G. Ball Ltd, Anchor Road, Stoke-on-Trent

Flower Making

reading:

Flowers from Feathers, Pamela Wood, David & Charles

Making Paper Flowers, Suzy Ives, Batsford

suppliers:

In Flower, Caundlemarsh, Sherborne, Dorset

Paperchase, 216 Tottenham Court Road, London W1

Handspinning

See Weaving and Handspinning

Jewellery

Jewellery Advisory Centre, 30 St Georges Street, London W1

Jewellery Summer School, Mill Wynd, Lundin Links, Fyfe, Scotland

assay offices:

Goldsmiths Hall, Gutter Lane, London EC2V 8AQ

Newhall Street, Birmingham B3 1SB

137 Portobello Street, Sheffield S1 4DR

15 Queen Street, Edinburgh EH2 1JE

reading:

Jewellery Making, Gordon Stokes, Pelham

Lapidary for Pleasure and Profit, Eric Shore, John Gifford

Lapidary Publications, 84 High Street, Broadstairs, Kent

Step-by-Step to Jewellery Making, Avril Redway, Hamlyn

Leatherwork

British Leather Carvers' Association, 24 Kelston Grove, Hanham, Bristol, Avon

reading:

Leathercraft by Hand, Jan Faulkner, Pelham

Making Clothes in Leather, B. & E. Morris, Studio Vista

suppliers:

Cotswold Craft Centre, 5 Whitehall, Stroud, Glos

The Tannery Shop, Gomshall, Guildford, Surrey GU5 9LE

Taylor & Co Ltd (Tools), 54 Old Street, London EC1V 9AL

Macramé

reading:

Introducing Macramé, Eirian Short, Batsford

Macramé: A Comprehensive Guide,

Heidy Willsmore, Faber

suppliers:

E. J. Arnold, Butterley Street, Leeds LS10 1AX

Arthur Beale, 194 Shaftesbury Avenue, London WC2

Atlas Handicrafts Ltd, PO Box 27, Laurel Street, Preston PR1 3XS

The Rope Shop, 26 High Street, Emsworth, Hants

Mosaics

reading:

A Course in Making Mosaics, Joseph Young, Van Nostrand Reinhold

Stone Mosaics, Sylvia Spenser, Blandford

Moulding with Polyester Resin

reading:

Glass, Mosaics and Plastics, ed. Eric Shults, Marshall Cavendish

Ornamental Ironwork

British Artists Blacksmiths' Association, Rawhurst Forge, Leatherhead, Surrey

Claydon Forge, Claydon, Nr Ipswich, Suffolk

Creative Metalwork, Clapham and Balham Institute, 6 Edgeley Road, London SW4 6EL

West Dean College (*see* Repairs: Restoring China and Ceramics)

reading:

Edge The Anvil, Jack Andrews, Rodale Press

Metal Techniques for Craftsmen, O. Untracht, Robert Hale

Papermaking

reading:

The Art and Craft of Handmade Paper,

Vance Studley, Studio Vista

Design and Make Greetings Cards, J. & T. Arundel, Dent

History and Process of Papermaking, Paper and Paper Products Industry Training Board, Potters Bar, Herts

Papermaking at Home, Anthony Hopkinson, Thorsons

Papermaking as an Artistic Craft, John Mason, Twelve by Eight Press

suppliers:

Paperkit Ltd, Melbourn Bury, Royston, Herts

Papier Mâché

reading:

Art and Design in Papier Mâché, Karen Kuykendall, Kaye & Ward

Papier Mâché, Robin Capon, Batsford

Patchwork and Quilting

Embroiderers' Guild (*see* Embroidery)

Quilters' Guild, Oakington Corner, Girton, Cambridge

reading:

Making Patchwork for Pleasure and Profit, Pauline Burbidge, John Gifford

The McCalls Book of Quilts, John Murray

The Seven-Day Quilt, Josephine Rogers, Mills & Boon

suppliers:

Laura Ashley, 71 Lower Sloane Street, London SW1

Patchwork Dog & Calico Cat, 21 Chalk Farm Road, London NW1

Patchwork Papers, 12 Park Steps, St George's Fields, London W2 2YQ

Picture Framing
reading:
Mounting and Framing Pictures, Michael Woods, Batsford

Pottery
Craftsmen Potters' Association, William Blake House, Marshall Street, London W1
Small Potteries Trade Association, Haroldstone House, Clay Lane, Haverfordwest, Dyfed, Wales
reading:
Pottery, Glen Pownalls, Allison & Busby
The Reader's Digest Manual of Handicrafts
suppliers:
Briar Wheels and Supplies Ltd, Arch Farm Industrial Estate, Whitsbury Road, Fordingbridge, Hants
Fulham Potteries Ltd, Burlington House, 184 New Kings Road, London SW6 4PB
Podmores (for kick-wheels), Stoke-on-Trent, Staffs

Silkscreen Printing
reading:
The Art of Screen Printing, Anthony Kinsey, Batsford
Silk Screening, Maria Termini, Prentice-Hall
suppliers
Selectaskine, 22 Bulstrode Street, London W1
Sericol Group Ltd, 24 Parsons Green Lane, London SW6

Soft Toys
British Toymakers' Guild, 240 The Broadway, London SW19
British Toys and Hobbies Association,
80 Camberwell Road, London SE5
BSI Test House, Hemel Hempstead, Herts
reading:
Good Toy Guide, Toy Libraries Association
How to Make Soft Toys, Anne Hulbert, John Bartholomew
Making Furry Toys, M. Foster, Paul Elek
Soft Toy Making, G. & K. Greenaway, Pelham
suppliers:
Harveson Surplus Co Ltd, 170 High Street, Merton, London SW19
Service Trading Co Ltd, 57 Bridgman Road, London W4
C. W. Wheelhouse Ltd, 11 Bell Road, Hounslow, Middlesex

Stained Glass
(*See* Decorating Glass)
reading:
How to Work in Stained Glass, A. Isenberg, Chilton

Weaving and Handspinning
Association of Guilds of Weavers, Spinners and Dyers, 10 Stancliffe Avenue, Manford, Wrexham, Glwyd LL12 8LP
British Wool Marketing Board, Kew Bridge House, Kew Bridge Road, Isleworth, Middlesex
The Handweaver Studio, 29 Haroldstone Road, London E17 7AN
reading:
Country Crafts, W. I. Home Skills, Macdonald
Handspinning, Eliza Leadbeater, Studio Vista
The Off-the-Loom Weaving Book, Naumann and Hull, Pitman

Rugs From Rags, John Hinchcliffe, Orbis

Spinning Wheels, Patricia Barnes, Batsford

The Weaving, Spinning and Dyeing Book, Rachel Brown, Routledge & Kegan Paul

suppliers:

British Wool Marketing Board (*see* above)

Craftsman's Mark Ltd, Trefnant, Denbigh, Wales

The Handweaver Studio (*see* above)

John Maxwell, Folders Lane, Burgess Hill, Sussex

The Weavers' Shop, King Street, Wilton, Salisbury, Wilts

Food

courses:

Cordon Bleu Cookery School, 114 Marylebone Road, London W1

Hotel and Catering Industry Training Board, Ramsey House, Central Square, Wembley, Middlesex HA9 7AB

Leith's School of Food and Wine, 36a Notting Hill Gate, London W11

agencies:

Alfred Marks, 84 Regent Street, London W1

Lucie Morton, 4 Paddington Street, London W4

reading:

The Book of Practical Preserving, Sonia Allison, David & Charles

Freezing Food at Home, Gwen Conacher, Electricity Council

Jams, Pickles and Chutneys, D. & R. Mabey, Macmillan

Menu Planner Series, Audrey Ellis, Sampson Low

Michael Smith's Book of Sandwiches, BBC Publications

National Federation of Fruit & Potato Trades' annual handbook, from 308 Seven Sisters Road, London N4

Furniture and Soft Furnishings

London College of Furniture, 41–47 Commercial Road, London E1

City and Guilds of London Institute (*see* General Courses and Training)

Caning

The Cane Centre, Jacobs, Young & Westbury Ltd, Bridge Road, Hayward's Heath, Sussex

The Cane Shop, 377 Seven Sisters Road, London N4

reading:

Canework, Charles Crampton, Dryad Press

French Polishing
reading:
Furniture Doctoring and French Polishing, Charles Harding, Foulsham

Gilding
Crafts Council (*see* General Courses and Training)
Guild of Master Craftsmen, 10 Dover Street, London W1
The Orton Trust (*See* Crafts: Courses)
reading:
How to Gold Leaf Antiques, Donald L. Chambers, Allen & Unwin
Practical Woodcarving and Gilding, Wheeler and Hayward, Evans
suppliers:
Stuart R. Stephenson, 22 Newland Court, Old Street, London EC1

Lampshades
reading:
Lampshades to Make, E. Doeser, Marshall Cavendish
The Modern Lampshade Book, D. Cox, Bell & Hyman
suppliers:
Lampshades Crafts Ltd, 110 Regent Street, Leamington Spa, Warks

Making Wooden Furniture
Lambeth Women's Workshop, Unit C22, Parkhall Trading Estate, Martell Road, London SE21
reading:
Woodwork For You, David M. Willacy, Hutchinson
suppliers:
Ashley Iles, East Kirkby, Lincs
Alex Tiranti, 21 Goodge Place, London W1
Craft Supplies, The Mill, Miller's Dale, Brixton, Derbyshire SK17 8SN

Roger's Mail Order Catalogue, 47 Walsworth Road, Hitchin, Herts

Marquetry
The Marquetry Society, 2a The Ridgeway, St Albans, Herts
reading:
The Art and Practice of Marquetry, W. A. Lincoln, Thames and Hudson
Introducing Marquetry, Marie Campkin, Batsford

Mirrors
reading:
Glass, Mosaics and Plastics, Marshall Cavendish

Restoring Furniture
Brass Tacks Workshop, 18 Ashwin Street, London E8 (workshops countrywide)
The British Antique Dealers' Association, 20 Rutland Gate, London SW7
reading:
Antique Furniture Repairs, C. Hayward, Hamlyn
Care and Repair of Furniture, Desmond Gaston, Collins
Restoring Old Junk, Michele Brown, Lutterworth

Upholstery
Association of Master Upholsterers, Dormar House, Mitre Bridge, Scrubs Lane, London NW10 6QX
reading:
Simple Upholstery, Hart & Halliday, Dryad Press
Soft Furnishing, A. V. White, Routledge & Kegan Paul
suppliers:
Porter Nicholson Ltd, Portland House, Norlington Road, London E10

Health and Beauty

Beauty Salon

British Association of Beauty Therapy and Cosmetology, 5 Greenways, Winchcombe, Cheltenham, Glos

Confederation of Beauty Therapy, 3 The Retreat, Nidwells Lane, Goudhurst, Cranbrook, Kent

Society of Beauticians, 29 Old Bond Street, London W1

Wendover House College of Beauty Therapy, Wendover House, Beaconsfield Road, London N11 3AB

Chiropody

London Foot Hospital, 33 Fitzroy Square, London W1

Society of Chiropodists, 8 Wimpole Street, London W1

Hairdressing

Hairdressing Council, 17 Spring Street, London W2

Hairdressers' Insurance Bureau, 16 Selhurst Road, London SE2 5QF

Keep Fit Classes

Keep Fit Association, 16 Upper Woburn Place, London WC1

Slimnastics, 14 East Sheen Avenue, London SW14 8AS

Natural Beauty Products

The Herb Society, 34 Boscobel Place, London SW1

College of Natural Therapies and Aesthetic Treatments, 22 Bromley Road, London SE6 2TP

(*See also* Plants: Herbs)

reading:

Lotions and Potions, Gwynned Lloyd, National Federation of Women's Institutes

Herbal Cosmetics, Liz Sanderson, Latimer Press

Feed Your Face, D. D. Buchman, Duckworth

Plants

Flowers and Plants Advisory Council, Agriculture House, London SW1X 7NJ

Royal Horticultural Society, Horticultural Hall, Vincent Square, London SW1

Women's Farm and Garden Association, Courtauld House, Byng Place, London WC1

Dried Flowers

National Association of Flower Arrangement Societies of Great Britain, 21a Denbigh Street, London SW1

Society of Floristry, 6 Arnold Lane, Whittlesey, Cambs PE7 1QR

reading:

Handbook for Flower Arrangers, Phyllis Page, Blandford

Herbs

The Herb Society (*see* Health and Beauty)

reading:
> The Complete Book of Herbs, Kay N. Sanecki, Macdonald
> Herbs for All Seasons, Rosemary Hemphill, Angus & Robertson
> Herb Growing for Health, D. Law, John Gifford

Indoor Plants
reading:
> The Complete Indoor Gardener, ed. Michael Wright, Pan
> Indoor Gardening, Violet Stevenson, Arthur Barker

Landscape Gardening
Landscape Institute, Nash House, Carlton House Terrace, London SW1
TOPS, Manpower Services Commission (*see* General Courses and Training)
reading:
> Patio Gardening, Robert Pearson, Hamlyn

Market Gardening
Agricultural Development Advisory Service, Great Westminster House, Horseferry Road, London SW1
National Farmers' Union, Agriculture House, London SW1X 7NJ
reading:
> The Complete Vegetable Grower, W. E. Shewell-Cooper, Faber
> Grow Your Own Fruit and Vegetables, L. D. Hills, Faber
> Making Money from Garden Produce, Keith Mossmay, Witherby

Mushroom Growing
Mushroom Growers' Association, Agriculture House, London SW1X 7NJ
reading:
> Mushroom Growing for Everyone, R. Genders, Faber
> Mushroom Growing Today, F. C. Atkins, Faber

Repairs

Bicycle Repairs
Cycling Touring Club, 69 Meadrow, Godalming, Surrey
reading:
> Building Bicycle Wheels, Robert Wright, World Publications (Selpress Books)
> Richard's Bicycle Book, R. Ballentine, Pan

Car Repairs
DIY Car Maintenance Centre, Milton Keynes, Bucks

reading:
> Low-Cost Car Repairs, J. Mills, Faber

Clock and Watch Repairs
British Horological Institute, Upton Hall, Upton, Newark, Notts NG23 5TE
reading:
> Clocks: Their Working and Maintenance, E. Smith, David & Charles
> Practical Watch Repairing, Donald De Carle, Norfolk Books

General Repairs
reading:
How to Clean Everything, A. C. Moore, David & Charles
How To Restore and Repair Practically Everything, Lorraine Johnson, Michael Joseph

Restoring Antique Dolls
The Costume Society (*see* Clothes and Accessories: Theatrical Costumes)
reading:
How to Repair and Dress Old Dolls, Audrey Johnson, Bell & Hyman

Restoring China and Ceramics
Robin Hood's Workshop, 18 Bourne Street, Sloane Square, London SW1
West Dean College, West Dean, Chichester, West Sussex PO18 0QZ
reading:
China Mending and Restoration, Parsons and Curl, Faber
Restoring Ceramics, Judith Larney, Barrie & Jenkins
suppliers:
Frank W. Joel, The Manor House, Wereham, Kings Lynn, Norfolk PE33 9AN

Services

Accountancy
Association of Certified Accountants, 29 Lincoln's Inn Fields, London WC2
Hatfield Polytechnic, Hatfield, Herts
School of Accountancy and Business Studies, Intertext House, 160 Stewarts Road, London SW8
reading:
Introduction to Accountancy for Business Studies, Langley, Butterworth
Modern Financial Accounting, G. A. Lee, Nelson

Astrology
Astrological Association, 57 Woodside, London SW19 7QB
Astrological Counselling Forum, c/o Frizco, 59 Twyford Avenue, London N2 9NR
Faculty of Astrological Studies, 20 Ensor Mews, London SW7
Mayo School of Astrology, 8 Stoggy Lane, Plympton, Plymouth, Devon
reading:
The Modern Textbook of Astrology, Margaret Hone, Fowler
The Complete Astrologer, Julia Parker, Mitchell Beazley
The Tarot, Alfred Douglas, Penguin
Wilhelm's Translation of I Ching, Routledge and Kegan Paul
suppliers:
Atlantis Bookshop, 49 Museum Street, London WC1A 1LY
W. Foulsham and Co Ltd, Yeovil Road, Slough, Bucks
Watkins, 19–21 Cecil Court, Charing Cross Road, London WC2N 4HB

Bed and Breakfast
reading:
Doing Bed and Breakfast, Audrey Vellacot and Liz Christmas, David & Charles

Book-keeping
reading:
Accounting Terms and Book-keeping Procedures Explained, Houghton and Wallace, Gower
Book-keeping and Accounts, D. J. Coakley, Cassell
Fred learns Book-keeping, Fredbook Productions Ltd

Computers
British Computer Society and British Computer Society Committee for the Disabled, 13 Mansfield Street, London W1N 0BP
Computer Sciences Personnel, 235 Rail Exchange, Manchester
Freelance Programmers, 16 Station Road, Chesham, Bucks
Microsystems Centre, 11 Fetter Lane, London EC4
National Computing Centre, Oxford Road, Manchester M1 7ED

Graphology
Bell House Study Centre, Swanton Novers, Melton Constable, Norfolk
reading:
Graphology, Patricia Marr, Teach Yourself Books
A Manual of Graphology, Eric Singer, Duckworth

Graphic Design
London College of Printing, Elephant and Castle, London SE1
reading:
Basic Typography, John Lewis, Studio Vista
Designing With Type, James Craig, Pitman
Lettering for Reproduction, David Gates, Pitman

Production for the Graphic Designer, James Craig, Pitman
suppliers:
C. J. Graphics, 4 Ganton Street, London W1
Cowling & Wilcox Ltd, 26 Broadwick Street, London W1

Home Economics
Association of Home Economists, 192 Vauxhall Bridge Road, London SW1V 1DX
reading:
A New Look at Careers in Home Economics, National Advisory Centre on Careers for Women

Imports and Exports
British Overseas Trade Board, 1 Victoria Street, London SW1
CoSIRA (*See* General Contacts)
Mantor Export Services, 26 Hockerill Street, Bishops Stortford, Herts
reading:
Croner's Reference Book for Importers and Exporters, Croner Publications
Export and Import Without Capital, James Pike, E. J. P. Publications
Export: A Manual of Instruction, A. W. Mason, Business Books

Indexing
Rapid Results College, 27–37 St George's Road, London SW19 4DS
Society of Indexers (J. Ainsworth Gordon), 28 Johns Avenue, London NW4 4EN

Minicab Driving
Public Carriage Office, Penton Street, London W1

Model Making
reading:
Constructing Model Buildings, John
Cleaver, Academy Editions
The Craft of Model Making, Thomas
Bayley, Dryad Press
suppliers:
Modelmakers' Materials Supply Co, 12
Macriss Road, London W14

Nursing
British Nursing Association, Freepost
32, London W1E 3YZ
British Red Cross Society and Joint
Committee of the Order of St John,
9 Grosvenor Crescent, London SW1
Nursing and Health Service Careers
Centre, 121–123 Edgware Road,
London W2
Royal College of Nursing and National
Council of Nurses of the UK, Hen-
rietta Place London W1M 0AB

Painting and Illustrating
Arts Council of Great Britain, 105 Pic-
cadilly, London W1V 0AM
Association of Illustrators, 10 Barley
Mow Passage, London W4 4PH
National Society for Art Education,
Champness Hall, Drake Street,
Rochdale, Lancs
Society of Miniaturists, 26 Conduit
Street, London W1R 9TA
reading:
The Complete Guide to Painting and
Drawing, C. Hayes, Phaidon
The Writers' and Artists' Yearbook, A.
& C. Black

Photographic Processing
See Photography

Photography
Artlaw Services, 358 The Strand,
London WC2
Arts Council of Great Britain, 105 Pic-
cadilly, London W1
Bureau of Freelance Photographers,
Focus House, 497 Green Lanes,
London N13 4BP
Institute of Incorporated Photogra-
phers, Amwell End, Ware, Herts
SG12 9HN
Photographic Information Centre, 84
Newman Street, London W1
Photographic Training Centre, 18
Grosvenor Street, London W1
reading:
Photography for Profit, G. Greenlaw,
Lyle Publications

Printing
Adana Ltd, Pier Road, North Feltham
Trading Estate, Feltham, Middlesex
TW14 0TW
London College of Printing (*see*
Graphic Design)
St Bride Printing Library, Bride Lane,
London EC4
reading:
Introduction to Printing: The Craft of
Letterpress, H. Simon, Faber
Printing for Pleasure, John Ryder,
Bodley Head

Proofreading
Book House Training Centre, 45 East
Hill, London SW18
British Standards Institution, 2 Park
Street, London W1
Editorial and Translating Services, 30
Gondar Gardens, London NW6
reading:
First Course in Proof Correcting,
Dellow, Northgate Publishers

The Writers' and Artists' Yearbook, A. & C. Black

Public Relations/Promotions
Institute of Public Relations, 1 Great James Street, London WC1

Creative Handbook Ltd, 100 St Martin's Lane, London WC2

Publishing
Independent Publishers Guild, 52 Chepstow Road, London W2 5BE

National Book League, Book House, 45 East Hill, London SW18

Publishers Association, 19 Bedford Square, London WC1B 3HJ

St Bride's Printing Library, (*see* Services: Printing)

reading:
   The Business of Book Publishing, Clive Bingley, Pergamon
   Publishing and Book Selling, Mumby and Norrie, Jonathan Cape
   The Truth About Publishing, Stanley Unwin, Allen & Unwin

Research
Association of Special Libraries and Information Bureaux, 3 Belgrave Square, London SW1

British Library (bibliographic services), 7 Rathbone Street, London W1

College of Arms, Queen Victoria Street, London EC4

Institute of Information Scientists, Harvest House, 62 London Road, Reading RG1 5AS

Library Association, 7 Ridgmount Street, London WC1E 7AE

Public Records Office, Chancery Lane, London WC2

Publishers Association (*see* Publishing)

Science Reference Library, Southampton Buildings, 25 Chancery Lane, London WC2

Society of Genealogists, 37 Harrington Gardens, London SW7

Office of Population Censuses and Surveys, St Catherine's House, 10 Kingsway, London WC2B 6JP

reading:
   Picture Researchers' Handbook, Hilary and Mary Evans, David & Charles
   Profit for Information, Martin S. White, Andre Deutsch

Sign Writing
Eltham Institute, Haimo Road, London SE9 6DZ

School of Building, Lime Grove, London W12

Vauxhall College of Building, Belmont Street, London SW8

reading:
   A Book of Scripts, A. Fairbank, Faber

Spray Painting Cars
reading:
   Panel Beating and Body Repairing, David Wait, Angus & Robertson

Taking In Lodgers
Department of the Environment, Building 3, Victoria Road, South Ruislip HA4 0NZ

Tourist Guide
British Tourist Authority, 64 St James's Street, London SW1

English Tourist Board, 4 Grosvenor Gardens, London SW1W 0DU

Guild of Guides and Lecturers, 7 Blackfriars Lane, London EC4V 6ER

London Tourist Board (Guide Activities Dept), 26 Grosvenor Gardens, London SW1

Transcribing Braille
National Library for the Blind, Cromwell Road, Bredbury, Stockport, Greater Manchester SK6 2SG
Royal National Institute for The Blind, Braille House, 338 Goswell Road, London EC1
Scottish Braille Press, Craigmillar Park, Edinburgh 9

Translating
Institute of Linguists, 24a Highbury Grove, London N5 2EA
Linguists Club, 68 Newington Causeway, London SE1
Translators Association, Society of Authors, 84 Drayton Gardens, London SW10

Typing
Joan Wilkins Associates, 37a Maida Vale, London W9 1TP
Pam Haybittle Business Services, 73 The Glade, Shirley, Croydon, Surrey CRO 7QJ
Pitmans Correspondence College, Worcester Road, London SW19
Unique Freelance Secretaries, 4 Hill Top, London NW11 6EE
reading:
Business Typewriting, Sylvia E. Parks, Macdonald & Evans
Typewriting by Programmed Instructions, R. Kesteven, Cassell

Word Processing
Institute of Word Processing, 173–175 Cleveland Street, London W1
Word Processing Training Services, 16 Regency Street, London SW1

Teaching

Dancing Classes
Council for Dance Education and Training, 5 Tavistock Place, London WC1
Dance Teachers' Association International, 76 Bennett Road, Brighton
Royal Academy of Dancing, 48 Vicarage Crescent, London SW11

Driving Instruction
Department of Transport, 2 Marsham Street, London SW1

Foreign-language Conversation
Centre for Information on Language Teaching and Research (CILT), 20 Carlton House Terrace, London SW1
Language Studies, 10 James Street, London W1
Linguaphone Institute, 207 Regent Street, London W1

Music Teaching
Incorporated Society of Musicians, 10 Stratford Place, London W1N 9AE
Royal Academy of Music, Marylebone Road, London NW1
Royal College of Music, Prince Consort Road, London SW7
Rural Music Schools Association, Little Benslow Hill, Hitchin, Herts

Teaching English: EFL and ESL
Association of Recognised English Language Schools (ARELS), 125 Holborn, London WC1

International House, 106 Piccadilly, London WC1

National Association for the Teaching of English as a Second Language to Adults (NATESLA), 38 Church Street, Stony Stratford, Milton Keynes MK11 1BD
reading:
> *Kernal Lessons*, O'Neil, Kingsbury & Yeadon, Longman
> *Scope*, Sealey and Skirrow, Books for Schools

Teaching Lipreading
Centre for the Deaf, Keeley House, Keeley Street, London WC2B 4BA

City Literary Institute, Stukeley Street, London WC2

LINK (short courses for deaf people), 19 Hartfield Road, Eastbourne, East Sussex

Manchester Polytechnic, Hilton House, Hilton Street, Manchester
reading:
> *Lipreading*, H. Burchett, National Institute for the Deaf
> *Speechreading*, Jeffers & Barley, Charles C. Thomas

Teaching Literacy and Numeracy
Adult Literacy Unit, 52 High Holborn, London WC1

Cambridge House and Talbot, 131 Camberwell Road, London SE5
reading:
> *On The Move*, BBC Publications

> *The Teaching of Reading*, Gordon Pemberton, Hutchinson
> *The Teaching of Numeracy*, Michael Pollard, Hutchinson

Teaching Sports
British Horse Society Equestrian Centre, Stoneleigh, Kenilworth, Warks CV8 2LR

Teaching Yoga
The Rambler, 22 New Road, Sandhurst, Camberley, Surrey GU17 8EF
reading:
> *Teaching Yoga*, Donald G. Butler, Pelham
> *Yoga Today* (monthly magazine)

Tutoring
Council for the Accreditation of Correspondence Colleges, 27 Marylebone Road, London NW1

Writing
National Council for the Training of Journalists, Carlton House, Hemnal Street, Epping, Essex CM16 4NL

National Union of Journalists, 314 Gray's Inn Road, London WC1

Society of Authors, 84 Drayton Gardens, London SW10 9SD

Writers' Guild of Great Britain, 430 Edgware Road, London W2 1EH
reading:
> *Preparing your Manuscript for Typing*, Joanna Johnson, Thornhill Press
> *The Writers' and Artists' Yearbook*, A. & C. Black

INDEX

233